D0524625

GREEN THUMBS IN THE KITCHEN

"When It's Smokin' It's Cookin' & When It's Burnt It's Done"

green thumb

Service ♦ Employment ♦ Training

2000 North 14th Street
Suite 800
Arlington, Virginia 22201
703-522-7272
Homepage: http://www.greenthumb.org

ACKNOWLEDGMENTS

Green Thumb is grateful for the contributions of the following individuals and companies:

CORPORATE SPONSORS
First Union National Bank of Virginia
EWA Travel, Inc., Arlington, Virginia

Title Suggested By
Patricia Metz, North Bend, OR
Elsie Troutman, Hiram, ME
Pat Koronis, Picher, OK

Written and Edited By
Alice Ann Toole
Green Thumb Director of Public Affairs

Jannell Khu
Public Affairs Assistant

Cover and Graphic Design By
Schum & Associates, McLean, Virginia

Special Thanks for Production Assistance, Research,
Proofreading, and Technical Expertise To
Judy Davis, Atlantic Beach, Florida;
Eula Mae Combs, Beattyville, Kentucky;
Pat Langreck, Wisconsin State Director;
Sally Boofer, Jan Dickey, Lauren Fyfe, Mike Gardner, and
Andrea Wooten in Green Thumb's National Office

ISBN: 0-9652554-0-9

Copyright 1996, Green Thumb, Inc.

1st Printing   October 1996   40,000 copies

Printed in the United States of America
TOOF COOKBOOK DIVISION

STARR ★ TOOF

670 South Cooper Street
Memphis, TN 38104

TABLE OF CONTENTS

*Cooking comes from the heart
as well as the hearth.*

"Green Thumbs in the Kitchen" reminds readers
that cooking is an art, not a science.
Every effort has been made to ensure the accuracy of recipes,
but we encourage creativity and experimentation.
We also suggest cooks consider the peculiarities of their stoves
and other kitchen appliances for best results.

Green Thumb is a

national nonprofit organization that provides low-income older workers with training opportunities and meaningful community service jobs. Each year 27,000+ "Green Thumbers" work more than 22 million hours in 12,500 municipal and nonprofit agencies. Like a treasured patchwork quilt, the contributions of workers, staff, and their host agencies form pieces of a whole that cover the U.S. from California to Maine, from Washington to Florida.

A VISION FROM CAMELOT
Green Thumb's story begins in the summer of 1963 when John F. Kennedy decided to make poverty a focus of his 1964 presidential campaign. Jim Patton, president of the National Farmers Union and a

White House advisor on labor issues, encouraged the President to develop policies that would help disadvantaged residents of America's rural communities. In the last Cabinet meeting before his ill-fated

trip to Dallas, the president doodled "poverty, poverty, poverty" on his note pad.

THE WAR ON POVERTY

Less than thirty days after the assassination of
President Kennedy, Lyndon Johnson invited
several national leaders to the White House to
discuss an agenda for his new administration.

Johnson needed to quickly
develop a theme that
would heal a badly shaken
country.

Jim Patton and Secretary
of Agriculture Orville Freeman remained after
the meeting at the President's request. When
the President asked for their ideas, Patton imme-

diately replied, "I think you
ought to declare war on
poverty!" Moments later,
the President officially
announced his "war" to
the press.

With the Economic Opportunity Act
stalled in Congressional debate,
however, it took the personal interest
of Lady Bird Johnson to help the
initiative press forward. A memo to
the first lady outlined the proposal to
"take the green thumbs of poor, older,
and retired farmers and put them to
work to beautify our highways." Mrs.

Johnson responded, "What an opportunity is presented here to provide [older farmers] with useful employment for which they are fully qualified, and at the same time, to beautify highways for the benefit of all our people."

On October 5, 1965, President Johnson at last signed the Nelson Amendment to the Economic Opportunity Act which funded the "green thumb" project of the National Farmers Union. Ten days later, Green Thumb, Inc., was launched as the first non-profit organization created to run a jobs program for disadvantaged rural Americans. The following spring, crews of farmers went to work on beautification projects in Arkansas, New Jersey, Oregon, and Minnesota.

Green Thumb Today

The small demonstration program initially launched by Green Thumb is now one of our nation's success stories—the Senior Community Service Employment Program—which annually provides community service training and employment opportunities for the almost 100,000 seniors across the country. Through this "Green Thumb Model," the organization has firmly established itself as the nation's leader in the field of older worker employment and training.

Today, Green Thumb workers continue to serve their communities in a variety of public service capacities. You'll find them reading to children at the library, running the local blood bank, caring for the sick and disabled, assisting teachers and students in elementary schools, operating recycling centers, staffing emergency hotlines, cooking meals at senior centers, clerking at Veterans Administration offices, giving tours in local museums, and yes, still building parks and working on beautification projects.

Organizations that host Green Thumb participants find that workers have much to contribute because of their years and their experience, not despite them. As a result of their experience on

Green Thumb community service assignments, about 30 percent of the workers annually move to better-paying, unsubsidized jobs.

Will Green Thumb rest on its laurels? Not a chance! Green Thumb evolved into a national presence by anticipating the needs of older workers and developing programs and services to meet them, including:

• Experience Works!, a new nationwide staffing service specifically targeting mature employees, to meet the temporary and permanent employment needs of local businesses, and

• Training programs that provide older workers with the opportunity to update or learn new technical skills so they can successfully re-enter the workforce, pursue new jobs, and even start second careers.

As the premiere provider of mature-worker training and employment, Green Thumb will continue to empower a rapidly aging population—one that both wants and needs to work in order to remain productive, contributing members of their communities.

GREEN THUMBS IN THE KITCHEN
The recipes in this book, spiced with traditions, anecdotes, and memories, come from the kitchens of Green Thumb workers and staff. Profits from the sale of *Green Thumbs in the Kitchen* will support continued training and community service employment opportunities for older workers.

With a thousand dollar smile, Mrs. Bernard Derousseau of 15 W. Bracklin st., keeps in trim in her kitchen for the national Pillsbury baking contest she'll compete in at New York City Dec. 11. Already winner of an electric stove and food mixer and a free trip to New York, the 17 year old Rice Lake housewife is eligible for a $5,000 cash prize for her "secret" cookie recipe.

—Woodward-Skrupky

THE COVER STORY

A newspaper photographer knocks on the front door of Ruth Derousseau's modest home in Rice Lake, Wisconsin. It's November 1950, and the life of this young wife and mother is about to change. Ruth has just been named a finalist in the junior division of the Second Grand National Pillsbury Bakeoff.

"Things were financially difficult for us at the time," Ruth remembers. Married at 15, the 17-year-old mother of two (with another baby on the way) prayed for a miracle. As a finalist, Ruth received a $1,000 prize, a new stove, and a trip to New York City to compete. "This was the answer to my prayer."

Raised by a grandmother who taught her to bake, by age eight Ruth was already accomplished at breadmaking.
"I experimented with a basic cookie dough recipe of my grandmother's and dressed it up a little." Then she submitted her recipe for Cherry Winks to Pillsbury.

Ruth and her husband board a train for New York where the December bakeoff event will be held. She's never been away from home, never had a honeymoon, never stayed in a hotel, much less a posh one like the Waldorf Astoria.

"We were treated like royalty for the three days of competition" she says. Contestants were told to be ready to depart for home at the conclusion of the awards luncheon. But a curious calm settled over Ruth that last morning. "I knew packing was unnecessary. I knew I was going to win."

And win she did! "It was a dream come true."

Emerging movie star glamorous from a make-over, Ruth is the toast of New York for the next few days, followed by press and photographers wherever she goes. A Life Magazine photographer rides the train back to Rice Lake with her. She is met at the depot by local dignitaries, receives a key to the city, and gifts and congratulations from the people of her hometown.

Life was a whirlwind during the next year. Working around the birth of her third child, Ruth made guest appearances, attended the openings of new stores featuring GE appliances--the official ovens of the Bakeoff, and pasted newspaper clippings and national magazine articles into her scrapbook.

With her family rapidly increasing, Ruth wants to invest the $5,000 prize money in a way that will allow her to look after her children and provide long-term financial stability. She puts her winnings into a telephone answering business she can operate at home. This proves a wise decision because Ruth's family ultimately numbers 16--nine girls and seven boys.

Over the years, Ruth developed other small businesses—home parties, wedding services—which gave her time to be with the children. She shut down her last venture, a small shop, when a giant national discount chain opened in the area and made it difficult to compete.

But Ruth still wanted and needed to work. She heard about Green Thumb through a local office on aging, enrolled in the program, and took a job at a senior center where she helped with bookkeeping, assisted in the office, and publicized activities. Because of her can-do attitude and excellent people skills, Ruth was hired as an aide by the Wisconsin Green Thumb program. She recently left for a better-paying unsubsidized job. If you happen to stop in Rice Lake some weekend, look for Ruth meeting and greeting customers, handing out coupons and samples, or demonstrating new products at local stores.

Would she change anything in her life? "I don't really think so," Ruth says. "I have understanding, patience, and I built character by experience." In addition to her job, Ruth also enjoys playing the piano ("I never had time to develop hobbies") and cooking. "I like to do soups and stews—things I can share. I enjoy using my imagination and creativity in developing recipes." And she still bakes the recipe that started it all--Cherry Winks. (Look for the recipe in the Desserts section.)

On behalf of Ruth Derousseau and hundreds of other contributors, Green Thumb invites you to share this collection of recipes and recollections of Green Thumbs in the Kitchen. Enjoy!

greenthumb

Service • Employment • Training

Beverages & Appetizers

BEVERAGES & APPETIZERS

CONTENTS

FRUITY ICED TEA

4-5 tea bags
2 quarts boiling water
1 quart white grape juice
1 quart Crystal Light lemonade
1 cup sugar (or 8-12 packages low-cal sweetener)

Steep tea in water for 30 minutes. Mix all ingredients except sugar in a large pitcher or punch bowl. Sweeten to taste. Serve over ice in tall glasses. Yield: 1 gallon

BONNIE STALEY, Green Thumb National Office

This iced tea is a standard, always-requested item for "pitch-ins" at the Green Thumb national office in Arlington, Virginia. Refreshing all seasons of the year.

AMAZING GINGER ROOT TEA

Large ginger root, peeled
2 cinnamon sticks
1 gallon water
1/4 cup brown sugar
3 tablespoons honey
Pine nuts for garnish (optional)

Boil ginger root and cinnamon sticks in water for about 45 minutes to an hour. The longer the root is boiled, the stronger the ginger potency. Sweeten tea with brown sugar and honey. Garnish with a few pine nuts. To be enjoyed hot or cold. Yield: 4-6 servings

JANNELL KHU, Green Thumb National Office

This is my mother's recipe from Korea. She swears by this tea to purify and cleanse the body, aid digestion, and treat colds. Take two aspirins, add a shot of brandy and this tea is better than commercial hot drinks for colds.

SPICED TEA

3 cups water
3 cups sugar (adjust to taste)
Grated rind of 1 lemon
4-5 cinnamon sticks
2 tablespoons whole cloves
1 large can pineapple juice
1 large bottle apple juice
1 large bottle lemon juice (or to taste)
1 16-ounce can frozen orange concentrate, thawed
1 gallon strong tea

Mix water, sugar, lemon rind, cinnamon, and cloves. Boil 10 minutes. Add juices and tea to the syrup. Yield: about 2 gallons

ANDREA WOOTEN, Green Thumb National Office

*My parents
worked hard,
especially during
the spring and
summer months,
but they believed
in taking breaks.
What we loved
the most were my
mother's improptu
outings that she
called "lemonade
picnics." It was an
occasion to enjoy
eating our midday
meal outdoors,
but what made it
extra special was
her sweet
lemonade. The
secret was the
water. We had our
picnics beside our
well, and the
water drawn from
that well was ice
cold and tasted
somehow fragrant
and sweet.*

*Emma Walker,
Wynnewood, OK
Age 75*

FRONT PORCH LEMONADE

1 cup sugar
1 cup water
Rind of 2 lemons, cut into pieces
1 cup lemon juice
4 cups iced water
Lemon wedges and sprigs of mint for garnish

In a medium saucepan, stir sugar, water, and rinds over low heat until
sugar is dissolved. Boil about 7 minutes. Cool; add lemon juice and
iced water. Pour over ice in pitcher or tall glasses. Garnish with a
lemon wedge or a sprig of mint. Yield: 6-8 servings

J. TURNER, Age 70

MINT FRUIT COOLER

4 cups unsweetened grape juice, chilled
4 cups unsweetened orange juice, chilled
1 1/2 cups lime juice from concentrate
1/2 cup sugar
1/2 teaspoon peppermint extract
Mint sprigs for garnish

Combine all ingredients in a large pitcher; stir until sugar dissolves.
Serve over ice and garnish with mint sprigs. Yield: about 2 quarts

GUY R. NORTON, Age 66

RASPBERRY SHRUB

3 pints raspberries, washed and hulled
1 1/2 cups sugar
2 cups water
1 cup lemon juice
2 quarts water

In a medium sauce pan, mix raspberries, sugar, and water. Cook 10
minutes over medium heat. Strain and cool mixture. Add lemon
juice and water. Pour into a pitcher. Serve over crushed ice. Yield:
about 2 1/2 quarts

ELIZABETH BOWEN, Age 63

FESTIVE SANGRIA

My husband proposed to me over this sangria--naturally it's our favorite!

2 oranges
2 lemons
2 fifth-bottles rosé, burgundy, or other red wine (1.5 liters)
1/4 cup sugar
1/4 cup brandy (2 ounces)
1 apple
1 28-ounce bottle carbonated water, chilled

Chill one orange and one lemon for garnish. Squeeze juice from the second orange and lemon. Place juices, wine, sugar, and brandy in a large pitcher or bowl. Stir to dissolve sugar; chill. Just before serving, divide mixture into 2 pitchers or pour into punch bowl. Cut chilled orange into wedges. Slice chilled lemon into cartwheels. Core apple and cut into wedges. Thread fruit on 2 long skewers to stand in pitchers or float in punch bowl. Slowly add carbonated water. Yield: 24 4-ounce servings

NANCY CANNON, Green Thumb National Office

ORANGE SLUSH

1 6-ounce can frozen orange juice concentrate
1 cup water
1 cup milk
1/2 teaspoon vanilla
1/4 cup sugar
1 cup ice cubes

Mix all ingredients in a blender until smooth. Serve immediately. Mixture may be frozen; defrost until slushy before serving. Yield: 4-6 servings

HELEN PENDERGRASS

Home Brews

My grandfather was one of those men who knew how to do just about anything. One thing he did best was make beers and root beers. He called them home brews. When the beers were ready to be sampled, it was an excuse for a small social gathering. Good friends, good food, and good brews were the ingredients for a party. Some things really don't change, do they?

*Adeline Urban,
Kimball, SD
Age 67*

The Cocoa Specialist

My mother became a hot cocoa specialist in the 1930's. Back then the government sent Extension Agents to educate and introduce farming communities to everything from new agricultural developments to nutrition. One day an agent made a house call and introduced my mother to canned milk. Mother experimented with various recipes using canned milk, but her greatest success turned out to be a rich hot cocoa. As a child, it was always hard to go inside when you were having fun playing, but it was worth it for this cocoa.

Tamlin Turner, Owensville, MO Age 62

HOT CHOCOLATE

2 ounces unsweetened chocolate
1 cup water
Pinch salt
3-4 tablespoons sugar
3 cups milk
Whipped cream for garnish

In a medium sauce pan over low heat, mix together chocolate and water, stirring until chocolate melts. Add salt and sugar and boil 4 minutes, stirring occasionally. Slowly stir in milk and heat until scalded. Do not boil. Just before serving, beat with whisk until smooth. Top with whipped cream. Serve hot. Yield: 6 servings

ICED CHOCOLATE
Cool chocolate mixture. Serve in tall glasses full of crushed ice. Top with sweetened whipped cream.

ALICE MARY HAAS, Age 74

SPICED APPLE CIDER

32 ounces cranberry juice
32 ounces apple juice or apple cider
1/2 cup orange juice
1 tea bag
1 cup cold water
Cinnamon sticks for garnish

Heat juices to boiling point in a large kettle. Allow the tea bag to steep in the juice mixture and then add the cold water. Serve in mugs and garnish with a cinnamon stick. Yield: 2 quarts

FRANCES CHAILLARD, Kennett, MO Age 76

HOT BUTTERED RUM

Straight from a ski resort in the Pocono Mountains.

1/2 stick unsalted butter
1 1/2 cups brown sugar
1 tablespoon ground nutmeg
1 tablespoon ground cinnamon
Pinch ground cloves
1 cup honey
1 shot rum per drink
Boiling water

In a medium bowl, beat butter, sugar, spices, and honey to form a fluffy batter. Pour a shot of rum into a mug, top with a heaping tablespoon of batter, and cover with boiling water. Yield 6-8 servings

CHERYL CROSBY

BOB'S CHILLED MANHATTAN

4 shots bourbon or blended whiskey
A few drops bitters
1 teaspoon maraschino cherry juice
1 shot sweet vermouth
Maraschino cherries for garnish

Pour all ingredients into a pitcher and stir lightly. Place two cocktail glasses and the pitcher in the freezer for an hour. When ready to serve, pour the mixture into glasses and garnish with cherries. Yield: 2 cocktails

BOB ZENTNER, Bismarck, ND Age 64

Aaaah. . .

I use this recipe just about every Friday night. It is an excellent sipping drink to enjoy just before dinner. The secrets are the cherry juice and the bitters.

FRUITED ICE RING

Rule of Thumb:

Boil water before freezing. It helps to keep ice clear as it freezes.

3/4 cup sugar
1 8-ounce bottle lime juice from concentrate
3 cups water
Grapes
Apple slices or wedges

In a 1-quart pitcher or bowl, dissolve sugar in lime juice. Add water. Pour 3/4 cup of mixture into a 5-cup ring mold; arrange small clusters of grapes and apples in mixture. Freeze. Pour remaining mixture on top; freeze. To unmold, quickly dip mold into water. Float in punch bowl.

DOROTHEA MONTAGUE, Age 84

APPLE GRAPE PUNCH

Fruited Ice Ring (See above)
1 quart apple juice, chilled
3 cups unsweetened white or red grape juice, chilled
1 8-ounce bottle lime juice from concentrate, chilled
1 cup vodka (optional)
1/2 cup sugar

Prepare fruited ice ring in advance. Combine all ingredients in a punch bowl; stir until sugar dissolves. Add ice ring. Yield: 2 quarts

GENEVA CRUSE, Age 66

MOCK CHAMPAGNE PUNCH

1 quart sparkling water or seltzer
1 quart ginger ale
1 quart unsweetened white grape juice

Mix all ingredients in a large punch bowl. Serve in chilled glasses. Yield: 20 servings

FRANCES B. LUKER, Lake City, FL Age 78

CHAMPAGNE PUNCH

2 bottles champagne, chilled
1 bottle Sauterne wine, chilled
1 pint apricot brandy
1 quart ginger ale, chilled

Combine all ingredients in a punch bowl. Yield: 24 servings

ALICE ANN TOOLE, Green Thumb National Office

Use the least-expensive available ingredients. For some reason, this champagne punch is just as good when made with the "cheap stuff." But it looks and tastes like a million bucks when we serve it in my sister's silver punch bowl. (She's toted that bowl all over the country for special family occasions!)

FRUIT PUNCH

This is the punch we serve at graduation teas, baby showers, and other "non-alcoholic" occasions.

12 ounces frozen lemonade concentrate, defrosted
6 ounces frozen orange juice concentrate, defrosted
2 cups cranberry juice
2 quarts ginger ale

Combine all ingredients in a large punch bowl. May be served over an ice mold or garnished with flowers. Yield: about 3 quarts

ALICE ANN TOOLE, Green Thumb National Office

BANANA PUNCH

This is a family favorite at Christmas time.

4 cups water
4 cups sugar
1 46-ounce can pineapple juice
Juice of 6 oranges
Juice of 2 lemons
6 ripe bananas mashed
3 1-liter bottles of ginger ale

In a large kettle or dutch oven, boil water and sugar for 3 minutes. Remove from heat and cool. Add the juices and bananas and stir. This mixture may be frozen in a ring mold or small containers. When ready to serve, run hot water over container to release mold. Place mold in a punch bowl and cover with ginger ale. Yield: 36 servings

DAISY COUCH, Springdale, AR Age 73

Everything Old is New Again

The Waterloo Library and Historical Society found this recipe in the archives and decided to revive the old Wassail Bowl tradition. The recipe was dated 1703, but wassail and its traditions are much older.

ENGLISH WASSAIL BOWL

1 teaspoon whole cloves
1 teaspoon whole allspice
2 sticks cinnamon
2 quarts apple cider
1/2 pint brandy
Brown sugar to taste
Apple slices studded with cloves

Place cloves, allspice, and cinnamon in a piece of muslin. Combine cider, brandy, and brown sugar in a large saucepan. Add the spice "bag" to the mixture, and bring to a boil over medium heat, stirring to dissolve sugar. Simmer 10-15 minutes. Stick whole cloves into slices of apple. Serve punch in heated mugs, garnished with apple slices. Yield: 8 8-ounce servings

JUDITH WHEATON, Waterloo, NY Age 61

PARTY POTION SPARKLE

1 cup rum
1/2 cup sugar
1 package raspberry or strawberry unsweetened soft drink mix
    (2-quart size)
4 cups cold water
1/2 cup lime juice from concentrate
1 10-ounce package frozen raspberries or strawberries in syrup,
    partially thawed
1 32-ounce bottle lemon-lime carbonated beverage, chilled
Maraschino cherries for garnish

In a large pitcher or small punch bowl, stir together rum, sugar, and drink mix; add water, stirring until sugar dissolves. Add lime juice and berries. Just before serving, add carbonated beverage. Serve over ice. Garnish with maraschino cherries. Yield: 2 1/2 quarts

MOLLY BRAULT, Green Thumb National Office

PINEAPPLE PUNCH

1 small package lemon or lime jello
1 cup hot water
2 cups sugar
2 quarts cold water
1 46-ounce can pineapple juice
3 1-liter bottles lemon-lime soft drink

In a large bowl, dissolve jello in hot water, add sugar, cold water, and pineapple juice. Pour into freezer-safe container, cover, and freeze solid. Remove frozen mixture from freezer about three hours before serving, place in punch bowl, and pour in lemon-lime soft drink. Alternative: allow ice mold to thaw to slushy consistency and serve undiluted. Yield: about 3 1/2 quarts

BONNIE CAWTHORN, Ozark, MO Age 76

PINK FROST CUBES
Make these special cubes and add them to your favorite fruit punch.

1/2 cup currant jelly
2 tablespoons lemon juice
1/4 cup water
1 16-ounce bottle ginger ale or lemon-lime soda, chilled

In a small saucepan, melt jelly in lemon juice over low heat; stir until jelly melts completely. Pour into ice cube tray and set aside. When jelly mixture is cool, pour in about 1/2" of chilled ginger ale or soda and freeze. Yield: one ice cube tray

JANNELL KHU, Green Thumb National Office

Rule of Thumb:

Store ice cubes in a brown paper bag and they won't stick together.

DECORATIVE ICE CUBES

Well-drained maraschino cherries, mint sprigs, pineapple chunks, citrus wedges or curls of peel, berries

Fill ice cube tray one-third full with water. Place in freezer; remove tray when water is partially frozen. Place items of your choice in each cube section. Fill tray with water and freeze. Variation: use sparkling water or carbonated lemon-lime drinks instead of water. The cubes keep drinks or punch lively and will not dilute beverages as they melt.

KATHRYN DANA

SNACK MIX

1 12-ounce package chocolate chips
1 cup peanut butter
1 stick margarine
1 box Crispix cereal
3 cups powdered sugar

In a medium saucepan, melt chips, peanut butter, and margarine over medium heat. Pour cereal into a large bowl; pour in melted chocolate mixture, stirring to coat well. Put powdered sugar in a large paper bag. Add cereal mix and shake to coat well. Spread on cookie sheet to set. Store in tightly covered container. Yield: 8-12 servings

DAISY COUCH, Springdale, AR Age 73

OYSTER CRACKER NIBBLES

3/4 cup cooking oil
2 tablespoons dill
12 ounces oyster crackers
1 package dry ranch dressing mix

In a jar or small bowl, mix oil and dill. Pour crackers into a large bowl and mix with dry dressing. Add oil mixture and stir to completely coat crackers. Spread on a cookie sheet to dry, stirring often. Store in jars or tins when completely dry. Yield: 4-6 servings

ROY A. WILEY, Cape Vincent, NY Age 72

BACON BREAD STICKS

24 packaged bread sticks
12 slices bacon, cut in half
1/2 cup Parmesan cheese

Preheat broiler. Wind bacon around bread sticks, candy-cane fashion. Place on cookie sheet cook 10-12" from broiler, turning bread sticks frequently to cook bacon evenly. Sprinkle with Parmesan. Serve hot. Yield: 24 bread sticks

MARY PARKER, Age 60

CEREAL MIX TREAT

This is great to take to parties and on trips. Everyone raves about it.

1/2 cup brown sugar
1/2 cup dark Karo syrup
1/2 stick margarine
Pinch salt
4 cups Chex cereal
1/4 cup raisins
1/2 cup peanuts
1 cup Chinese noodles
1 cup Ritz Bits or Goldfish crackers

Preheat oven to 325 degrees. Bring sugar, syrup, margarine, and salt to a boil in a saucepan over medium heat. Mix cereal, raisins, peanuts, noodles, and crackers in a large bowl. Add the syrup mixture and stir to coat well. Pour onto a cookie sheet and bake for 15 minutes. Store cereal mix in a tightly covered container. Yield: 8-12 servings

DELORES DEVORE, Davenport, NE Age 64

CHEESE STRAWS

4 cups grated cheddar cheese
1 stick margarine
2 cups plain flour, sifted
2 teaspoons salt
2 teaspoons baking powder
Dash cayenne pepper

Rules of Thumb:

Four ounces of block cheese equal one cup of grated cheese.

Preheat oven to 350 degrees. Place cheese and margarine in a large bowl to soften. Mix well; add flour that has been sifted with salt, baking powder, and pepper. Mix thoroughly--knead with hands, if necessary, as dough will be stiff. Put dough in cookie press. Pipe onto cookie sheet and bake 12-15 minutes until golden. Do not overbake. Cut into 2 1/2 inch lengths. Cool on a rack. Store in tightly covered container or tin. Yield: 8 servings

Wrap block cheese in a cloth dampened with vinegar to keep it from drying out.

MARY SUSAN SPILMAN, Dawson, GA Age 68

SPICY DILL DIP IN A BREAD-BOWL

DIP
- 1 pint sour cream
- 2 tablespoons horseradish
- 4 ounces pastrami, cut into small pieces
- Dillweed to taste

In a small bowl, combine sour cream, horseradish, and pastrami. Mix well and sprinkle with dill to taste. Chill until ready to serve.

BREAD
- 1 unsliced round loaf of dark bread
- 1 loaf any other desired bread (rye, white, pumpernickel), cut into cubes

Scoop out round loaf to form a bowl. Cube excess bread. When ready to serve, place bread-bowl on a tray and fill with dip. Arrange cubes around "bowl." Yield: 10-12 servings

MARTY ROSE, Georgetown, TX

CRABMEAT DIP

- 1 can lump crabmeat (do not use claw meat)
- 1 8-ounce package cream cheese, softened
- 1 tablespoon horseradish
- 1 teaspoon lemon juice
- 2 tablespoons grated onion
- Salt and pepper to taste
- Dash Worcestershire sauce
- Dash hot sauce
- Few drops milk
- Slivered almonds for garnish
- Crackers

Preheat oven to 300 degrees. In a medium casserole dish, combine all ingredients except almonds. Blend with a fork to mix. (Do not use a food processor.) Use milk to achieve desired consistency. Top with slivered almonds and bake 15-20 minutes. Serve with crackers. Yield: 8-10 servings

DR. CHARLES TOFTOY, Arlington, VA

SALMON LOG

1 8-ounce package cream cheese
2 teaspoons dried onion
1 tablespoon lemon juice
1 teaspoon prepared horseradish
1/2 teaspoon liquid smoke
1 7.5-ounce can salmon, deboned, drained, and flaked
1/2 cup chopped pecans
Watercress for garnish
Crackers

Soften the cream cheese in a medium mixing bowl. Add remaining ingredients except pecans and blend thoroughly. Shape mixture into log, wrap in foil and chill at least two hours. Before serving, roll in chopped pecans. Garnish with watercress. Serve with crackers. Yield: 12 servings

EDITH ANN SALB, Ottawa, KS Age 63

Rule of Thumb:

If the weather turns humid or damp before your party, store tightly-wrapped crackers in the refrigerator to keep them fresh and crisp.

SHRIMP MOLD

1 can cream of mushroom soup, undiluted
1 8-ounce package cream cheese
1 cup mayonnaise
1 package unflavored gelatin
3 tablespoons cold water
1 cup finely chopped celery
1/4 cup chopped green onion tops
2 cans small shrimp, drained (or 7 ounces frozen shrimp)
Crackers

Blend soup, cream cheese, and mayonnaise in a saucepan over medium heat. Cool. Add cold water to gelatin in a cup and stir until blended. Pour into cooled soup mixture. Add celery, onion tops, and shrimp. Pour into a lightly oiled mold and chill 4 hours to overnight. Serve with crisp crackers. Yield: 10-12 servings

HELEN McINTYRE, Tracy, CA Age 71

SHRIMP DIP

2 6-ounce cans shrimp
16 ounces sour cream
1 8-ounce package cream cheese
2 packages dry Italian dressing mix
2 tablespoons lemon juice

Drain shrimp and mix all ingredients together in a medium bowl. Chill before serving. Yield: about 3 cups

MARGERY M. COMPTON, Homer, LA Age 67

GARLIC COCKTAIL OLIVES

1 7-ounce jar pitted green olives, drained
1 7-ounce jar ripe olives, drained
2 tablespoons chopped parsley
4 cloves crushed garlic
3 tablespoons olive oil
1/4 teaspoon salt
Dash pepper

Combine all ingredients. Refrigerate covered several days to develop flavor. Yield: 2 1/2 cups

ANDREA WOOTEN, Green Thumb National Office

PIZZA SPREAD

1/2 pound pepper cheese, grated
1/2 pound sharp cheddar cheese, grated
2 small cans tomato paste
6 tablespoons dehydrated onions
Garlic salt to taste
2 teaspoons oregano
1 1/2 cups mayonnaise
Crackers, English muffins, or crustless bread

Combine all ingredients in a medium mixing bowl, blending well. Store in a covered container in the refrigerator. To serve, spread on crackers, English muffins, or crustless bread and toast until bubbly. Yield: 4-5 cups

DIANE CHAPMAN, Magnolia, AR Age 58

CHILI RELLENOS APPETIZERS

1 brick (1/2 to 1 pound) Monterey Jack cheese
1 brick (1/2 to 1 pound) mild cheddar cheese
3 4-ounce cans whole green chilies
3 eggs
2 5.33-ounce cans evaporated milk

Grate both bricks of cheese. Open and remove seeds from inside of chilies. Combine egg and milk in a small bowl, beating with a fork to blend. Place chilies on the bottom of a 13 x 9 baking pan, cover with cheeses, and pour egg mixture over the top. Bake 35-40 minutes until top is golden brown. Let stand 5-10 minutes before cutting into squares. Yield: 18-24 squares

HELEN McINTYRE, Tracy, CA Age 71

TORTILLA PINWHEELS

8 ounces sour cream
1 8-ounce package cream cheese
1 4-ounce can diced green chilies, well drained
2 tablespoons minced onion
1 4-ounce can chopped black olives, well drained
1 cup grated cheddar cheese
1/2 cup chopped green onion
Garlic powder to taste
Seasoned salt to taste
1 package (5) 10" flour tortillas
Salsa

Combine all ingredients except tortillas in a large bowl. Divide the mixture and spread evenly over the tortillas. Roll up and tightly cover each tortilla with plastic wrap, twisting the ends. Refrigerate for several hours; unwrap; cut in slices 1/2" to 3/4" thick. Serve with salsa. Yield: about 40 pieces

PAT LANGRECK, Neillsville, WI

Food for Thought

I work with children in an after-school program sponsored by the local Boys & Girls Club. "Food for Thought" helps establish good homework habits by rewarding children for completing their assignments. I monitor their progress, and when they meet their goals I order grocery bags full of kid-pleasing foods like cereal, cake mixes, and fruit drinks from a local food bank. I love my job.

Helen McIntyre

Hometown
Saturday
Night

When I was growing up, my mother belonged to a "card club." Several friends took turns hosting rummy and pinochle on Saturday evenings. These ladies had sons and daughters who dropped them off at the hostess' house before going out on their dates. This arrangement discouraged breaking curfews because the teenagers had to pick up their mothers! The hostess always served refreshments. When it was my mother's turn, she would bake her famous coffee cake, but during the lean Depression years she served less-expensive-to-make, but equally famous, yam puffs (recipe on page 174).

Lillian Brouzouski, Urbana, NY Age 72

OPEN-FACE CUCUMBER SANDWICHES

8 slices sandwich-style bread, crusts removed
1/2 cup mayonnaise
2 medium cucumbers, peeled
Shaker of lemon-pepper seasoning

Spread mayonnaise on bread slices; cut into quarters. Cut cucumbers into 1/4" slices. Place a cucumber slice on each bread quarter. Shake lemon-pepper over cucumber. Yield: 48 pieces

ALICE ANN TOOLE, Green Thumb National Office

TEA SANDWICH SPREAD

1 8-ounce package cream cheese
1 bell pepper, minced
1 medium onion, minced
1/2 cup chopped nuts of choice
Dash hot sauce
1/2 teaspoon lemon juice
1/4 teaspoon salt
1/2 cup mayonnaise
Cucumbers or paprika for garnish
Crackers or toast points

Combine all ingredients in a medium mixing bowl, blending well. Store in a covered container. Spread on crackers or toast points. Garnish with a thin slice of cucumber or paprika. To use as a dip, thin with milk to desired consistency. Yield: about 3 cups

DIANE CHAPMAN, Magnolia, AR Age 58

SPICY PECANS

1/3 cup margarine, melted
1 tablespoon Worcestershire sauce
1/2 teaspoon Tabasco sauce
1/4 teaspoon freshly ground pepper
1 teaspoon salt
1 pound pecans or peanuts

Preheat oven to 300 degrees. Combine all ingredients except nuts in a small bowl. Place nuts on a jelly roll pan; pour spiced mixture over; toss to coat. Spread nuts in a single layer and bake 20 minutes, stirring frequently. Drain on paper towels. Yield: 1 pound

ANDREA WOOTEN, Green Thumb National Office

COCONUT-CRANBERRY CHEESE SPREAD

1 8-ounce package cream cheese, softened
1/4 cup whole berry cranberry sauce
1 teaspoon grated orange zest
1/8 teaspoon salt
2 tablespons flaked coconut
Ginger snaps

Combine cream cheese, cranberries, orange zest, and salt in a small bowl, stirring until well blended. Spoon into a serving dish and sprinkle with coconut. Serve with ginger snaps. Yield: 1 1/4 cups

ANNE PERHAM, Neptune Beach, FL Age 65

COCKTAIL MEATBALLS

2 pounds hamburger or ground turkey
2 eggs
1 cup corn flakes, crushed
2 teaspoons catsup
1 teaspoon parsley
2 teaspoons minced onions
2 teaspoons soy sauce
1/4 teaspoon pepper

SAUCE

1 cup jellied cranberry sauce
1 bottle chili sauce
2 teaspoons brown sugar (packed)
1 teaspoon lemon juice

Rule of Thumb:

To freeze meatballs, place them on a cookie sheet until frozen. Place in a plastic bag and they will stay separated so that you may remove as many as you want. This also works well for strawberries and other small fruits.

Preheat oven to 350 degrees. Combine all meatball ingredients in a large mixing bowl, blending thoroughly. Shape meat mixture into balls the size of a walnut. Place in a single layer in a large baking dish. Bake uncovered until brown. Drain off fat. Combine sauce ingredients in a sauce pan. Stir over medium heat until cranberry sauce melts. Pour sauce over meatballs. May be placed in a crock pot or chafing dish for serving. Yield: about 75 meatballs

WANDA M. RHODES, Hillsboro, OH Age 75

Shivaree

Friends and neighbors used to wake up a newly-married couple on their first night home from their honeymoon. We would surprise them in the middle of the night by banging and clanging pots and pans. Then we would have a refreshment party with light snacks, cakes, pies, and beverages. It was our fun way of wishing them well for their future married life.

Adeline Urban, Kimball, SD Age 67

BARBECUED MEATBALLS

3 pounds ground beef
1 cup oats
2 eggs
1/2 teaspoon garlic powder
1 1/2 teaspoons pepper
1 small can evaporated milk
1 cup cracker crumbs
1/2 chopped onion
2 teaspoons salt
2 teaspoons chili powder

SAUCE

2 cups catsup
1/2 teaspoon liquid smoke
1/2 cup chopped onion
1 cup brown sugar
1/2 teaspoon garlic powder

To make meatballs, combine all ingredients in a large mixing bowl (mixture will be soft). Shape into walnut-sized balls. Place meatballs in a single layer on wax paper-lined cookie sheets. Freeze until solid, then store in freezer until ready to cook. Preheat oven to 350 degrees. To make sauce, combine all ingredients and stir until sugar is dissolved. Place frozen meatballs in a 13 x 9 baking pan, cover with sauce, and bake for one hour. Yield: about 80 meatballs

VIRGINIA F. BILLINGTON, Kennet, MO Age 71

BURNING BUSH

1 8-ounce package cream cheese
1 package finely-chopped dried beef
1 grapefruit for serving base

Divide cream cheese into 24 pieces and shape into balls. Roll in dried beef. Insert one end of toothpick into ball, the other end through the grapefruit. Yield: 6-8 servings

ANNE PERHAM, Neptune Beach, FL Age 65

-34-

QUICKIE HAM ROLL-UPS

8 thin slices boiled or baked ham
1 8-ounce package cream cheese, softened
1/4 cup each chopped sweet pickle, onion, and parsley

Spread ham slices with softened cream cheese. Combine pickle, onion, and parsley. Sprinkle over cream cheese. Roll up ham slices, wrap in foil, and refrigerate overnight or until firm enough to slice. Cut in quarter-inch wide slices. Yield: about 8 servings

ANNE PERHAM, Neptune Beach, FL Age 65

SAUSAGE STUFFED MUSHROOMS

1 pound whole fresh mushrooms, cleaned
2 sausage links
1 small onion, chopped
1 clove of garlic
3 tablespoons margarine
1 1/2 cups bread crumbs
1/2 teaspoon salt
Pepper to taste
1/2 teaspoon basil
2 tablespoons oil
2 tablespoons lemon juice

Rule of Thumb:

Store mushrooms in your refrigerator. If you do not use all the mushrooms in a container, crumple a paper towel and put it next to the mushrooms. They will not turn brown for days.

Preheat oven to 300 degrees. Remove and reserve stems from mushrooms. Remove casings from sausage. Saute crumbled sausage, chopped onion, garlic, and mushroom stems in margarine until sausage is cooked. Blend in bread crumbs, seasonings, oil, and lemon juice. Melt 1 tablespoon margarine in a shallow baking dish. Fill mushroom caps with stuffing mixture and place filled side up in dish. Bake uncovered about 15 minutes. Refrigerate until serving. When ready to serve, broil mushrooms about 2 minutes. Serve hot. Yield: 4-6 servings

LUCILLE PETRALIA, Vero Beach, FL Age 67

BEEF TORTILLA PIZZA

1 pound ground beef
1 medium onion, chopped
1 teaspoon oregano
1 teaspoon salt
4 10" flour tortillas
Small amount cooking oil
1 medium tomato, chopped
1 tablespoon fresh basil
1 cup mozzarella cheese, shredded
1/4 cup Parmesan cheese

Brown ground beef and onions in skillet; pour off drippings. Stir in oregano and salt. Preheat oven to 400 degrees. Lightly brush tortillas with oil, place on two cookie sheets and bake for 3 minutes. Spoon beef mixture over tortillas. Place one-quarter of chopped tomato over each tortilla. Sprinkle with basil and cheeses. Return to oven and bake 12-14 minutes or until light brown. Yield: 24 servings

SALLYANN ISBELL, Carey, OH Age 57

VEGGIE PIZZA

This is a really good recipe and it gives a body all the vegetables you could want.

2 8-ounce packages cream cheese, softened
2/3 cup Miracle Whip
2 packages (8 count) crescent rolls
Vegetables of choice: tomato, onion, broccoli,
cauliflower, etc., chopped
1 cup grated cheddar cheese
Dill to taste

Preheat oven to 350 degrees. Mix cream cheese and Miracle Whip in a medium bowl; set aside. Unroll crescent dough; pat together in the bottom of a 13 x 9 casserole dish. Bake 10 to 12 minutes until light golden in color; cool. Cut up vegetables. Spread cream cheese mixture over cooled crust. Generously sprinkle with vegetables; top with cheddar cheese, sprinkle with dill. Cut to serve, refrigerate leftovers. Yield: 24 slices

RUTH HULL, Dexter, MO Age 72

SPINACH-CHEESE BITES

4 tablespoons butter
3 eggs
1 cup flour
1 cup milk
1 pound Monterey Jack cheese, grated
1 teaspoon baking soda
2 8-ounce packages frozen spinach
1/8 teaspoon salt
Parmesan cheese, sour cream, or salsa

Preheat oven to 350 degrees. Spread butter in a 9 x 13 pan. Mix remaining ingredients in a large bowl and pour into pan. Bake 35 minutes. Allow to cool and cut into bite-sized pieces. Serve with Parmesan cheese, sour cream, or salsa. Yield: 20 servings

GLYNCORA WILBURN, Pittsburg, KS Age 79

SWEET & SOUR CHICKEN WINGS

3 pounds chicken wings

MARINADE
3 tablespoons vinegar
3 tablespoons brown sugar
3 tablespoons granulated sugar
2 teaspoons garlic salt or garlic powder
1/3 cup soy sauce (lite is best)
1/3 cup cooking oil
1 teaspoon ginger

Cut chicken wings at joint; do not use tips. Trim off as much fat as possible but leave skin on. Mix marinade ingredients in a small bowl. Place wings and marinade in sealable plastic bag(s) and refrigerate overnight, turning occasionally to distribute marinade. Preheat oven to 350 degrees. Place chicken pieces on a rack over a cookie sheet or broiling pan. Bake 1 hour or until brown. May be served hot or cold. Yield: 10-12 servings

BLANCHE A. SLAUGHTER, Darwin, MN Age 58

Juke Box at the Pine Ridge Diner

When I was a teenager, the Pine Ridge Diner was a favorite local hangout that was especially popular on weekends with the younger crowd. I met my future husband there when I was sweet sixteen. I can remember how we used to work up a thirst dancing to the jukebox that blared out the latest hits. The next best thing to dancing was to take a soda pop break in one of the cozy booths. My husband always ordered the orange crush, but I loved cola pop. I sipped it slowly so that it would last a long time.

Jean C. Davis, Horse Cave, KY Age 70

Breakfasts
& Breads

BREAKFAST AND BREADS

CONTENTS

FRUIT JUICE SPARKLERS

These beverages are refreshing starters for breakfast or brunch.

1 part juice (orange, apple, cranberry, grape, etc.)
2 parts sparkling water (club soda, seltzer, etc.)
Fresh fruit or mint sprigs for garnish

Combine juice and sparkling water in a pitcher, or prepare by the glass. Pour over ice in tall glasses. Garnish with fresh fruit or mint sprigs.

LAUREN FYFE, Green Thumb National Office

FRUIT JUICE FREEZE

Try some of the exotic juice blends: orange/pineapple or strawberry/ kiwi.

2 bananas
1 1/2 cups whole strawberries, hulled
1 cup ice cubes
1 cup fruit juice of choice
2 tablespoons honey

Place all ingredients in a blender. Process until smooth. Yield: 3 1/2 cups

MEDA BAXTER, Pine Hills, FL

A GOOD CUP OF TEA

1-1 1/2 teaspoon tea leaves per cup of water

Heat the teapot just before making tea by filling it with boiling water. Let it stand a few minutes, pour off water, and put tea leaves in the heated pot. Pour 'furiously boiling' fresh water over tea leaves. *Take the teapot to the kettle, never the kettle to the pot.* Cover pot and let tea steep 3-5 minutes. Strain into another heated pot or into cups.

JEANNIE PARKER, Age 75

Rule of Thumb:

"Until the kettle boiling B, filling the pot will spoil the T."

1 pound of bulk tea yields 150-200 cups.

-41-

Rules of Thumb:

*Coffee loses flavor
quickly when
exposed to air.
Keep it tightly
covered and buy it
often.*

*Start with fresh
COLD water.*

*Use one more
spoonful of coffee
than the number
of cups of water.*

OLD-FASHIONED EGG COFFEE

4 cups cold water
1 egg
5 heaping spoonsful of ground coffee

Break the egg, shell and all, into a small non-aluminum mixing bowl.
Mix in coffee grounds and a little cold water. In a non-aluminum
pot, bring the water to a boil. Stir in the coffee mixture. Bring the
coffee back to a boil and turn off the heat immediately. Let sit for
five minutes before serving. The egg mixture is an old-time trick that
causes the grounds to settle on the bottom of the pot, but you may
prefer to strain the coffee through a fine-meshed sieve when pouring
it. Yield: 4 servings

LAUREN FYFE, Green Thumb National Office

MOCHA COFFEE
This is good hot or cold.

2 cups of prepared cocoa
2 cups brewed coffee
1 teaspoon vanilla or 1/4 teaspoon almond extract
Pinch of ground nutmeg
Whipped cream for garnish

*In the 1950's, the
art of making
good coffee was
considered "an
asset to successful
homemaking."*

Mix equal parts of hot cocoa and coffee in a pot or carafe. Add
vanilla extract and ground nutmeg. Pour into cups or mugs and top
with a teaspoon of whipped cream. To save time, instant coffee and
cocoa mixes may also be used for preparation. Use 1% or skimmed
milk when making cocoa to keep calories down. To serve cold,
refrigerate mixture until icy; stir and add a slightly sweetened dollop
of whipped cream just before serving. Yield: 4 servings

LAUREN FYFE, Green Thumb National Office

CINNAMON COFFEE

1 3" stick of cinnamon, crushed
2 cups water
1-2 heaping tablespoons finely ground coffee

Combine the cinnamon and water in a small saucepan and bring to a
boil. Simmer 1 minute. Add coffee and let water come back to a
rolling boil. Remove from heat, cover, and let steep for 2 minutes.
Strain coffee into cups and serve. Garnish with cinnamon sticks.
Yield: 2 servings

LAUREN FYFE, Green Thumb National Office

HOT FRUIT COMPOTE

This is good served at brunch with egg and cheese casseroles or quiches. It is also a delicious complement to poultry.

2 pounds mixed dried fruit (pitted prunes, apricots, pears, peaches, apples, cherries, etc.)
2 20-ounce cans chunk pineapple with natural juice
1 16-ounce can cherry pie filling
1/4-1/2 teaspoon cinnamon

Preheat oven to 350 degrees. Place dried fruit in a decorative oven-to-table crock or casserole dish. Pour pineapple and juice over dried fruit, sprinkle with cinnamon and mix thoroughly. Spoon cherry pie filling over top of fruit mixture. Cover and bake 30-45 minutes. Serve hot. Yield: 8-12 servings

LITA LEVINE KLEGER, Green Thumb National Office

FROSTY FRUIT COMPOTE

3 medium peaches, peeled and sliced
1 cup strawberries, halved
1 cup carbonated lemon-lime beverage
2 tablespoons sugar
1 teaspoon lemon juice
2 tablespoons flaked coconut

Place peaches and strawberries in a 1-quart freezer container. Blend carbonated beverage, sugar, and lemon juice; pour over fruit, seal container, and freeze. Before serving: thaw 3 hours. Spoon slushy mixture into compote dishes and top with coconut. Yield: 6 servings

ANN LIVERS, Loogootee, IN Age 81

BERRY AMBROSIA

This ambrosia belongs to the Scandanavian fruit-soup family, and can be made from several varieties of fresh, canned, or frozen berries. It's best in summer when berries are fresh. Freezes well.

4 cups blueberries or other berries, preferrably fresh
Thin-cut peel of one lemon
1 teaspoon grated orange rind
2 quarts water
1/2 cup sugar
2 tablespoons cornstarch
1/2 cup water
Whipped cream
Ground cinnamon for garnish

Set aside a few berries for garnish. Simmer the remaining berries, lemon peel and orange peel in 2 quarts of water until berries are soft, about 2 minutes. Add sugar and stir until dissolved. Reserve liquid. Strain and put the berries through a sieve or puree them in a blender. Return to reserved juice. Mix cornstarch in about 1/2 cup of water and add to mixture. Simmer 5 minutes. Chill to iciness and serve with whipped cream. Dust the cream lightly with ground cinnamon and garnish with reserved berries. If substituting frozen or canned berries that are packed in sugar, do not add sugar to recipe. Yield: 16 punch servings or 8 cold soup servings

LAUREN FYFE, Green Thumb National Office

SUNNY DAY SOUP

6 whole fresh oranges, peeled, seeded, and sectioned
2 bananas
1 8 1/2-ounce can crushed pineapple
1 small bottle maraschino cherries
1/2 cup sugar
2 ounces grated coconut and mint leaves for garnish

Puree oranges in a blender; pour into a bowl. Puree bananas, pineapple with juice, and cherries; add to orange mixture. Add sugar and stir to combine. Chill. Pour into soup bowls and sprinkle with coconut. Garnish with mint leaves. Yield: 6 servings

MARTIN de BLANK, Age 65

SOUTHERN AMBROSIA

*Do not be tempted to experiment with the simple perfection
of this recipe!*

12 oranges, peeled and sectioned
4 bananas, sliced
8 ounces coconut

Peel and section the oranges over a bowl; squeeze the remaining
orange membranes to capture as much juice as possible. Sprinkle
with coconut and stir to blend; cover and refrigerate until ready to
serve. Add bananas just before serving. Yield: 8 servings

HELEN BERRY, Age 77

BAKED APPLE SLICES

2 1/2 cups flour
1 cup shortening
1 tablespoon sugar, 1 cup sugar
1/2 teaspoon salt
1 tablespoon water
1 egg yolk
1/2 cup milk (approximately)
2/3 cup cornflakes, crushed
6 apples, pared and sliced
1 teaspoon cinnamon

GLAZE

1 cup powdered sugar
Enough water to thin sugar
1/2 teaspoon vanilla

Preheat oven to 400 degrees. Mix flour, shortening, 1 tablespoon of
sugar, and salt in a large bowl. Put egg yolk in a measuring cup and
add milk to make 2/3 cup. Stir egg and milk to combine, then add to
flour mixture. Blend to form dough. Roll half of dough to fit 9 x 13
baking dish, and cover with corn flakes. Lay the apples on top of the
cornflakes, and sprinkle with 1 cup of sugar and cinnamon. Roll out
the rest of of the dough and cover the apples, sealing the edges. Beat
egg white until stiff and spread on top. Bake 1 hour. Combine
powdered sugar with enough water to form a thin frosting; add
vanilla. Drizzle glaze over warm pastry. Yield: 24 servings

JOAN NOAH, Neillsville, WI

Florida Fresh

*My children are
fifth-generation
Floridians. We
made this
ambrosia with
oranges we picked
in our back yard.
These were the
old-fashioned
oranges, though--
the kind with
seeds--so it was
labor intensive to
prepare and we
usually had it on
special occasions.
Although our
family is spread
out now, this is
always one of the
most-requested
menu items when
the kids are home.
They still think
it's special.*

Helen Berry

I visited the Green Thumb exhibit at the Indiana State Fair to learn more about raising plants. What I found was a way to put myself and my bookkeeping skills back to work. I am assigned to the Wells County Veterans Service Office as a secretary. I like to think of myself as a "spicy spinster," and I confess that I'm addicted to romance novels. I also like to feed and watch the birds outside my window. I still make these dumplings on occasion. Without Green Thumb, I could exist, but my job gives me the means to enjoy life.

Lucile Arnold

APPLE DUMPLINGS

2 cups flour
3 tablespoons sugar
1/2 cup milk
2 teaspoons baking powder
1/2 cup butter-flavored shortening
8 medium apples, peeled and sliced
Milk or ice cream, optional

TOPPING

2 cups sugar
2 tablespoons cinnamon
1 cup flour
1/4 cup brown sugar
1 stick butter or margarine

CINNAMON SAUCE

1 1/2 cups sugar
1/2 cup white Karo syrup
3 cups water
1/4 pound red-hot cinnamon candies

Preheat oven to 375 degrees. Mix flour, sugar, milk, baking powder, and shortening in a medium bowl. Place the dough in waxed paper, pat it into a long roll, and divide it into eight portions. In a small bowl, combine sugar, cinnamon, and flour for topping. Roll each dough section into an eight-inch circle and top with 1/8 of the apples. Cover with a heaping tablespoon of topping, add a teaspoon of brown sugar and a teaspoon of butter. Bring up the sides of the dough and moisten with water to seal. Place dumplings on a cookie sheet sprayed with vegetable oil and bake 30 minutes or until golden brown.

To make sauce, combine sugar, syrup, water, and cinnamon candies in a medium saucepan. Cook over medium heat until mixture comes to a boil. Serve over dumplings with milk. Serve with ice cream for a dessert. Yield: 8 servings

LUCILE ARNOLD, Bluffton, IN Age 76

-46-

MOTHER'S DOUGHNUTS

3 tablespoons shortening
2/3 cup sugar
2 eggs
4 cups flour
4 teaspoons baking powder
1/4 teaspoon cinnamon
1/4 teaspoon cloves
1/8 teaspoon mace
1 tablespoon salt
2/3 cup milk

In a large bowl, cream the shortening and sugar. Add the eggs and beat well. Sift together the flour, baking powder, cinnamon, cloves, mace, and salt. Add to creamed mixture, alternating with milk. Turn the dough onto a floured board. Pat to a one-inch thickness and cut with a floured doughnut cutter or floured drinking glass. Fry in deep fat (370 degrees). Brown both sides and drain on absorbent paper. Sprinkle with powdered sugar or a mixture of granulated sugar and cinnamon. Yield: 30 doughnuts

MARGERIE M. CLAYTON, Lapeer, MI Age 65

AUNT LIZZIE'S DOUGHNUT HOLES

1 cup sugar
3 eggs, beaten
6 tablespoons melted shortening
1 1/2 teaspoons vanilla
3 cups all purpose flour
2 teaspoons baking powder
1 teaspoon baking soda
1 teaspoon salt
1/2 teaspoon nutmeg
1 cup buttermilk

Combine sugar, eggs, shortening, and vanilla in a large mixing bowl. Sift all dry ingredients together. Add the sifted ingredients to the first mixture, alternating with buttermilk. Drop scanty teaspoonfuls of the batter, a few at a time, in 370 degree hot oil, turning once. Drain on paper towel and roll in granulated sugar. Yield: 4 dozen

BARBARA LUCAS, Lewisville, OH Age 68

There weren't any nearby "donut shops" in the rural area where I grew up. The ingredients for these doughnuts are all pantry items, so we made our own. It's also a fun rainy day activity.

Rule of Thumb:

Add a tablespoon of vinegar to the oil for frying doughnuts to keep them from becoming soggy and greasy.

-47-

MILK TOAST

This was always the first meal we had after being sick with flu. One old cookbook says milk toast is "guaranteed to cure anything."

1 1/2 cups milk
1/4 teaspoon salt
4 slices white bread
Butter, optional

Heat milk in a small saucepan over low heat until hot but not boiling; add salt. Toast bread and place a single slice in a soup bowl. Pour milk over toast to cover. Add a dot of butter, or butter toast before adding milk. Yield: 4 servings

BLANCHE A. SLAUGHTER, Darwin, MN Age 58

COCOA GRAVY

Serve over hot buttered biscuits or toast for an unusual breakfast.

1/4 cup powdered cocoa
2 tablespoons flour or 1 1/2 tablespoons cornstarch
1/2 cup sugar
2 cups milk
1 teaspoon vanilla

In a medium saucepan, combine cocoa, flour, and sugar, and mix well. Add milk and stir to dissolve. Cook over medium heat, stirring constantly until mixture is thick. Add vanilla. Yield: about 2 1/2 cups

MARY ANN RESCH, Texas/New Mexico Green Thumb

WHEATQUICK PANCAKE MIX

4 cups whole wheat flour
4 cups unbleached white flour
1/3 cup baking powder
4 teaspoons salt
1/2 cup sugar
1 1/4 cups powdered milk
2 cups shortening

Mix dry ingredients in a large bowl. Add shortening and mix well. Store in a plastic container in the refrigerator. For pancakes: mix 1 egg, 2 cups wheatquick, 2 cups water. Yield: 4 servings. For waffles: add 2 tablespoons salad oil to pancake recipe. Yield: 4 servings

FREDERICK LANBAUGH, Niagara Falls, NY Age 69

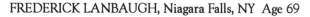

FINNISH PANCAKES (PANNU KAKKU)

2 eggs, well beaten
2 cups milk
1/3 cup sugar
1 cup sifted flour
1 stick margarine or butter, melted
Powdered sugar

Preheat oven to 400 degrees. Mix eggs, milk, sugar, and flour in a large bowl and beat well. Pour 1/2 cup melted margarine in each of two 9" cake pans. Pour half of batter into each pan and bake about 40 minutes. Cool; sprinkle with powdered sugar and slice. Yield: 8-12 servings

HELEN HARRIS, Hancock, MI Age 67

OLD-FASHIONED BUTTERMILK PANCAKES

1 cup old-fashioned oats
1 cup buttermilk
1 beaten egg
1/4 cup flour
1 tablespoon sugar
1/2 teaspoon baking powder
1/2 teaspoon baking soda
1/8 teaspoon cinnamon
1 tablespoon melted butter

Mix oats and buttermilk. Cover and refrigerate overnight. Add egg, flour, sugar, baking powder, baking soda, and cinnamon. Stir in butter. Cook on hot griddle. Yield: 12 servings

MARION CARD, Owego, NY Age 65

Finnish Hospitality

My parents were Finnish immigrants who raised their children with their native customs and traditions. One custom we learned at an early age was always to have refreshments on hand for visiting friends and relatives. This meant strong sweet coffee and baked goods. During WWII when sugar was severely rationed, my sister and I (we were the youngest of 13 children), drank our coffee unsweetened and saved our sugar to bake this Finnish pancake on Sunday mornings.

Helen Harris, Hancock, MI

When my grandson got married, the groomsmen met at my daughter's house to dress. We quadrupled this recipe for their breakfast. The boys loved it and didn't leave a crumb. I work in the kitchen of a local school and really enjoy the young people. I plan to keep working as long as my health holds. Green Thumb is a great service for older folks.

SPECIAL OCCASION FRENCH TOAST

1 cup brown sugar
1 stick butter
2 tablespoons Karo syrup
1 loaf French bread, uniformly sliced
5 eggs
1 1/2 cup milk
1 teaspoon vanilla

Combine sugar, butter, and syrup in a medium saucepan, and heat until sugar is dissolved. Oil an 8 x 8 pan, and pour in the syrup mixture. Layer bread slices over syrup. In a blender, combine eggs, milk, and vanilla. Pour over bread layer. Tightly cover pan with plastic wrap and refrigerate 8 hours. When ready to serve, preheat oven to 350 degrees. Remove plastic wrap; place pan on highest oven rack and bake 30 minutes. Yield: 8 servings

ROSEMARY KAMPA, Grenville, SD Age 70

The Spirit of Green Thumb

I've been a Green Thumb field coordinator for fifteen years. Nothing is more rewarding than seeing the transformation of enrollees when they are placed in jobs--low self-esteem is replaced by confidence, doubt is replaced by hope. To me, this positive transformation is the real spirit of Green Thumb.

Jan McCarron

WISCONSIN FRENCH TOAST

4 eggs
2/3 cup orange juice
1/3 cup milk
1/4 cup sugar
1/4 teaspoon nutmeg
1/2 teaspoon vanilla extract
1/2 loaf Italian bread (cut in 1" slices)
1/3 cup butter, melted
Ground orange peel to taste
3/4 cup pecan pieces

Using a wire whisk, beat together eggs, juice, milk, sugar, nutmeg, and vanilla in a large bowl. Place bread, edges touching, in a single layer in a large baking dish. Pour milk mixture over bread; cover and refrigerate overnight, turning once. When ready to cook, preheat oven to 400. Pour melted butter on a jellyroll pan, spreading evenly. Arrange soaked bread slices in a single layer on pan. Sprinkle evenly with orange peel and pecans. Bake until golden, 20-25 minutes. Check slices during last 5 minutes to avoid burning. Serve with maple syrup and butter. Yield: 4 servings

JAN McCARRON, Plainfield, WI

POTATO PATTIES

Add diced ham or crumbled sausage to this dish for brunch
or a light supper.

    1 medium potato, shredded
    1 egg, beaten
    3 tablespoons flour
    1/2 teaspoon garlic powder
    1/2 teaspoon salt
    1/2 teaspoon pepper
    Chopped green onions (optional)
    Oil for frying

Squeeze juice from the shredded potato; place potatoes in a medium
bowl. Add egg, flour, garlic, salt, and pepper; mix well and shape into
patties. Sprinkle with green onions (or blend into potato mixture).
Fry patties in a small amount of oil in a medium skillet, turning
frequently until brown. Yield: 4 patties

FREDERICK LANBAUGH, Niagara Falls, NY Age 69

Rule of Thumb:

Store leftover
potatoes in a
straight glass;
pack tightly. Run
a knife blade
around the edge
of the glass to
loosen; slice and
fry for potato
patties.

BREAKFAST POTATOES

    6 medium white potatoes
    2 tablespoons butter or margarine
    1 onion, chopped
    2 sweet red peppers, diced
    2 green peppers, diced
    1/2 teaspoon garlic powder
    1/2 teaspoon seasoned salt
    1/2 teaspoon black pepper

Bake potatoes with skins on. Refrigerate until cold. Slice unpeeled
potatoes. Melt butter in a large skillet, and saute onions, red and
green peppers until tender. Add garlic powder, salt, and pepper. Add
sliced potatoes and saute until flavors blend and potatoes are tender.
Yield: 8 servings

MARTHA M. TAYLOR, Breckenridge, MO Age 68

CHEESE AND NOODLE OMELET

8 eggs
1 teaspoon salt
1/8 teaspoon pepper
2 cups cooked noodles
4 ounces grated cheddar cheese
2 tablespoons chopped bell pepper
1 tablespoon minced pimento
2 tablespoons melted margarine

Beat eggs in a large bowl with salt and pepper. Stir in noodles, cheese, bell pepper, and pimento. In large skillet, melt margarine and pour in the egg mixture. Cover and cook over medium heat for 15-20 minutes. <u>Do not stir.</u> Cut into wedges and serve. Yield: 6-8 servings

DIANE CHAPMAN, Magnolia, AR Age 58

CHICKEN OMELET OVER RICE (OYAKO DOMBURI)

Domburi, kona sansho, and nori are found in oriental markets.

3 cups cooked rice
2 scallions, including about 2 inches of the green stems
About 4 ounces chicken breast, skinned and boned
1/2 cup domburi ni shiru
4 eggs
Dash of kona sansho (Japanese pepper)
1 sheet nori, crumbled

Place 1 1/2 cups of steamed rice in each of 2 serving bowls. Cover and keep warm in a 250-degree oven while preparing omelets. Cut scallions in half lengthwise, then into 1 1/2" long pieces. Divide chicken and scallions in half and place in 2 separate bowls. Add 1/4 cup domburi ni shiru to each bowl. Pour the contents of one bowl into a 5 or 6" skillet or crepe pan. Bring to a boil over high heat; reduce to medium heat; cover and cook for 2 minutes. Meanwhile, break 2 eggs into a bowl, stirring just enough to combine yolks and whites. Stir in kona sansho. Add egg mixture to the pan. Cover pan and cook 2 to 3 minutes, or until eggs are lightly set. Slide the omelet on top of one of the bowls of rice and garnish with the crumbled nori. Quickly make the second omelet with the remaining ingredients and serve at once. Yield: 2 servings

JUNKO CLYMER, Owego, NY Age 65

After my husband died, the pastor at my church told me about Green Thumb. Through Green Thumb's job training I have improved my potential for obtaining employment. I work for the American Red Cross at Tioga, New York. I have many native Japanese recipes to share, but I chose this one because both Asians and Americans love it.

Junko Clymer

OMELET A LA RIQUISIMA

1 large potato
4 tablespoons cooking oil
3 slices of cooked ham
1/3 green pepper
6 fresh eggs
6 tablespoons milk
Garlic powder and salt to taste
2 tablespoons catsup
2 rings of medium onion, diced
3 slices American cheese, cut in 1" pieces

Peel and cut the potato into small pieces. Fry in oil in a medium-sized non-stick skillet over medium heat, turning potatoes until all sides are golden in color. Cut up ham and green pepper; add to the potato mixture, stirring to heat through. Beat eggs and milk in a mixing bowl; mix in garlic powder, salt, and catsup. Add the onions and cheese. Pour the egg mixture into the frying pan over the potatoes. Add more oil if necessary. Turn omelette so that it cooks on both sides. Remove from heat and serve with toasted bread, butter, and jelly. Yield: 2-3 servings

MIRIAM D. ROMAN, Cabo Rojo, Puerto Rico Age 60

SPECIAL K LOAF

Slice cold leftovers and use for sandwiches.

3 eggs
1/4 cup margarine
2 cups cottage cheese
1/2 envelope dry onion soup mix
1/2 cup chopped walnuts
3 cups Special K or similar cereal
1 cup shredded cheese

Preheat oven to 350 degrees. In a large bowl, beat eggs; add margarine, cottage cheese, soup mix, walnuts, cereal, and cheese. Pour into a loaf pan and bake 45 minutes or until set. Let stand a few minutes before serving. Yield: 6 to 8 servings

CAROLINE G. SAGE, Zephyrhills, FL Age 71

Farmer's Breakfast

My father was a wheat farmer. As a young girl, I would wake up at 5:30 a.m. to help my mother prepare breakfast for our family of 10. A typical morning meal included pancakes, bacon, ham or sausage, eggs, grits, oatmeal or porridge, and thick slices of homemade bread that Mother toasted on our trusty black range. This seems like a lot of food, but a big hearty breakfast was a must for a farming family that had a long day of work ahead of them.

Betty Lewis, Minatare, NE, Age 72

-53-

This is a very tasty recipe, and it's quick and easy to make. I am mostly a vegetarian and have thousands of vegetarian books and recipes.

DELICIOUS VEGETARIAN QUICHE

1/2 cup cashews
1/2 cup water
1/2 pound tofu
1/8 teaspoon garlic powder
1 teaspoon basil
1 teaspoon salt
2 tablespoons cornstarch
1/2 cup chopped green bell pepper
1/2 cup chopped red bell pepper
1/2 cup chopped onions
1/2 cup finely diced carrots
1/2 cup sliced olives
1 9" whole-wheat pie shell, unbaked

Preheat oven to 350 degrees. In a blender or food processor, puree cashews and water until creamy smooth. Add tofu, garlic, basil, salt, and cornstarch to cashew mixture and blend until smooth. Saute peppers, onions, and carrots. Add vegetables and olives to the creamy mixture. Mix and pour into pie shell. Bake 35 minutes. Yield: 4 servings

ELSIE CLEVELAND, Greeley, CO Age 70

CHICKEN BROCCOLI QUICHE

Variation: substitute ham, tuna, or crumbled bacon for the chicken.

1/2 package frozen chopped broccoli,
    partially thawed and drained
1 1/2 cups boneless cooked chicken, cubed
1 cup grated cheese of choice
1 9" pie shell
3 eggs
1 cup milk
2 tablespoons lemon juice
Salt and pepper to taste

Preheat oven to 375 degrees. Sprinkle broccoli, chicken, and cheese in the pie shell. Blend eggs, milk, lemon, salt and pepper until mixed well but not frothy. Pour over chicken mixture. Bake 40-50 minutes until center is set. Remove from oven and let sit about 10 minutes before serving. Yield: 6-8 servings

FAITH SHERLOCK, Lancaster, OH Age 58

EASIEST, CHEESIEST QUICHE EVER

This rich dish is great for Christmas morning or other once-in-a-while occasions.

4 eggs
2 cups heavy whipping cream
1/4-1/2 teaspoon cayenne pepper
1/2 teaspoon salt
1 tablespoon butter or margarine
1 frozen 9" deep-dish pie crust
1 pound Swiss cheese, grated
6-8 slices bacon for garnish

Preheat oven to 425 degrees. Combine eggs and cream in a medium bowl, and whisk until foamy. Add cayenne and salt. Drop butter into the bottom of the pie crust and fill with cheese. Pour egg mixture over cheese, filling to the top of the crust. Fry bacon until partially cooked. Roll tightly into rosettes and secure with a wooden toothpick. Position rosettes at intervals around edge of pie crust. Place pie on a cookie sheet and bake on middle oven rack for 10 minutes. Reduce temperature to 300 degrees and bake 1 hour. Remove from oven. Quiche should set about one hour before cutting. Variations: add sauted vegetables--onions, asparagus, etc.--to the egg mixture before filling the crust. Yield 6-8 servings

MIKE TOOLE, Manassas, VA

Exotic Fruit for Breakfast

When I was growing up in the late 30's, no one had to prod me to wake up on Sunday mornings. As part of the welfare produce program, the USDA introduced grapefruit to North Dakota and my family (especially me) took to this fruit right away. Mother saved ours for Sunday breakfast. I loved mine with sugar on top.

Hjordis M. Campbell, Valley City, ND Age 67

SAUSAGE STRATA

1 pound hot sausage
1/3 cup chopped onions
6 slices bread
2 cups mozarella cheese
6 eggs
1 12-ounce can evaporated milk
2 teaspoons prepared mustard
Salt and pepper to taste

Preheat oven to 325 degrees. Brown sausage and onions, drain on paper towel and crumble. Place bread slices in bottom of 9 x1 3 baking dish. Cover with a layer of sausage and onions, then mozarella cheese. Combine eggs, milk, mustard, salt and pepper in a medium bowl; pour over layers. Bake for 35 minutes. Yield: 8 servings

BERNICE L. PRIVETT, Beckley, WV Age 71

Annie Baxter's Breakfast Theory

I came from a large family. When I say large, I mean LARGE. My parents had 17 children, but they had enough love for all of us. Every morning, my mother, Annie Baxter, religiously prepared a hot breakfast. She had a theory that school children who started off the day with a hot, hearty morning meal became better students. Her specialty was hot hominy grits with red tomato gravy. We didn't need any urging to scrape our bowls clean before running off to school. In exchange, my mother expected nothing less than A's on our report cards.

Solomon Baxter, Reading, PA

SOUTHERN BAKED GRITS

A favorite breakfast served with crisp bacon and fresh fruit.

5 cups water
1 1/2 teaspoons salt
1 cup regular (not instant) grits
1/2 pound grated sharp cheese
2 eggs, beaten
1 tablespoon butter or margarine

Preheat oven to 350 degrees. Bring water to a boil in a medium saucepan. Add salt and grits and bring to a slow boil and cook for 20 minutes. Set aside 2/3 cup cheese. Add the rest of the cheese, butter, and eggs to the cooked grits and mix well. Pour into a buttered casserole dish and top with the remaining 2/3 cup cheese. Bake 30 minutes. Yield:10-12 servings

DAVID BOGER, Green Thumb National Office,
from his grandmother Martha Anne France

HOMINY EXPRESS

My children would not eat hominy, so, I started to experiment by adding lots of tasty things to it. This is the way they liked it best.

4 strips of bacon
1/2 onion, chopped
1/2 green bell pepper, chopped
1 can white or yellow hominy
Velveeta cheese

Fry bacon until crisp; drain off excess fat and break into bits. Add onion and green pepper to skillet with bacon. Drain hominy and add to skillet mixture. Fry until onion and green pepper are soft. Pour mixture into microwave dish. Spread Velveeta cheese on top and put in microwave to melt (about 1 minute or less). Serve. Yield: 4 servings

FLORENCE W. REEDER, Stratton, CO Age 62

SAUSAGE TWIRLS

Biscuit dough for 8-10 biscuits
1 pound bulk sausage

Mix enough biscuit dough for about 8-10 biscuits; roll out on a floured board to about the same thickness as pie crust. Crumble the sausage over the dough. Pick up one edge of dough and roll. Chill 1 hour or overnight. Preheat oven to 350 degrees. Cut roll into one-inch slices and place on a cookie sheet. Bake 10-12 minutes or until brown. Yield: 8-10 servings

IRENE DAVIS, East Prairie, MO

I made this receipe when the children were small. Quick and easy and no messy skillet to clean. It's good with scrambled eggs.

SAUSAGE BISCUITS

Mixture will blend easily if the sausage is at room temperature.

1 pound hot (spicy) bulk sausage
3 cups biscuit mix
1 pound sharp cheddar cheese, grated

Preheat oven to 350 degrees. Mix all ingredients in a large bowl. Shape into small balls and place on a cookie sheet. Bake about 15 minutes or until golden brown. Yield: about 30 biscuits

WILLIE E. KNIGHT, Sicily Island, LA Age 85

WASP CAKE

1 3-ounce box vanilla pudding
1 box yellow cake mix
1 6-ounce package butterscotch morsels

Preheat oven to 350 degrees. Cook the pudding according to package directions, then add the cake mix. Stir to mix thoroughly and pour into a greased and floured 9 x 13 pan. Sprinkle the butterscotch morsels over the top and bake for 30 minutes. Yield: 24 servings (this cake is so rich, it should be cut into smaller servings)

MADORA F. HETRICK, Williamsport, IN Age 75

I work at a senior center and often make this cake to share with my co-workers over coffee.

*I came to
America from
Worcestershire,
England. I work as
an aide at the
Prospect Avenue
Elementary
School in
Salamanca, New
York--the only
U.S. city located
on an Indian
reservation. I am
a widow, and I
would go mad
alone. This is a
job I can do that
serves a useful
function. The
money I earn
means a lot to me.*

Catherine Spako

COFFEE RING

3 1/2 cups flour
1/3 cup sugar
3/4 teaspoon salt.
1 package dry yeast or 1 tablespoon bulk yeast
2/3 cup warm milk
3 eggs
1/3 cup vegetable oil
1/2 cup brown sugar
1 teaspoon cinnamon

FROSTING

1 1/2 cups powdered sugar
1/2 cup milk
1/4 to 1/2 teaspoon maple extract

Sift 1 1/2 cups flour, sugar, and salt into a large mixing bowl. Add the dry yeast, then the warm milk and beat well. Add the remaining flour, eggs, and oil and beat well. Cover the bowl and allow dough to rise until double in size. Roll dough into an oblong on a lightly-floured surface. Mix the brown sugar and cinnamon and sprinkle over the dough. Roll the dough, jellyroll fashion; place it on a cookie sheet, form it into a circle, and press the ends together. With scissors, snip the top at intervals. Cover the ring and let it rise. Preheat the oven to 350 degrees and bake for about 15 minutes or until browned. To make frosting, add small amounts of milk to the powdered sugar until it is the desired consistency. Add maple flavoring to taste. Pour over cooled coffee ring. Yield: 8-10 servings

CATHERINE SPAKO, Salamanca, NY Age 69

PIKELETS (DROP SCONES)

This pancake-like recipe comes from a sheep station I once visited in Queenstown, New Zealand.

1/2 cup flour
4 tablespoons sugar
1/4 cup milk
1 egg
Pinch of salt

Mix all ingredients in a medium bowl. Use a teaspoon to drop batter onto a hot griddle. Keep them small. Serve with butter, jellies, honey, or syrup. Yield: 4-6 servings

DORINE BLANCHARD, Oswego, NY

CINNAMON PASTRIES

1 loaf sandwich bread (white or wheat)

COATING
    1/2 cup butter or margarine, melted
    1 8-ounce package cream cheese, softened
    2/3 cup granulated sugar
    1 egg yolk
    1/2 teaspoon vanilla
    1/4 cup granulated sugar
    1 teaspoon cinnamon
    1/2 cup melted margarine or butter

Cut crusts from bread slices. Mix cream cheese, 2/3 cup sugar, egg yolk, and vanilla until smooth. Spread cheese mixture thinly over bread. Roll each slice like a jelly roll. Mix 1/4 cup granulated sugar and cinnamon. Dip top of bread rolls into melted margarine and then into sugar mixture. Wrap in wax paper or plastic wrap and freeze at least overnight. When ready to bake, preheat oven to 350 degrees; place frozen rolls on a cookie sheet and 20-25 minutes. These can be frozen indefinitely. Yield: 18 pastries

FERN L. LAWLOR, Miles City, MT Age 80

I operated a bakery for 30 years and baking is still one of my favorite hobbies. This recipe was given to me by an old friend. I have used it often and received loads of compliments.

CHOCOLATE ZUCCHINI BREAD

    3 eggs
    1/2 cup vegetable oil
    1/2 cup applesauce
    2 cups sugar
    1 tablespoon vanilla
    2 cups shredded zucchini
    2 1/2 cups flour
    1/2 cup cocoa
    1 teaspoon cinnamon
    1 teaspoon salt
    1/4 teaspoon baking powder
    1 teaspoon baking soda

Preheat oven to 350 degrees. Mix eggs, oil, applesauce, sugar, and vanilla in a large bowl. Stir in zucchini. Mix the dry ingredients in a separate bowl. Add to the zucchini mixture and blend well. Pour into two greased loaf pans. Bake for one hour. Let loaves sit for at least five minutes before removing from the pans. Yield: 2 loaves

ROSE O'NEIL, St. Regis Falls, NY Age 67

Cooking is what I like to do best, although I don't do as much now as in the past. I brought some of this bread to the school where I work and the little ones loved it--until they heard about the zucchini!

*I inherited a
wonderful
pumpkin roll
recipe from my
mother that I
baked every
Thanksgiving
until a few years
ago when it just
disappeared.
While helping
Green Thumb
sort out recipes
for this cookbook,
I saw my mother's
recipe. I couldn't
believe my eyes! It
had been
submitted by a
lady from
Brownsville,
Pennsylvania,
which is near the
town where I was
born and raised. I
couldn't resist
giving her a call.
Judy True not
only knew my
family, but she
had gotten this
recipe from my
maternal aunt!
This year, thanks
to Green Thumb
and an old family
friend, we will
reinstate our
pumpkin roll
tradition.*

*Judy Davis,
Atlantic Beach,
FL
Age 56*

PUMPKIN ROLLS

3 eggs
1 cup sugar
2/3 cup canned pumpkin (not pie filling)
1 teaspoon salt
1 teaspoon baking soda
2 teaspoons cinnamon
3/4 cup flour
1/2 cup chopped nuts, optional
Powdered sugar

FILLING

1 8-ounce package cream cheese, softened
2 tablespoons margarine
1 teaspoon vanilla
1 cup powdered sugar

Preheat oven to 375 degrees. In a large mixing bowl, beat eggs and gradually add sugar. Blend in pumpkin, salt, soda, cinnamon, and flour. Spread onto a cookie sheet which has been greased and lined with waxed paper. Sprinkle batter with nuts if desired. Bake 15 minutes. While still warm, turn out onto a tea towel covered with powdered sugar. Roll both towel and "cake" into a long roll and cool. Mix filling ingredients; unroll "cake" and spread filling edge to edge. Reroll and chill. Slice before serving. Yield: 8 servings

JUDY TRUE, Brownsville, PA Age 56

PEANUT BUTTER MUFFINS

2 cups whole wheat flour
1 tablespoon baking powder
1/2 teaspoon salt
1/4 cup crunchy peanut butter
1/4 cup vegetable oil
1 1/2 cups milk
4 tablespoons molasses or honey

Preheat oven to 350 degrees. In a medium bowl, stir flour, baking powder and salt together. Cut in peanut butter with a fork or pastry tool until the mixture is like small grains. Add the oil, milk, and molasses and stir just until well mixed. Do not beat. Fill oiled muffin tins 2/3 full and bake 12 to 15 minutes. Yield: 24 muffins

JOSEPHINE TUTTLE, Olean, NY Age 83

BANANA CRUNCH MUFFINS

3 cups all-purpose flour
1 cup packed brown sugar
1 tablespoon baking powder
1 teaspoon salt
3/4 teaspoon baking soda
1/4 teaspoon ground nutmeg
4 large bananas
3/4 cup refrigerated no-cholesterol egg substitute
1/3 cup salad oil
1 8-ounce container strawberry-banana low-fat yogurt
1 1/2 cups banana nut cereal

Preheat oven to 375 degrees. Spray 10 3" by 1 1/2" muffin-pan cups
with non-stick cooking spray. In a large bowl, mix flour, brown sugar,
baking powder, salt, baking soda, and nutmeg. Coarsely chop 1
banana and set aside. In bowl, mash remaining 3 bananas with a fork.
Stir in egg substitute, salad oil, yogurt, and chopped banana. Stir
banana mixture into flour mixture just until flour is moistened.
(Batter will be lumpy.) Spoon half of batter into muffin cups and
sprinkle with 3/4 cups banana nut cereal. Spoon remaining batter
into cups and top with remaining cereal and reserved banana. Bake
muffins about 25 minutes or until golden. Cool on wire rack. Yield: 10
jumbo muffins

MARY A. SMITH, Jackson, MI Age 78

SUGAR TOPPED MUFFINS

1/2 cup oil
3/4 cup brown sugar
1 egg, beaten
3/4 cup milk
1 cup quick oats
1 cup flour
3/4 teaspoon baking soda
3/4 teaspoon baking powder
Sugar/cinnamon mixture to taste

Preheat oven to 375 degrees. Mix all ingredients except cinnamon/
sugar in a large bowl. Pour batter into muffin pan and top with mixed
cinnamon and sugar. Bake for 20 minutes. Yield: 12 muffins

MABEL E. LANE, Dresden, OH Age 85

Sweet Bread

*I am a coal
miner's daughter--
my father worked
mines in Pennsyl-
vania for almost
50 years. We
didn't have much
money, but we
were a happy and
close family.
During the
Depression when
times were
especially hard,
the government
would send sacks
of flour, oats, and
other staples to
mining towns. At
times, plain old
bread was the
only thing we had
to eat for weeks. I
guess that's why
my favorite breads
are the sweet
ones--good
enough to eat as
dessert.*

*Catherine L.
Cavany,
Tunkhannock, PA
Age 72*

Rule of Thumb:

*To keep the edges
of muffins from
burning during
baking, fill one
compartment of
your muffin pan
with water.*

MELT IN YOUR MOUTH BISCUITS

4 cups self-rising flour
3 heaping tablespoons sugar
1 tablespoon baking soda
1/2 cup butter-flavored Crisco
1 1/2 cups buttermilk

Rules of Thumb:

Bake biscuits in the middle of the oven. A heavy or shiny pan helps prevent overbrowning bottoms. If using a pan with sides, turn it over and bake biscuits on the bottom.

Place biscuits close together for soft sides. Place about an inch apart for crisp, crusty sides.

Preheat oven to 400 degrees. In a large bowl, mix all dry ingredients with Crisco until crumbly. Slowly add buttermilk, mixing with hands. (Hint: wrap your hands in plastic sandwich bags.) Mix until dough holds together. Remove dough to a floured board and knead 6-8 times. Let stand 10 minutes. Roll dough to 1/2" thickness. Cut with biscuit cutter that has been dipped in flour. Place biscuits close together on an ungreased cookie sheet. Bake 10-12 minutes until golden brown. While hot, pull biscuits apart and insert a small pat of butter or margarine. Yield: 26-28 biscuits

ANNE PERHAM, Neptune Beach, FL Age 65

SOUTHERN BISCUITS

2 cups all purpose flour
2 teaspoons sugar
2 teaspoons baking powder
1 teaspoon salt
1/2 teaspoon baking soda
1/3 cup shortening
2/3 cup buttermilk

Preheat oven to 450 degrees. Measure flour, sugar, baking powder, salt, and soda into a large bowl. Cut in shortening until mixture looks like cornmeal. Stir in almost all the buttermilk. If dough is not pliable, add just enough milk to make a soft, puffy, easy-to-roll dough. Round up dough on a lightly floured board. Knead lightly 20 to 25 times, about 30 seconds. Roll to slightly less that 1/2" thick. Cut with a floured biscuit cutter and place on ungreased baking sheet. Bake 10 to 12 minutes or until golden brown. Yield: about 12 biscuits

SHIRLEY HEATON, Seneca Falls, NY Age 56

QUICK & CHEESY BISCUIT FINGERS

Everyone is suprised when they bite into the biscuits and meet cheese. These can be prepared 2 hours ahead, covered, refrigerated and then baked.

    2 8-ounce tubes round biscuits
    4 ounces cheese cut in strips
    2 tablespoons butter, melted
    1/2 teaspoon Worcestershire sauce
    1/4 teaspoon garlic salt
    Sesame seeds or 1/2 cup finely crushed potato chips

Preheat oven to 400 degrees. Grease an 8" or 9" square pan. Separate each can of biscuits. Pat each biscuit into a 3 1/2" oval. Place a strip of cheese on each oval, and wrap dough around cheese strip, pressing edges to seal. Place rolls, seam side down, in two rows in lightly greased pan. In a small bowl, combine butter, sauce, and salt. Brush over top of rolls; sprinkle with seeds or chips and gently press into rolls. Bake 18-22 minutes until golden. Yield: 20 biscuits

DIANE CHAPMAN, Magnolia, AR Age 58

QUICK LUNCH ROLLS

    1 cup milk, scalded and cooled
    1 1/2 cups warm water
    1 tablespoon sugar
    3 packages active dry yeast
    2 cups flour
    3 eggs, well beaten
    1/2 cup sugar
    1/3 cup cooking oil
    1 teaspoon salt
    5 cups flour

I was raised on a farm and homemade rolls were a family favorite. Several batches of these were made weekly to feed our farm appetites.

In a large mixing bowl, combine milk, warm water, 1 tablespoon sugar, yeast, and 2 cups flour. Add beaten eggs, 1/2 cup sugar, cooking oil, and salt. Work in remaining flour, and knead dough until springy and smooth. Set aside to rise until doubled. Punch down and cut rolls with a biscuit cutter or a glass dipped in flour. Place rolls on a greased cookie sheet. Let rise until light. Preheat oven to 375 degrees. Bake 12 to 15 minutes. Yield: 24 rolls

SYLVIA WILLOUGHBY, Velma, ND Age 68

SPOON ROLLS

2 packages active dry yeast
2 cups warm water (110-115 degrees)
1 1/2 sticks margarine
1 egg
1/4 cup sugar
4 cups flour

Combine yeast and water in a small bowl. Set aside. Melt the margarine. In a large bowl, cream the margarine with the sugar. Add egg, then stir in yeast until well mixed. Add flour, one cup at a time. Place the dough in a container that can be tightly closed and store it in the refrigerator. Pinch off a "spoonful" of dough, roll it in a ball, and place in muffin pan. Bake at 400 degrees for 15-20 minutes. Yield: 24 rolls

JEAN ADAMS, Albany, KY Age 59

SWEET POTATO ROLLS

2 packages active dry yeast
1 cup cooked mashed sweet potato
3 tablespoons melted butter or margarine
1 egg
1 teaspoon salt
3 tablespoons sugar
5 cups all purpose flour
1/2 cup warm water
1/4 cup melted butter or margarine

Dissolve yeast in warm water per package instructions. In a large mixing bowl, blend sweet potatoes and butter; add the dissolved yeast. Add egg, salt, sugar and blend well. Add flour alternately with warm water. Knead dough on a floured board until smooth. Place dough in a greased bowl and let rise about 2 hours. Punch down and roll to desired thickness. Cut with biscuit cutter or shape into rolls. Brush with melted butter. Place on a greased pan and let rise 1 hour. Preheat oven to 425 degrees. Bake 15-20 minutes. Yield: 30 medium rolls

FRANCES B. LUKER, Lake City, FL Age 78

BOSTON BROWN BREAD

1 cup rolled oats
1/2 cup molasses
1 yeast cake
1/2 cup warm water
1 tablespoon salt
7 cups flour
1/4 cup melted butter or margarine

Pour boiling water on oats and let stand until lukewarm; add molasses. Dissolve yeast cake in warm water; add to oat mixture. Add salt and about 7 cups of flour. Knead. Let stand overnight. Knead down; shape into 2 loaves; let rise until double in size. Bake at 325 degrees for 1 hour. Brush with butter and serve. Yield: 2 loaves

MILDRED M. ZIEGLER, Traverse City, MI Age 87

IRISH SODA BREAD

4 cups flour, sifted
3 teaspoons baking powder
1 teaspoon baking soda
1/2 teaspoon salt
1 stick butter or margarine
1 cup sugar
1 cup raisins
1 cup currants
2 teaspoons caraway seeds
1 cup sour cream
1 cup buttermilk

Preheat oven to 350 degrees. In a large bowl, mix flour, baking powder, baking soda, salt, butter, sugar, raisins, currants, and caraway seed. Add sour cream and buttermilk to make a soft dough. Add more buttermilk, if necessary, to make the dough workable. Knead lightly, divide in two, shape, and place each loaf in a 9" pie pan. Place a cut in the top with a knife or scissors. Bake about 45 minutes. Yield: 2 round loaves

ELEANOR EIGNOR, Phoenicia, NY

Brown Bread & Beans for Breakfast

I grew up in Massachusetts, and every Wednesday and Saturday morning we had hot beans and brown bread for breakfast. This wasn't just any brown bread, but B & M--a commercial brand that comes in a can. You can still buy it. Mother sliced and buttered the raisin-studded bread. It tasted so good with the hot beans!

Louise M. Milstead, Albany, GA, Age 71

Monkey bread is a sweet bread formed by arranging small chunks of dough in several overlapping layers in a pan. Pans of almost any shape may be used. When baked, the chunks cling together to form a solid loaf.

MONKEY BREAD

4 packages refrigerator biscuits
2/3 cup sugar
2 teaspoons cinnamon
1 teaspoon nutmeg
1 1/4 sticks butter or margarine
1 tablespoon vanilla
2/3 cup sugar
2 teaspoons cinnamon
1 teaspoon nutmeg

Preheat oven to 350 degrees. Cut each biscuit in quarters with kitchen shears. Mix sugar, cinnamon, and nutmeg in a plastic bag. Drop cut biscuits, a few at a time, into the bag and shake well. In a greased bundt or tube pan, layer and overlap the coated biscuit clumps. Melt butter; add vanilla, sugar, cinnamon, and nutmeg. Pour mixture over biscuits. Bake at 350 degrees for 35 minutes. Yield: 1 loaf

GLADYS E. BROUARD, Kingston, NY Age 74

BRATSEN

1 cup milk
1/2 cup sugar
1 teaspoon salt
1 package active dry yeast
1 cup lukewarm water
6 cups flour
6 tablespoons shortening, melted

Scald milk in a saucepan over medium-high heat; add sugar and salt. Let milk mixture cool to lukewarm. Dissolve yeast in water per package instructions, and add to milk mixture. Add 3 cups flour. Beat until smooth. Add shortening and balance of flour. Knead until smooth and place in a greased bowl. Cover, let rise until double in size. Roll into 1/2" ropes and make braids. Put in cake pans, forming braided dough into a ring, and let rise about 1 hour. Preheat oven to 425 degrees. Bake 20 minutes. Yield: 2 rings

ED G. ESCHENBACHER, Brainerd, MN Age 67

INDIAN CORNBREAD

1 1/2 cups cornmeal
1/2 cup all purpose flour
4 teaspoons baking powder
1/2 teaspoon salt
1/4 cup milk
1 egg, beaten
1/4 cup melted bacon drippings, 2 tablespoons bacon drippings
3/4 cup fresh tomatoes, chopped
1 tablespoon green chilies, chopped

Preheat oven to 425 degrees. Mix cornmeal, flour, baking powder, and salt in a large bowl. Add milk, egg, 1/4 cup bacon drippings, tomatoes, and chilies to the cornmeal mixture. Stir only enough to mix. Pour into a 10-inch iron skillet that has been heated with 2 tablespoons of bacon drippings over high heat for one minute, then place in oven. Bake 25-30 minutes. Yield: 6-8 servings

MARILYN R. THOMASON, Kingston, TN Age 66

BROCCOLI CORNBREAD

1 10-ounce package chopped broccoli, thawed and drained
2 7-ounce packages cornbread mix
1 large onion, chopped
1 cup cottage cheese
4 eggs, slightly beaten
1 1/2 sticks margarine, melted

This is my family's favorite cornbread. It was prepared it at the County 4-H show, and won the "Intermediate Bread & Cereal" category.

Preheat oven to 325 degrees. Set broccoli out to thaw about 30 minutes before prior to preparing. In a large mixing bowl, add all ingredients and stir to comgine. Pour into a greased 9 x 13 pan and bake 30-45 minutes. Serve hot or cold. Yield: 12 servings

GLORIA CRUMP, Canyon, TX Age 69

GREEN TOMATO BREAD

I love this delicious bread for breakfast. If you wrap it well, it keeps frozen for months.

3 eggs
1 1/4 cups sugar
3/4 cup vegetable oil
1 teaspoon salt
1 tablespoon vanilla
2 cups green tomatoes, grated and drained
3 cups flour
1/4 teaspoon baking soda
1/2 teaspoon baking powder
3/4 cup raisins or currants
1 cup chopped nuts

Preheat oven to 350 degrees. In a large bowl, beat the eggs well; add the sugar, oil, salt, vanilla, and tomatoes. Sift the flour, baking soda, and baking powder together and gradually add to the tomato mixture. Beat well after each addition. Stir in the raisins and nuts. Pour the batter into two greased pans and bake for 45 minutes. Yield: 2 loaves

ELSIE CLEVELAND, Greely, CO Age 70

POTATO BREAD

Rule of Thumb:

Bread dough is considered "doubled in size" when you can press two fingers into the dough and they leave indentations.

2 cups mashed potatoes
3 cups scalded milk
1 cup oil
1 1/8 cups sugar
3 packages active dry yeast
4 eggs
12 cups all purpose flour

Place potatoes in a large mixing bowl. Add milk, oil, and sugar; beat until fluffy. Dissolve yeast in warm water per package directions and add to potato mixture. Add eggs, one at a time. Add flour gradually to make a soft dough. Knead on floured board until dough is shiny. Repeat kneading process. Place in a bowl, cover, and let stand 1 hour or until dough is double in size. Divide dough into 2 loaves and place in regular bread pans. Let rise 1 hour. Preheat oven to 325 degrees. Bake 45 minutes. Yield: 2 loaves

LILLIAN A. PARKER, Lawrenceburg, IN Age 69

ONION BREAD

1 package yeast
2 teaspoons sugar
2 tablespoons minced onion
1 cup warm water
1 teaspoon salt
3 cups flour, hold 1/2 cup for kneading
1 medium onion, diced
Paprika

Mix yeast, sugar, onion, and warm water together. Add flour and mix well. Put in a warm place and let rise until double in size. Shape into loaf (or buns), place in pan and let rise until doubled. Sprinkle with paprika. Bake for 25 minutes at 375 degrees. Yield: 1 loaf

MARGE KLOASTER, Little Falls, MN Age 65

IN-A-HURRY WHITE BREAD

I love to give my family hot home-made bread, but it is just too time consuming. Using a food processor to mix ingredients and letting the bread rise in a plastic bag speeds the process.

1 cup milk
1 package dry yeast
1 1/2 tablespoons sugar
3 cups all purpose flour
1 teaspoon salt
2 tablespoons chilled butter or margine

In a small saucepan, heat milk to lukewarm; add yeast and sugar. Stir and let stand for 5 minutes. Mix flour, salt, and butter together in a food processor. Add liquid ingredients and mix until dough forms a ball. Remove from processor and knead by hand for 30 seconds. Put dough in a one gallon plastic bag; close bag tightly and let dough rise until double in size. Remove from bag and either make one large loaf, or 2 small loaves. Put into loaf pans and let rise until double in size; bake at 400 degrees for 25-30 minutes. This whole process takes about 1 to 1 1/2 hours. Yield: 1 large or 2 small loaves

THEDA MINER, Craig, CO Age 59

Yeast Bread for Special Days

When I was growing up on a farm in Arkansas, cornbread and biscuits were the everyday breads. Yeast-leavened bread was baked for special days. My brother and I always knew when Mother was preparing a yeast bread because we weren't allowed in the house while it was baking in the oven. "Noisy naughty children ruin a yeast bread," she'd say as she shooed us out of the house.

Florene Coogen, Mena, AR

BREAKFAST BREAD

This nutritious bread is very moist and delicious.

2 cups sifted flour
2 1/2 teaspoons baking powder
1/2 teaspoon baking soda
1 teaspoon salt
1/2 cup brown sugar
1 cup quick rolled oats
1/2 cup finely chopped nuts (optional)
1/2 cup buttermilk or sour milk
1 cup applesauce
2 tablespoons oil

Preheat oven to 350 degrees. Sift flour, baking powder, soda and salt together in a large bowl. Stir in brown sugar, rolled oats, and nuts. Combine buttermilk, applesauce and oil. Add to dry ingredients, mixing only enough to blend. Grease and flour loaf pan. Bake for 55 minutes. Yield: 1 loaf

ELSIE CLEVELAND, Greeley, CO Age 70

OATMEAL BREAD

2 1/3 cups boiling water
1 cup dry oatmeal
2 tablespoons butter or margarine
2 packages active dry yeast
1/3 cup warm water
1 tablespoon salt
1/2 cup honey
1/2 cup sunflower seeds, hulled
2 1/2 cups all purpose flour
2 1/2 cups whole wheat flour
Egg yolk
1/4 cup sesame seeds

Pour boiling water over oatmeal and butter in a large bowl and let stand 30 minutes. Soak yeast in 1/3 cup warm water. Add yeast, salt, honey, and sunflower seeds to oatmeal mixture. Add flours to make dough. Knead for 10 minutes. Return dough to bowl and let rise until double in bulk. Preheat oven to 350 degrees. Divide dough in half and place in 8" loaf pans. Mix a few drops of cold water with egg yolk and coat tops of loaves. Sprinkle with sesame seeds. Bake for 45 minutes. Yield: 2 loaves

DAISY COUCH, Springdale, AR Age 73

RHUBARB SUNFLOWER BREAD

1 1/2 cups brown sugar
2/3 cup sunflower oil
1 egg
1 cup sour milk
1 teaspoon salt
1 teaspoon soda
1 teaspoon vanilla
2 1/2 cups all-purpose flour
1 1/2 cups diced fresh rhubarb
1/2 cup roasted sunflower seeds

TOPPING

1/2 cup sugar
1/4 cup sunflower seeds
2 tablespoons butter, softened

Preheat oven to 325 degrees. In a large mixing bowl, combine bread
ingredients in order given. Divide batter between two well-greased 9
x 5 loaf pan. Mix topping together and sprinkle over batter in pans.
Bake 50 minutes. Yield: 2 loaves

ETHEL C. HALVORSON, Aneta, ND Age 72

SWEDISH RYE BREAD

2 packages active dry yeast (2 tablespoons)
1 quart lukewarm water
1 teaspoon sugar
1/2 cup molasses
1/2 cup brown sugar
4 teaspoons salt
1/2 cup vegetable oil
3 cups rye flour
9 cups white flour

Mix yeast, lukewarm water, and sugar well; let stand for 10 minutes.
Stir yeast mixture; add molasses, brown sugar, salt, and vegetable oil.
Mix in rye flour well; add white flour. Knead until smooth; place ball
in a greased bowl, turning once to bring greased side to the top. Cover
and let rise until double in size. Shape into four loaves; place in
greased bread pans. Let rise until double in size. Bake at 375 degrees
for 10 minutes; reduce heat to 350 and bake for 35 minutes. Yield: 4
loaves

BLANCHE SLAUGHTER, Darwin, MN Age 58

Typical Dakota

We apply the term "typical Dakota" to recipes that use North Dakota ingredients. For instance, to bake this bread, I take my wheat to the town of Grand Forks to be milled into flour. My garden provides all the fresh rhubarb I need, and my fields are rich with sunflowers. We take pride in growing, harvesting, cooking, and eating what North Dakota provides for us.

Ethel Halvorson

Soups & Salads

SOUPS & SALADS

CONTENTS

VEGETARIAN LENTIL SOUP

2 medium onions, diced
2 teaspoons olive oil
2 quarts water
1 pound lentils
6 peppercorns
4 carrots, diced
1 tablespoon cajun seasoning
1/2 cup celery
1 medium potato, grated
2 bay leaves
Salt to taste

In a kettle or dutch oven, saute onions in oil. Add water, lentils, seasonings, and vegetables. Bring mixture to a boil, then simmer until vegetables are tender. Add water, if necessary, to reach desired consistency. Yield: 6-8 servings

MARY HODGES, Port Huron, MI Age 64

EASY VEGETABLE SOUP

1 pound stew meat, browned
1 can tomatoes
1 can mixed vegetables
1 can string beans
1 can early peas
1 small can carrots
Salt to taste
1/2 cup water
3-4 white potatoes, cubed

Mix ingredients, including liquids, and cook about 2 hours. Yield: 4-6 servings

E. LANE, West Paint, MS Age 63

Flour Sacks & Bean Soup

My mother was a young house wife during the Depression years. She always said she would never have survived the "lean, mean '30s" if not for flour sacks and bean soup! In those days flour came in huge printed cloth sacks. When times were especially hard, Mother made dresses out of them. She used to smile and say that they were so nice no one ever guessed their humble origin. And as for beans, nothing was cheaper, tasted better, or was more filling and nutritious than bean soup. No one ever complained when she served bean soup three or four times a week.

Sandra Fincher, Moultow, IA Age 56

VEGETABLE DUMPLING SOUP

4 pounds short ribs
3 cups diced celery
3 cups diced carrots
4 cups diced cabbage
3 cups diced potatoes
4 fair sized onions, diced
1 can tomatoes, cut up
2 cans vegetable soup

DUMPLINGS
2 cups flour
1 cup butter
2 cups boiling water
8 eggs

Fill an 8-quart soup pot about 3/4 full of water, add the short ribs and cook over medium heat until meat is completely cooked. Remove meat and set aside. Add carrots, onions, and celery; simmer about 15 minutes. Add cabbage and potatoes. When all vegetables are cooked, add the tomatoes and vegetable soup. Skim and season to taste. To prepare dumplings, melt butter in an iron skillet on low heat, add 2 cups boiling water. (Pour water in fast or it splatters.) Add flour to the mixture, and using a spoon or flat wire whisk, stir together, turning over and over. A ball will form. Continue to stir and cook for 5 minutes. Let cool. Add 1 egg at a time, folding over and over. Drop by tablespoonsful into soup. Cover and boil slowly 20 minutes. Add cut meat. Yield: about 1 gallon

DOROTHY OMEN, Hammond, WI Age 83

CHINA CHOWDER

1 can whole spear baby corn
2 cans mushroom soup
1 can sliced bamboo shoots
1 can sliced water chestnuts
1 can cream style corn

Combine all ingredients in a kettle and add one soup-can of juices from baby corn, water chestnuts, and bamboo shoots. Heat through and serve. Yield: 4-6 servings

ELSIE CLEVELAND, Greeley, CO Age 70

HEARTY POTATO VEGETABLE SOUP

6 medium potatoes, peeled and sliced
6 celery stalks, diced
2 carrots, diced
2 quarts water
1 onion, chopped
6 tablespoons butter
6 tablespoons flour
Salt and pepper to taste
1 1/2 cups milk

Cook potatoes, celery, and carrots in water until tender. Drain, set vegetables aside, reserving liquid. Saute onion in butter. Stir in flour, salt, and pepper. Gradually add milk. Stir constantly until thick. Gently stir in vegetables. Add reserved cooking liquid until soup is desired consistency. Yield: 8-10 servings

SARAH LAWHORN, Albany, GA Age 58

POTATO SUPPER SOUP

1 pound ground beef
4 cups potatoes, cubed and peeled
1 small onion, chopped
3 8-ounce cans tomato sauce
4 cups water
2 teaspoons salt
1/2 teaspoon pepper
Frozen peas or carrots (optional)

Brown ground beef in dutch oven or large kettle. Drain the meat and add potatoes, onions, and tomato sauce. Stir in the water, salt, and pepper and bring to a boil. Reduce heat and simmer 1 hour. Frozen peas or carrots may be added if desired. Yield: 4-6 servings

STANLEY ETELMAN, Jensen Beach, FL

Country School Lunch Program

During the 30's I went to a country school in North Dakota. Back then, we called lunch dinner and dinner was supper. By the time it was noon, my stomach growled and I couldn't wait for the dinner bell to ring. As soon as it did, I tore out of the school house and ran the 1/2 mile distance home. I was so hungry by the time I got there anything would taste good, but my favorite was potato soup. When Mom made potato soup, I declare I could smell it all the way from school!

Patricia Sabot, Washburn, ND Age 65

Bone Broth

*Fall was slaughter-
ing time at our
farm. This was
actually a
neighborhood
social affair and
close friends
helped out. In
return, they took
home a chunk of
our good meat.
My father looked
forward to the
smoked meat,
cured ham, and
the seasoned
sausages. But my
mother loved the
bones. She had a
way of making the
most fragrant rich
broth out of those
bones! I loved it
best when she
dropped home-
made dumplings
into the broth.--it
sure put canned
soups to shame.*

*Eleanor A.
Gierke,
Hutchinson, MN
Age 74*

ZUCCHINI SOUP

Delicious hot or cold--quick too.

2 zucchini, wash and cut ends (do not peel)
1 medium onion
Pinch of parsley
1 regular can chicken broth
10 ounces cream cheese
Dash pepper

Chop zucchini, onion, and parsley. Combine vegetables and chicken broth in a medium saucepan and cook over medium heat for 25-30 minutes. Puree the mixture in a blender. Add cream cheese and pepper, and puree again. Yield: 4 servings

SUZANNE A. WESTERMAN, St. Cloud, FL Age 69

CHEESE VEGETABLE SOUP

*My recipes are tried and true. This family favorite is especially good
when served in a store-bought "bread bowl."*

1 1/2 quarts (6 cups) water
3 chicken bouillon cubes
1 small onion, chopped
3 potatoes, diced
Pepper to taste
1 16-ounce package frozen mixed vegetables, cut in small pieces
2 cans cream of chicken soup
1 pound Velveeta cheese

Dissolve bouillon cubes in water; add onion and potatoes and simmer until partially cooked. Add pepper to taste (no additional salt), mixed vegetables, soup, and cheese. Cook on low heat until vegetables are thoroughly done. Yield: 6-8 servings

CLEVA KERR, Carlisle, IA Age 69

BROCCOLI SOUP

This is a recipe that can also be used with cauliflower. It is a good way to get the nutritional benefits of broccoli even if you don't much care for the taste of it.

3 stalks fresh broccoli
1/2 stick butter
1 cup Velveeta cheese
Milk
Salt and pepper to taste

Clean, dice, and cook broccoli in salted water until tender; do not overcook. Mash the cooked broccoli, add butter and enough milk to cover the broccoli. Add the Velveeta; salt and pepper to taste. Heat until cheese is melted. Serve hot. Yield: 4 servings

DONNA WHITLEY, Eporia, KS Age 70

OLD-FASHIONED CREAM OF TOMATO SOUP

32 ounces canned diced tomatoes
9 ounces chicken broth
1 tablespoon butter
2 tablespoons sugar
1 tablespoon chopped onion
Pinch of baking soda
2 cups cream

Combine tomatoes, broth, butter, sugar, onions, and soda in a kettle or dutch oven. Simmer 1 hour. Heat cream in double boiler and add to hot tomato mixture. Yield: 6-8 servings

KAY WILES, Torrington, WY Age 59

Renaissance Man

I remember thinking how unique my father was compared to the fathers of my school friends. For instance, while my friends' fathers were farmers, my father was a truck driver. Whereas most men wouldn't be caught dead doing "woman's work" in the kitchen, my father prided himself on being an excellent cook. When times were hard and meat was scarce, he came up with an incredible vegetarian black-eyed pea "sausage." But his specialty was chili. Saturday supper was always a big deal at our house. That was the day when Father came home from trucking to cook up his famous chili.

Johnnie Lou Benton, Foreman, AR Age 69

LUSCIOUS LEEK SOUP

Add a thinly sliced red tomato or a sliver of sweet red pepper for color. Make the soup a little thicker and use it as a deliciously different sauce on thin pasta.

1 tablespoon butter
2 cups chopped leeks (substitute green onions or asparagus)
1 quart whole milk (or substitute low-fat non-dairy creamer)
1/4 cup oregano leaves (must be fresh!)
1 teaspoon salt
1/2 teaspoon black pepper
1/4 cup fresh chopped parsley
8 ounces cream cheese
4 ounces cream sherry

Melt butter in a large kettle or dutch oven. Add the chopped leeks and saute until tender, but not brown. In a separate saucepan, bring the milk to a boil. Add seasonings and herbs, and simmer 5 minutes. Add milk mixture to sauteed leeks and simmer 15 to 20 minutes. Cut cream cheese into cubes and add slowly, stirring constantly to blend. Simmer 20 minutes, or until the mixture is smooth and creamy in texture. Add the sherry and stir in to blend. Simmer at very low heat to reach desired consistency. Yield: 8 servings

ROSE L. LARSON, Glenmont, OH Age 64

SPLIT PEA SOUP (SNERT)

1 pound split peas
3 quarts water
1 ham bone with some meat
2 onions, quartered
1 teaspoon parsley
2 teaspoons Worcestershire sauce
Salt and pepper

Soak peas overnight per package directions; drain. Put water in a large kettle or soup pot, add all ingredients. Boil for 30 minutes, then simmer for 2 1/2 hours. Yield: 4-6 servings

HELEN J. DEMKO, Central, SC Age 80

SUPPER SOUP

This is a very filling soup. It freezes well and is easy to warm up in the microwave.

1/2 pound ground beef
1 10 1/2-ounce can consomme
2 soup cans water
2 cups coarsely chopped cabbage
1 large celery stalk, chopped
1 1/2 teaspoons salt
1 large onion, thinly sliced
1/8 to 1/4 teaspoon pepper
3 carrots cut in 1" pieces
1 1/2 teaspoons sugar
1 medium potato, cubed
1/2 can tomato paste
1 1-pound can tomatoes, chopped
1 10-ounce package frozen peas

Brown beef in a separate pan. Put all ingredients, except peas, in a large dutch oven or kettle. Add drained, browned beef and bring to a boil over medium heat, stirring occasionally. Simmer uncovered for 50 minutes. Add frozen peas, cover, and simmer 10 minutes, or until peas are tender. Yield: 6 hearty servings

H. VICTORIA BOYD, Vineland, NJ Age 70

GROUND BEEF AND RICE SOUP

1 pound ground beef
3 beef bouillon cubes
6 cups hot water
1-pound can tomatoes
1 envelope dry onion soup mix
1 cup diced celery
3/4 cup uncooked white rice
1/2 teaspoon oregano
1/2 teaspoon salt

Place the ground beef in a 4-quart saucepan. Cook over moderate heat until meat is lightly browned. Stir in the rest of the ingredients. Bring to a boil then reduce heat to low and simmer for 40 to 45 minutes or until rice is tender. Yield: 8-10 servings

CATHERINE F. RABIDEAU, Mooers Forks, NY

HOT RED CHILI

1 pound lean ground beef
1 20-ounce can hot chili beans
1 tablespoon chili powder
2 tablespoons instant coffee powder
1/4 cup picante sauce
1 14-ounce can diced tomatoes
1/2 teaspoon celery seed
1/4 teaspoon garlic powder or one clove garlic
1/4 cup chopped onion or 1 teaspoon onion powder

Brown ground beef in a large skillet; drain. Add remaining ingredients and spices. Cook in slow cooker or dutch oven over low heat for 2-8 hours. The longer it simmers, the better the flavor. Yield: 6-8 servings

JOAN MUSTER, Greeley, CO Age 63

MOM'S CHILI

I am the mother of four sons and one daughter. They are all grown and always liked "Mom's chili". Whenever I know some or all of them will be home, this is one of the dishes I fix. Not only is it tasty, but it stretches.

2 pounds brown beans (soak 2-3 hours or overnight)
2-3 pounds ground beef
1 small onion, diced
2 small cans of tomato sauce
2 teaspoons sugar
1 teaspoon salt
Pepper to taste
3 teaspoons chili powder (more if desired)
1-2 teaspoons catsup or taco sauce to taste

Cook beans in a kettle until tender, about 3 hours. Brown onion and ground beef together in a skillet over low heat until done (about 1 hour), and add to cooked beans. Add tomato sauce, sugar, salt, pepper, chili powder, catsup/taco sauce, and enough water to make the mixture soupy. Simmer at least 20 minutes. Eat with crackers. Yield: 10 servings

LORENE WANSING, Vienna, MO Age 66

DEPRESSION SOUP

I was young during the Depression, one of eight siblings, and food was not plentiful. My mother served this soup often.

3 strips bacon
3 cups water
2 medium potatoes, cubed
3/4 cup rice
1/2 cup tomato juice (or canned tomatoes)
1/2 teaspoon baking soda
Milk
1 tablespoon margarine
Salt and pepper to taste

Rule of Thumb:

Drop lettuce leaves or ice cubes into your soup or stew pot. Stir, and surface fat will cling. If using ice cubes, remove before they melt.

Cook bacon until crisp and crumble into small pieces. Pour bacon *and* drippings and 3 cups of water into a large soup pot. Add potatoes and rice, and boil 20-25 minutes, or until rice is cooked. Drain off most of the water and add tomato juice or tomatoes. Add soda and enough milk to reach desired consistency. Heat until hot but not boiling. Add margarine, salt and pepper to taste. Yield: 6 servings

BETTY L. LEWIS, Minatare, NE Age 71

SHRIMP RICE SOUP

2 cups sliced fresh mushrooms
1 1/4 cups sliced green onions
1 clove garlic, minced
2 tablespoons butter
4 cups chicken broth
3/4 cup dry white wine
1/2 teaspoon dried thyme, crushed
1/2 cup long grain rice
2 tablespoons corn starch
2 tablespoons cold water
12 ounces fresh or frozen shelled shrimp
2 tablespoons snipped parsley

Saute mushrooms, onions, garlic, and thyme in butter in a large saucepan until tender. Stir in broth, wine, thyme, and bring to a boil. Stir in rice; cover and simmer for 15 minutes. Blend cold water into corn starch and stir into hot broth. Stir in shrimp and bring to a boil. Reduce heat, cover and simmer 2 minutes. Stir in the parsley. Yield: 6 servings

MARION PIEPER, Three Rivers, MI Age 70

I have missed Manhattan clam chowder for years because they rarely serve it in West Coast restaurants. This recipe reminds me of life in the East, fall weather, leaves turning, the smell of woodsmoke, ice skating on ponds, and coming home to this hearty soup served with oysterette crackers.

MANHATTAN CLAM CHOWDER

2 carrots, diced
4 green peppers, diced
4 onions, diced
4 large celery stalks, diced
2 large potatoes, diced
4 tablespoons olive oil
8 cups water
1 16-ounce can tomato pieces
16 ounces marinara sauce
1 tablespoon Italian seasoning
2 8-ounce jars clam juice
4 cans minced and chopped clams
Pepper to taste
Chopped parsley or basil for garnish
Crackers/French bread

Saute all the vegetables in olive oil in a large skillet. Put water into a large kettle or soup pot and add tomatoes, marinara sauce, and Italian seasoning. Add sauteed vegetables and bring the mixture to a boil. Reduce heat and simmer about 25 minutes or until potatoes are tender. Add clam juice, clams, and pepper. Simmer 10-15 minutes. To serve, garnish with chopped parsley or basil, and pass crackers or slices of French bread. Yield: 20 servings

LAUREL MOSS, Mendocino, CA Age 68

LOBSTER CHOWDER

2 1 1/4-pound Maine lobsters
2 cups milk
2 cups whipping cream
1 stick butter

Cook lobsters in boiling water for 20 minutes. Remove lobsters and reserve cooking liquid. Cool lobster and remove meat from claws, bodies and tails. Discard veins from backs of tails. Place shell pieces in cooking water and boil to reduce to 2 cups. Melt butter in 2-quart saucepan over medium heat. Add bite-sized pieces of lobster; stir to coat. Alternately add strained lobster water, milk, and cream, stirring constantly. Cool, then refrigerate overnight to "blossom" and develop flavor. Reheat cautiously and serve with oyster crackers. May be seasoned with pepper or paprika to taste. Yield: 6 servings

JOHN J. WILLARD, Norway, ME Age 61

HARVEST SALMON CHOWDER

1 1-pound can salmon
1 tablespoon vegetable oil
1 cup chopped onion
1 cup chopped celery
1 cup diced potatoes
1 cup sliced carrots
2 cups chicken broth
1 1/2 teaspoon seasoned salt
1/2 teaspoon dill
1/2 cup diced zucchini or broccoli
1 13-ounce can evaporated milk
1 14-ounce can cream-style corn
Fresh chopped parsley for garnish

Drain salmon; reserve and strain liquid. Flake the salmon into a
bowl. In a medium saucepan, heat oil over medium heat and saute
onion and celery until translucent. Add salmon, salmon liquid,
potatoes, carrots, chicken broth, salt, and dill. Bring mixture to a
simmer; cook for 10 minutes, stirring occasionally. Cover and simmer
an additional ten minutes. Add zucchini or broccoli; simmer five
minutes. Add milk and corn. Continue cooking over low heat until
mixture is heated through. Garnish with fresh chopped parsley. Yield:
6-8 servings

JOAN W. LAWRENCE, Alfred, NY Age 63

**Sunday
Soup Supper**

*Every Sunday, we
had chicken soup
for supper. Sure,
every family has
chicken soup, but
my clever mother
had a special way
of serving hers.
She would first
pour the basic
soup broth in a
huge tureen. She
then set the table
with three big
bowls individually
filled with fluffy
rice, homemade
egg noodles, and
chicken meat.
When it was time
to eat, you helped
yourself to the
combination you
wanted. I could
never make up my
mind, so I took a
little of every-
thing.*

*Margerie Clayton,
Lapeer, MI
Age 65*

FRESH MUSHROOM CHICKEN SOUP

Prepared from scratch, this soup reheats very well.

3 cooked breast halves, skinned, deboned, and cut in 1" cubes
4 cups water
1 can chicken broth
1 1/2 tablespoons soy sauce
1/2 cup carrots, thinly sliced
1/2 cup celery, thinly sliced
8 ounces fresh mushrooms, sliced
1/3 cup green onions, sliced
2 ounces uncooked egg noodles
1/4 to 1/2 teaspoon thyme
Salt and pepper to taste

Combine chicken chunks, water, broth, and soy sauce in a large
dutch oven. Add carrots and celery and simmer 10 minutes. Skim top
and add mushrooms, onions, noodles, and thyme. Simmer until
noodles are cooked. Stir in salt and pepper to taste. Yield: 8-12
servings

MARY LOU MARVIN, Oscoola, IA Age 65

CHICKEN NOODLE SOUP

A tasty soothing soup to eat when you are feeling under the weather.

6 chicken thighs
8 cups water
4 carrots, grated
2 celery stalks, chopped
1 small onion, chopped
2 cups of dry noodles
Seasoning to taste

In a large pot, simmer chicken thighs in water until meat is tender
and well done. Remove chicken, reserving broth, and cool. Add
carrots, celery, and onion to broth and cook until soft, about 15
minutes. Bone and dice chicken meat and add to broth. Cook
noodles in separate kettle for about 15 minutes; drain and rinse and
add to broth mixture. Simmer to combine flavors; season to taste.
Yield: 4-6 servings

KAY MEREDITH, Great Falls, MT Age 79

SNEAKY CHICKEN SOUP

1 onion, chopped
1 cup sliced carrots
4 cups zucchini (butternut squash, or other vegetable), chopped
2 tablespoons butter
1 14-ounce can chicken broth
1/4 teaspoon sugar
1/4 teaspoon marjoram
1/4 cup whipping cream or 3 ounces cream cheese
Salt and pepper to taste
Nutmeg or parsley for garnish

In a large saucepan, saute chopped vegetables in butter. Add broth, sugar, and marjoram. Cover and simmer until tender. Pour mixture into a blender and puree. Return liquid to pan, add cream, salt, and pepper. Heat until steamy and garnish with nutmeg or parsley. Refrigerate to store. Yield: 2-4 servings

MAVIS HUFF, Fort Bragg, CA

I call this soup "sneaky" because it is a delicious way to get vegetables down a "meat and potatoes man" or the kids. Variations are unlimited as long as you use a chicken base. Use chicken concentrate for thicker soup. Serve it for a fancy lunch and call it bisque. It is!

SOUP ACCOMPANIMENTS

Green Thumb workers enjoy soups because they're easy to make, and left-overs are easily frozen for future enjoyment or when family and friends drop by. They recommend the following accompaniments to dress up this simple meal:

SPECIAL CRACKERS
Preheat oven to 350 degrees. Brush commercial crackers with soft butter; sprinkle with poppy seed, celery seed, onion salt, or paprika. Pop into the oven until lightly browned.

CHEESE TOAST
Turn oven to broil. Sprinkle toasted bread strips or triangles with grated American or Parmesan cheese. Place under broiler until cheese is melted.

GARNISHES
Drop a few pieces of white-cheese popcorn on top of tomato soup. Minced chives, sprigs of watercress, or chopped parsley are a nice finish to cream soups. Sliced radishes or a dusting of paprika add a touch of color.

The Herbalist's Salad

I developed an interest in herbs back in 1965. Every year, I maintain a beautiful herb garden and I have given many lectures at garden clubs. Once, when my five children were young, I decided to serve them an herb salad of dandelion greens, pods of day lilies, and wild onions. My kids absolutely hated it and accused me of feeding them yucky weeds! It wasn't really too bad, though. The lily pods taste exactly like asparagus and the dandelion leaves have a slighly bitter tangy taste. I liked it just fine.

Tamlin Turner, Ownsville, MO Age 62

CRANBERRY JELLO WALDORF SALAD

This is great to have in the refrigerator as a quick treat for drop in friends. Keep in a covered dish.

1 3-ounce package cherry or raspberry jello
1 cup boiling water
1/4 cup cold water
1 cup diced celery
1 cup diced apple
1 16-ounce can whole-cranberry sauce
1 cup mayonnaise or 1 cup whipping cream
1 cup miniature marshmallows
1/4 cup broken walnuts or pecans

Dissolve jello in boiling water in a large bowl. Add cold water and allow to gel. When cool, mix in celery, apple, and cranberry sauce. Stir in mayonnaise for a salad or whipping cream for a dessert, marshmallows, and nuts. Yield: 8 servings

DORTHY SIMON, Walla Walla, WA Age 81

RED HOT & APPLE COOL SALAD

2 3-ounce packages lemon gelatin
2 1/2 cups boiling water
1/2 cup red cinnamon candies
2 cups thick unsweetened applesauce

In a large bowl, pour boiling water into gelatin and stir until dissolved. Add candies and stir until melted. Blend in applesauce and refrigerate. When partially set, may be poured into a mold if desired. Yield: 8 servings

BLANCHE A. SLAUGHTER, Darwin, MN Age 58

FROSTED APRICOT SALAD

SALAD
    1 6-ounce package orange or lemon gelatin
    1 16-ounce can apricots, drained and chopped (reserve juice)
    1 9-ounce can crushed pineapple, drained (reserve juice)

Prepare gelatin as directed on package. Add fruit, pour into 9 x 13 glass dish, and chill until set.

TOPPING
    1/2 cup sugar
    2 tablespoons flour
    1 cup juice from fruit
    1 egg, slightly beaten
    2 tablespoons butter
    1 cup heavy cream or non-dairy whipped topping
    1/2 cup chopped nuts

In a saucepan, mix sugar, flour, and juice over medium heat. Stir in egg and cook until thick. Mix in butter. Chill mixture. Fold in whipped cream and spread on gelatin. Sprinkle with chopped nuts. Refrigerate until ready to serve. Yield: 8-10 servings

MARY N. BENNET, Clinton, MO Age 77

ICE CREAM SALAD
Holds outdoors for a long time, good at picnics.

    1 cup boiling water
    1 3-ounce box lime jello
    1 pint vanilla ice cream
    1 cup crushed pineapple (drained)
    1 cup grated longhorn cheese
    1 cup grated carrots

Add 1 cup boiling water to lime jello; stir until dissolved. Add ice cream and stir until dissolved. Mix other ingredients and refrigerate. Stir once to mix ingredients evenly. Ready to serve in 15 to 20 minutes. Cut into squares. Yield: 10-15 servings

LUCILLE BLACK, Shenandoah, IA Age 68

AUTUMN SALAD

1 large can crushed pineapple, including juice
1 cup sugar
1 3-ounce box lemon gelatin
1 8-ounce package cream cheese, room temperature
1 8-ounce container whipped topping
1 cup diced apples, unpeeled
1 cup chopped nuts

In a saucepan, bring pineapple (with juice) and sugar to a boil; simmer for 3 minutes. Stir in gelatin and let mixture cool for 10 minutes. Combine remaining ingredients and add to cooled pineapple mixture. Pour into 1 1/2-quart casserole dish and refrigerate until set. Yield: 8 servings

JUANITA EVANS, Dublin, GA Age 73

ORANGE-APRICOT SALAD

This salad is a little on the tart side. A not-so-sweet salad is best with some meals.

2 1-pound cans apricots
2 3-ounce packages orange or apricot jello
1 6-ounce can frozen orange juice concentrate
2 tablespoons lemon juice
7 ounces lemon-lime soda

Drain apricots and reserve juice. In a medium saucepan, bring 1 1/2 cups juice to boil. Add jello and stir until dissolved. Puree apricots in a blender. Add remaining apricot juice and apricot puree to jello mixture. Add orange juice and lemon juice, stir until completely combined. Add soda by pouring down side of kettle. Pour mixture into a mold and chill until set. Yield: 10-12 servings

NORMA LAYTON, Chester, MT Age 64

SALAD DRESSINGS

Green Thumbs in the Kitchen share favorite homemade dressings.

FRENCH DRESSING

    1 tablespoon sugar
    1 teaspoon salt
    1 teaspoon paprika
    1 teaspoon mustard
    1/4 teaspoon pepper
    1/4 cup mild vinegar or lemon juice
    3/4 cup salad oil
    Few drops onion juice or clove garlic

Mix all ingredients in a jar; shake well to combine. Keep refrigerated. Shake to remix before using. Yield: 1 cup

SWEET FRENCH DRESSING

To 1/2 cup commercial French dressing, add 2 tablespoons sifted powdered sugar or 2 tablespoons honey. Mix well. Yield: 1/2 cup

CITRUS DRESSING

    1/2 cup currant jelly
    4 tablespoons salad oil
    2 tablespoons lemon juice
    Dash of salt
    Few drops onion juice

In a small bowl, beat jelly with a fork until smooth. Add remaining ingredients; continue beating until smooth. Yield: 1/2 cup

CARROT SALAD

    1 8-ounce can crushed pineapple
    2 tablespoons mayonnaise
    1 1/2 cups shredded carrot
    1/4 cup coconut
    1 tablespoon sugar
    1/2 cup raisins

Drain pineapple, reserving juice. In a jar or small bowl, combine juice and mayonnaise; shake or mix until smooth. Combine all other ingredients in a salad bowl. Pour in juice mixture and toss gently to coat. Chill before serving. Yield: 4 servings.

FLOSSIE WILLIAMS, Charleston, MO

Grandma's Tennessee Poke Salad

As a little girl, I loved visiting my grandparents in Tennessee. My grandmother was a wonderful old-fashioned cook, and I always looked forward to eating a big plate of wilted greens that she called poke salad. She would go into the fields and gather poke, mustard, and turnip greens. She then boiled the greens and seasoned them with salt, black pepper, bits of bacon, and bacon drippings. Eaten with fresh butter, poke salad made a wonderful supper.

Betty Schlobohm, Marianna, FL Age 67

Pickles, the Winter Salad

During the spring and summer months we had plenty of garden greens to eat. My favorite was a baby lettuce salad dressed with my mother's cream dressing. She shook fresh cream, vinegar, salt, black pepper, and a dash of sugar, and coated the tender leaves. It was mouth-watering good. During the winter months, though, we weren't so lucky. We didn't have fancy grocery stores where we could buy lettuce. We did, however, have pickles. With the repetitive winter diet of canned and salted meat, potatoes, beans, and bread, pickles always had a way of waking up the tired taste buds. My mother called them her dependable winter salad.

Eleanor Gierke, Hutchinson, MN Age 74

CAULIFLOWER SALAD

DRESSING

    2 cups mayonnaise or salad dressing
    1/4 cup sugar
    1/3 cup grated Parmesan cheese

In a jar, combine ingredients and refrigerate overnight.

SALAD

    1 head cauliflower, sliced
    1 head lettuce, torn into bite size pieces
    1 medium onion, diced
    6-8 slices bacon, fried crisp and crumbled

In a salad bowl, toss vegetables to mix. Shake dressing to remix and pour over salad. Garnish with bacon. (Do not add dressing and bacon until ready to serve.) Yield: 8 servings

CAROLE KINCAID, Beattyville, KY

SUMMER GARDEN SURPRISE
Even grown kids still ask for it.

    2 onions
    3 cucumbers, peeled
    3 tomatoes, skin removed if desired
    1 cup salad dressing
    2 tablespoons vinegar
    1/2 cup milk

Dice all vegetables and place in a large bowl. In a jar or smaller bowl, mix salad dressing, vinegar, and milk. Blend thoroughly and pour over vegetables. Chill. Servings: 8-10.

BARBARA BEISNER, Oberlin, KS Age 62

7-LAYER SALAD

A wonderful summertime main dish.

10 ounces fresh spinach, washed and torn into bite-size pieces
1 head leaf lettuce, washed and torn into bite-size pieces
4-6 hard boiled eggs, sliced
1 1/2 cups frozen peas, thawed
1 pound bacon, fried and crumbled
4-6 green onions, chopped
1 pint mayonnaise
    (or equal parts mayonnaise and salad dressing)
6 ounces Swiss cheese, grated

Place ingredients in a clear bowl or oblong clear dish in the order given. (Each layer may be sprinkled with salt, pepper, and sugar for extra flavor.) Spread mayonnaise (or mayonnaise mixture) generously over top layer. Top with cheese and cover with plastic wrap. Refrigerate overnight. Servings: 8

LILLIAN BAUER, New Leipzig, ND Age 83

WARMED POTATO SALAD

6 bacon slices
6 red potatoes, peeled and cubed
2 cups onion, chopped
2/3 cup chopped celery
2 large carrots, chopped
1 cup water
1 1/2 teaspoons salt
1 teaspoon sugar
1/4 teaspoon pepper
1/4 cup flour
4 cups milk
1/2 pint whipping cream or 1 cup sour cream

In large skillet, fry bacon until crisp. Remove bacon from pan and crumble. Set aside. Add vegetables, water, salt, sugar, and pepper to bacon drippings. Cook covered 20-25 minutes until vegetables are tender. Blend flour with 1 cup milk until smooth. Add to cooked vegetables along with remainder of milk. Cook over medium heat 10-15 minutes, stirring occasionally. When thickened, add cream and bacon crumbles. Garnish with chives. Yield: 10 servings

FLORENCE E HEISLER, Pelican Rapids, MN Age 71

I am a Native American resident of South Dakota. I enjoy bowling, scrabble, card playing, and traveling--especially by air. I miss the scenery, but I need more time with my families. I have four daughters and 38 grandchildren, great grandchildren, and great-great grandchildren. I love them all. I also love my Green Thumb job as receptionist in a county nursing home.

NEW MEXICO POTATO SALAD

4 large potatoes, boiled until firm and diced
4 hard boiled eggs, diced
5 green onion stalks
6 large green chilies
2 cups mayonnaise
Salt and pepper to taste
Pimiento for garnish

Place diced potatoes and eggs in a large bowl. Add chopped onion stalks and chilies. Fold in mayonnaise and coat mixture well. Add salt and pepper to taste. Garnish with thin strips of green chilies and/or pimiento. Yield: 8 servings

TORY HOBBIT, Martin, SD Age 84

BARLEY AND BROCCOLI SALAD

2/3 cup quick barley
3 cups salted water
1 large bunch broccoli
1 cup raisins
1/2 cup diced red onion
1 cup roasted sunflower seeds
10 strips bacon, fried crisp and crumbled

DRESSING

1/2 cup sugar
2 teaspoons white vinegar
3/4 cup mayonnaise

Cook barley for 10 minutes according to package directions, drain and rinse. Chill. Cut broccoli into florettes. Combine barley, broccoli, raisins, onion, and sunflower seeds. In a small bowl or jar, combine dressing ingredients. Mix or shake. Just before serving, pour dressing over salad and top with bacon. Yield: 8 servings

MONNA NESTRUD, Mora , MN Age 67

TOMATO-AVOCADO SALAD

3 medium tomatoes
1 large avocado, peeled
2 teaspoons chopped onion

DRESSING

2 teaspoons vinegar
4 teaspoons oil
1/4 teaspoon ginger
1/2 teaspoon salt
2 teaspoon sugar

Cut tomatoes and avocados in thin wedges. In a small bowl or jar, mix or shake dressing ingredients to combine. Just before serving, toss salad with onion and dressing. Yield: 4 servings

EMILY SNOW, Age 66

Rule of Thumb:

To make avocados ripen faster, bury them in flour.

SOUTHWEST SALAD

1 can kidney beans with juice
1 8-ounce can chick peas
1 bottle Catalina dressing
1 onion, chopped
1/2 head lettuce
2 medium tomatoes
2 avocados
6 green onions
1 cup croutons
Corn chips, crumbled

Mix kidney beans and juice, chick peas, Catalina dressing, and chopped onion in a large salad bowl. Set aside. Tear lettuce into bite size pieces; chop tomatoes, avocados, and green onions and add to salad bowl mixture. Toss to coat; sprinkle croutons and corn chips on top.

KENNY HARRILL, Jesup, GA Age 32

MARINATED ORIENTAL SALAD

1 No. 2 can tiny peas
1 No. 2 can french-cut green beans
1 can water chestnuts (sliced)
1 can Chinese vegetables
1 jar chopped pimentos
1 cup chopped onion
1 cup chopped celery
1 cup sliced mushrooms
1 cup sugar
2/3 cup white vinegar
1/4 cup oil

In a colander, drain the peas, beans, water chestnuts, Chinese vegetables, and pimentos. Add onion, celery and mushrooms; put in large bowl and add sugar. Let sit for 1 hour; add vinegar and oil. Cover and refrigerate overnight. Yield: 6-8 servings

ELOISE CALVIN, Drunright, OK Age 75

CUCUMBER SALAD
This is good with any meal.

4 cucumbers
1 sweet Spanish onion, sliced
1 quart salted ice water
1 cup sugar
1 cup water
1/2 cup vinegar
1/2 cup oil
Pinch of celery seed

Rule of Thumb:

The salted ice water bath gives the cucumbers a pleasant transparency.

Peel cucumbers, and score lengthwise with tines of fork all around. Slice cucumbers thinly and place in salted ice water. Slice the onion, separate into rings, add to water with cucumbers, and let stand 1-2 hours. Cook sugar and water over low heat in a small saucepan until sugar is dissolved. Cool. Add vinegar, oil, and celery seed to cooled syrup and mix well. Drain and rinse cucumber and onion slices. Pour cooked mixture over vegetables and refrigerate 12 hours to overnight. Store in a wide mouth jar, crock, or covered casserole container. Yield: 8-10 servings

WANDA REEVES, Ada, OK Age 70

BROCCOLI SALAD

4 cups chopped broccoli
12 slices bacon, fried crisp and crumbled
1/2 cup red onion, chopped
1 cup red grapes, cut in half

DRESSING

1 cup salad dressing or mayonnaise
1 1/2 teaspoons vinegar
1/2 cup sunflower seeds or chopped nuts
2 teaspoons sugar

In a medium bowl, combine salad ingredients and toss gently. Mix dressing in a jar or small bowl and add to salad. Chill before serving. Yield: 4 servings

ROBERTA WARNER, Auburndale, FL Age 66

GERMAN SLAW

1 large head cabbage, shredded
1 large onion, sliced and separated into rings
1 cup sugar
1 teaspoon mustard
1 teaspoon celery seed
1 cup white vinegar
2 teaspoons sugar
3/4 cup salad oil

In a large bowl, mix cabbage and onions with sugar; let stand. In a saucepan, mix mustard, celery seed, vinegar, sugar ,and oil and boil 3 minutes. Pour over slaw. Allow to stand in refrigerator overnight. Yield: 6-8 servings

MARTHA LAMB, Aileen, SC Age 72

Sliced Salads

Today we have all sorts of green salads--Caesar salad, chef's salad, garden salad, Cobb salad, just to name a few. Back when I was growing up, I don't remember having leafy salads like these. We had what we called sliced salads. This was simply a big platter of garden vegetables seasoned with salt, black pepper, and sometimes a splash of vinegar. Our family's favorite sliced salad consisted of tomatoes, onions, and cucumbers. We would have this at supper with a meat dish. It was wonderfully plain and simple.

Louise Cox,
Waxahachie, TX
Age 73

-97-

FLUFFY FRUIT SALAD

2 20-ounce cans crushed pineapple
2/3 cup sugar
2 tablespoons all purpose flour
2 eggs, lightly beaten
1/4 cup orange juice
3 tablespoons lemon juice
1 tablespoon vegetable oil
2 17-ounce cans fruit cocktail, drained
2 cans mandarin oranges, drained
2 bananas, sliced
1 cup heavy cream, whipped

Drain pineapple, reserving 1 cup juice. In a small saucepan, combine reserved juice, sugar, flour, eggs, orange juice, lemon juice, and oil. Bring to a boil, stirring constantly. Boil for 1 minute, remove from heat and let cool. In a salad bowl, combine the pineapple, fruit cocktail, oranges, and bananas. Fold in whipped cream and cooled sauce. Chill several hours before serving. Yield: 12-16 servings

PAULINE SMITH, Ochlocknee, GA Age 74

CHERRY SALAD
Very rich.

1 8-ounce carton whipped topping
1 can cherry pie filling
1 8-ounce can crushed pineapple
1 14-ounce can sweetened condensed milk
1 cup chopped nuts
Optional: 1 cup miniature marshmallows, 1 teaspoon almond extract, 1/4 cup lemon juice

Combine all ingredients in a large bowl, stirring to mix well. Pour into a 9 x 13" pan; chill overnight. Yield: 8 servings

JANICE BRAMWELL, Buffalo, MO and
DOROTHY BREMNER, Redwing, MN Age 77

APPLE-SNICKER SALAD

The tartness and sweetness make a good combination in this novelty salad.

    1 8-ounce carton non-dairy whipped topping
    6-8 apples, peeled and diced
    4 (2.7 oz) Snicker Bars, diced

Combine all ingredients in a large mixing bowl. Chill and serve. Yield: 12 servings

LORNA SAND, Ellendale, ND Age 68

BANANA PINEAPPLE FREEZE

Also a great light dessert.

    5 bananas mashed
    4 tablespoons lemon juice
    1 1/2 cups sugar
    1 20-ounce can crushed pineapple, drained
    1 large carton whipped topping

In a large bowl, thoroughly combine the first 3 ingredients. Fold in pineapple and whipped topping. Pour into 13 x 9" glass dish and freeze. May be topped with pecans. Cut in squares to serve. Yield: 16-20 servings

JANIS STILWELL, Nocona, TX Age 64

ANYTIME ORANGE SALAD

    12 ounces dry cottage cheese
    6 ounces dry orange jello
    16 ounces mandarin oranges, drained
    9 ounces non-dairy whipped topping

Mix cottage cheese and jello in a medium bowl. Add oranges and fold in whipped topping. Chill before serving. Yield: 8 servings

MARION COVELL, Norwich, NY Age 75

Muskmelons

My mother was an amazing gardner. Every year she made a point of growing at least one new thing. One year, to our delight, she planted muskmelons and they turned out big and juicy. That summer, Mother served those melons in a variety of ways, but my favorite was with a scoop of vanilla ice cream. Muskmelons are actually cantaloupes.

Mildred Moen, Canton, SD, Age 78

LIME LOVER'S SALAD

1 large package lime jello
1 8-ounce carton cottage cheese
1 tablespoon mayonnaise
1 tablespoon sugar
1 small can crushed pineapple, drained
1 8-ounce package chopped pecans

Combine all ingredients in a large mixing bowl. Cover and refrigerate overnight. Yield: 8 servings

JEAN STARKEY, Pasgah, AL Age 55

APPLE BANANA SALAD

4 apples, peeled and chopped
2 bananas, sliced
1 cup chopped celery

LEMON DRESSING
1/2 cup water
1/2 cup lemon juice
1 egg, beaten
1/2 cup sugar

Toss fruit and celery together in a medium mixing bowl. In a sauce-pan, combine lemon dressing ingredients over medium heat; stir constantly until thick. Cool. Add to fruit, chill and serve. Yield: 6 servings

CATHERINE P. LAW, Rocky Mount, VA Age 74

CHERRY-CANTALOUPE SALAD

24 Bing cherries, pits removed
4 ounces cream cheese, softened
Lettuce cups
24 cantaloupe balls
Sweet French dressing, raspberry vinagrette, or poppy seed
    dressing
Sprigs of mint for garnish

Fill cherries with cream cheese. Refrigerate. Arrange in lettuce cups with equal number of cantaloupe balls. Drizzle with dressing; garnish with mint. Yield: 4 servings

HELEN BERRY, Age 77

BANANA SALAD

SAUCE
2 eggs, beaten
1 1/3 cups sugar
1 1/3 cups milk
2 tablespoons flour
1/2 stick margarine
1/3 cup vinegar

2 to 2 1/2 lbs. bananas
Crushed nuts

Rule of Thumb:

Put salad plates or bowls in the refrigerator to chill 15-20 minutes prior to serving.

Combine the sauce ingredients in a medium saucepan; cook over medium heat 15 minutes or until thick, stirring constantly. Cool. Slice bananas and layer with sauce and nuts in a serving bowl. Continue until all bananas are used. Yield: 6 servings

RUTH E. DAVIS, Crawfordsville, IN Age 63

POPCORN SALAD

1/2 cup sliced green onions
1 cup diced celery
3/4-1 cup mayonnaise
3/4 cup crisp fried bacon, or bacon bits
1 cup grated cheese of your choice
1/2 cup sliced water chestnuts
6 cups popped corn
Lettuce
Additional grated cheese for garnish

Combine first six ingredients in a large bowl. Mix in popcorn and stir to coat. Serve on a bed of lettuce, and garnish with additional grated cheese. Yield: 8-10 servings

WINONA SNIDER, Montrose, CO Age 65

STRAWBERRY-PRETZEL SALAD

CRUST
2 2/3 cups crushed pretzels
2 teaspoons sugar
3/4 cup melted margarine

CREAM CHEESE LAYER
1 8-ounce package cream cheese
1 cup sugar
1 large container non-dairy whipped topping

GELATIN/STRAWBERRY LAYER
1 6-ounce package strawberry gelatin
2 cups boiling water
2 16-ounce packages frozen strawberries

Rule of Thumb:

Store dry fresh strawberries, stems in place, in a colander in the refrigerator. Wash when ready to use; the berries will stay firm for several days.

Preheat oven to 375 degrees. Mix the crust ingredients together and press into a 9 x 13" pan. Bake for 10 minutes. Mix the cream cheese layer ingredients together and spread over the cooled pretzel crust. Dissolve gelatin in boiling water and add strawberries. When gelatin mixture is partially set, cover the cream cheese mixture with the gelatin mixture and chill for an hour. Yield: 6-8 servings

VIANNA BOGWELL, Covington, OH Age 72

FRUIT SALAD COMBINATIONS
Green Thumbs in the Kitchen recommend favorite fruit salad combinations that are both attractive and easy to prepare.

Roll banana slices in chopped nuts; arrange with orange slices.

Press pistachio nuts in cream cheese balls. Arrange on apricot halves.

Spread cream cheese on fresh pineapple spears and garnish with strawberries.

Stick salted almonds or peanuts into canned pear halves. Arrange on lettuce leaves.

Mix minced celery with mayonnaise. Spoon into the hollows of peach or pear halves. Sprinkle with paprika, chopped pistachios, or toasted almonds.

Combine balls of cantaloupe, watermelon, and honeydew melon.

Mix mayonnaise and cut-up dates in softened cream cheese. Spoon onto slices of pineapple.

SZECHUAN SHRIMP WITH PEA PODS

The tender shrimp contrast beautifully with the crisp green pea pods.

1 pound raw shrimp, shelled
3 tablespoons commercial stir fry sauce
2 teaspoons corn starch
2 tablespoons ginger stir fry oil
2 tablespoons minced garlic
1/4 pound fresh pea pods, stems and strings removed
1 5-ounce can sliced water chestnuts

Mix shrimp with stir fry sauce and corn starch. Heat oil in wok or frying pan over medium heat. Add shrimp mixture to oil and stir constantly for two minutes, or until shrimp is no longer translucent (add 1-3 tablespoons of water if mixture becomes too thick). Add garlic, pea pods, and drained water chestnuts; stir 2 minutes. Serve hot or cold. Yield: 4 servings

BETTIE ARMONTROUT, Pryor, OK Age 67

TUNA ANTIPASTO

1 6-ounce jar marinated artichoke hearts, undrained
1 8-ounce can garbanzo beans, drained
1/4 cup seedless raisins
1 teaspoon cider vinegar
1/8 teaspoon dillweed
1 7-ounce can chunk light tuna, drained
1/4 cup thinly sliced red onion
4 lettuce cups
4 hard boiled eggs, halved lengthwise

BLEU CHEESE DRESSING

1/3 cup dairy sour cream
2 tablespoons crumbled bleu cheese
1 teaspoon cider vinegar

In a medium bowl, combine and toss the artichoke hearts, garbanzo beans, raisins, vinegar, and dillweed. Add the tuna and onion, mixing gently. Chill 1 hour. In a jar, combine the salad dressing ingredients. Spoon the salad into lettuce cups and drizzle with dressing. Garnish each salad with egg halves. Yield: 4 servings

GLADYS E. BROVARD, Kingston, NY Age 74

AVOCADO-SEAFOOD SALAD

PER PERSON
1 avocado half, peeled
Lettuce cup
1/2 cup crab, shrimp, or other seafood salad
1 tablespoon mayonnaise
Garnish with sieved hard-cooked egg, watercress, radish roses,
Large ripe olives

Place avocado on lettuce. Spoon crabmeat into avocado cavity. Place mayonnaise to one side. Arrange garnishes. Pretty as a picture!

M.L. FAUST, Age 74

HEAVENLY TAHITIAN CHICKEN SALAD
California memories.

3 1/2 cups cold cooked chicken
2/3 cup sliced celery
2 sliced green onions
1 small apple, diced
3 tablespoons sliced almonds
2 tablespoons water chestnuts

DRESSING
2 tablespoons chopped chutney (Major Grey's)
1/2 teaspoon garlic salt
1/8 teaspoon cayenne pepper
1/2 teaspoon prepared mustard
2 teaspoons fresh lemon or lime juice
1 teaspoon curry powder

4 warmed croissants

In a medium bowl, combine salad ingredients. Mix dressing in a jar or small bowl and add to salad. Toss gently to coat. Serve on warm croissants. Yield: 4 servings

SHIRLEY J. ERICKSON, Mt. Holly Springs, PA Age 72

I think I keep youthful and energetic through my work at the Carlisle Senior Center. I am a kitchen supervisor, greet guests, teach line dancing on Mondays, crafts on Wednesdays, and Tai Chi on Fridays. You can say that I'm a jack of all trades. This Heavenly Tahitian Chicken is especially nice for a romantic picnic.

HOT CHICKEN SALAD

2 cups diced cooked chicken
1/4 cup sweet pickle relish
1 cup chopped celery
1/4 cup blanched slivered almonds
2 teaspoons chopped onion
1/2 cup crushed potato chips
1/2 cup grated cheese of choice
Parsley flakes for garnish

DRESSING

2/3 cup low-fat mayonnaise
1/2 teaspoon salt
1/4 teaspoon celery seed
2 teaspoons vinegar or lemon juice
1/8 teaspoon pepper
1/4 cup milk

Preheat oven to 350 degrees. In a medium bowl, toss chicken, pickle relish, celery, almonds, and onion. Mix dressing in a small bowl or jar. Put salad in 10 x 6" baking dish; toss gently with dressing; sprinkle with chips and grated cheese, and garnish with parsley flakes. Bake for 30 minutes. Yield: 6 servings

ALTA ROSALIE HAMILTON, Ava, MO Age 70

This dish may be frozen and baked later. When I serve this salad at luncheons, people really like it.

MEAT AND POTATO SALAD

3 cups cubed cold boiled potatoes
1 tablespoon finely chopped onion
1/2 teaspoon salt
Dash pepper
1/4 cup commercial ranch or French dressing
2/3 cup salad dressing or mayonnaise
2 cups cooked lean meat strips (beef, ham, veal, chicken)
Hard cooked eggs, tomato wedges, or parsley for garnish

Mix potatoes and onion in a large salad bowl. Sprinkle with salt and pepper; toss lightly with dressing. Refrigerate up to 2 hours. Fold in mayonnaise; add meat and toss gently. Yield: 6 servings

EMMA CRONYN, Age 83

Main Dishes &
Pot Luck

MAIN DISHES AND POT LUCK

CONTENTS

BASIC MEAT LOAF

I like to serve meatloaf because it's easy to prepare and great for leftovers. Good to eat with potatoes and green beans.

1 1/2 pounds ground beef
1 egg, beaten
2 teaspoons salt
Pepper to taste
1 medium onion, chopped
1 cup bread or cracker crumbs
1/2 cup tomato catsup

Preheat oven to 350 degrees. Combine all ingredients in a large mixing bowl. Shape in a loaf and place in greased baking dish. Bake 1 1/2 hours; test for doneness after 1 hour. Yield: 6 servings

MARY L. TOOLEY, Ralisbury, MO Age 61

BEA'S APPLESAUCE MEAT LOAF

The applesauce in this recipe makes it extra moist and adds a special flavor.

1 pound ground beef
1/4 cup cheese, cut up
2 cups whole wheat bread crumbs
1 cup applesauce
1 egg
3 green onions and tops, chopped
2 teaspoons salt
1/4 teaspoon pepper
1 can tomato sauce, divided in half

Preheat oven to 350 degrees. Mix all ingredients in a large bowl, using only half the can of tomato sauce. Form meat into a loaf and place in a baking pan. Spread remaining tomato sauce on top. Bake for 2 hours. Yield: 8 servings

BEULAH MORRIS, Versailles, MO Age 76

Meatloaf? Baloney!

During the Depression we ate an awful lot of beans, potatoes, and corn bread. Pork was the staple meat---I don't think I tasted beef until I was an adult. The meat dish I remember most was my mother's bologna meatloaf. Back then this deli meat was not sold in fancy packaged slices, it was sold in the butcher shop by the pound. While I don't have my mother's recipe, I believe she must have ground the chunk of bologna and followed a traditional meatloaf recipe. It was such a welcome change to our diet; no steak could have tasted better.

Mary Newton, Wheatland, MO, Age 74

-109-

MEAL IN A PUMPKIN

This recipe is fun to serve in the fall.
It's a great conversation piece at the table and kids really love it.

1 medium pumpkin
1 medium onion, chopped
2 tablespoons cooking oil
1 1/2 to 2 pounds ground beef
2 tablespoons soy sauce
2 tablespoons brown sugar
1 4-ounce can mushrooms, drained
1 can cream of mushroom soup
1 1/2 cups cooked rice

Preheat oven to 350 degrees. Cut an opening in the top of the pumpkin, clean it thoroughly and set aside. In a large skillet, saute the onion in oil; add ground beef and cook until browned; drain off the excess fat. Add soy sauce, brown sugar, mushrooms, and soup. Simmer the mixture 10 minutes, then add the cooked rice. Pour into prepared pumpkin. Place pumpkin on a cookie sheet and bake for 1 hour. Yield: 4-6 servings

MARION McANDREW, Green River, WY Age 66

TACO CASSEROLE

Rule of Thumb:

Shake soup cans before opening. The contents will have no lumps and combine easily with other ingredients.

1 pound ground beef
1 can cream of chicken soup
1 can cream of mushroom soup
1 can enchilada sauce
1 large can evaporated milk
1 can green chilies
1/2 large onion
1 1/2 cups grated cheese
1 large bag taco-flavored chips

Preheat oven to 350 degrees. Brown meat in a large frying pan; add other ingredients except cheese and taco chips. Spread half the chips in a baking dish; add half the meat mixture and half of the cheese. Spread the rest of the taco chips, top with remaining meat; sprinkle cheese over meat. Bake 30 minutes. Yield: 8 servings

JANICE ROBERTS, Bennington, OK Age 63

BARBECUED BEEF SHORT RIBS

4 pounds short ribs
1 cup water
1 teaspoon salt
2 tablespoons flour
1/2 teaspoon pepper
1/2 teaspoon cloves
2 tablespoons prepared mustard
2 tablespoons Worcestershire sauce
1 cup pickle juice
1/2 cup catsup
1/4 cup chopped onion

In a large kettle or dutch oven, add water and salt to short ribs. Cover and cook slowly for 1 1/2 to 2 hours or until tender. (May also be cooked in a pressure cooker.) Barbecue sauce: In a small bowl, mix flour, pepper, and cloves. Blend in mustard and Worcesterrshire sauce. Add pickle juice, catsup, and chopped onion; mix well. To grill over coals: Remove short ribs from cooking liquid and place on grill. Cook slowly, turning occasionally, and brushing with barbecue sauce. Cook until brown on all sides. May also be baked in oven at 350 degrees. Yield: 4-6 servings

DELORES CANNADY, Harrisonville, MO Age 62

BEEF TIPS VERONIQUE

2 pounds beef cubes
3 tablespoons oil
1 tablespoon dry mustard
1 tablespoon honey
1 teaspoon salt
1/2 cup water
2 tablespoons parsley
3 cups cooked rice
1/2 cup chopped nuts
1 cup seedless grapes or raisins

Brown beef cubes in oil. Remove meat and keep warm. In a small bowl, stir together mustard, honey, salt, and water. Add to meat drippings and simmer to blend. Mix in parsley and cooked rice. Add grapes or raisins and nuts. Heat well, then add meat. Yield: 6 servings

DIANE CHAPMAN, Magnolia, AR Age 58

The Minister's Daughter

We always made much ado about Sundays because my father was a minister. After service, the other ministers would invite us over for supper, or my parents invited them to our house for supper. I had mixed feelings about these Sunday suppers. On one hand, children of ministers had to be still as mice; if we made even the smallest squeak, we were told, "children should be seen, not heard." On the other hand, Sunday suppers meant roast beef, greens, creamed corn, mashed potatoes, cornbread, sweet potato pie, and egg custard. Egg custard was worth behaving for!

Bertha L. Williams, West Point, MS Age 62

Welcome Home, Son

I was 21 when I was drafted to serve in WWII, and I was stationed mostly in Southeast Asia. I've tasted spicy Burmese salads, hot Indian curries, and noodle soups of China, but I couldn't wait to come back home to my mother's good old-fashioned cooking. How did she know to make steak and mashed potatoes for my welcome home dinner? It was only after my first bite that it felt like I was truly home.

Melvin Renderman, Fond du Lac, WI Age 76

PEPPER STEAK

This dish is a must at our home. We serve it every other Sunday with salad and garlic toast. You can also use tough cuts of steak or venison for variety.

2 pounds round steak
Salt and pepper to taste
1/2 cup flour
1-2 tablespoons cooking oil
1 teaspoon garlic salt
1 can cream of mushroom soup
1 can cream of celery soup
1 4-ounce can green chilies, chopped

Preheat oven to 350 degrees. Cut steak into serving size pieces. Salt and pepper to taste and roll in flour. Sear both sides of steak in hot oil. Do not cook through. Place in baking dish, sprinkle with garlic salt. Spread undiluted soups and green chilies over steak strips. Cover and bake for 3 hours. Yield: 4 servings

MARGARITE K. HANCOCK, Maud, TX Age 75

LONDON BROIL

1 1/2 pounds flank steak
3/4 cup Italian dressing
2 teaspoons soy sauce
1/8 teaspoon lemon pepper
Salt to taste

Score flank steak on both sides and place in a shallow pan. Blend dressing, soy sauce, and lemon pepper; pour over steak. Cover and let stand at room temperature for 2-3 hours, turning several times. Place steak on a broiler pan and broil 5 minutes, season with salt, turn and broil 5 minutes for medium rare. Carve steak in very thin slices, carving diagonally across grain. Yield: 6-8 servings

JO ANN KAPPELL, Wadesville, IN Age 56

HAMBURGER-POTATO CASSEROLE

5 medium potatoes
1 pound hamburger
2 tablespoons chopped onions
Bread crumbs
1 can whole kernel corn, drained
2 cans cream of chicken soup
1/4 cup milk
Salt and pepper to taste

Pare and slice potatoes; place in a large pot, cover with water, and cook until done. Drain. Brown hamburger and chopped onions together in a skillet. Drain. In a greased 9 x 11 baking pan, layer hamburger and potatoes. Sprinkle bread crumbs over layered mixture. Combine corn, soup, and milk in medium bowl; stir well and add salt and pepper to taste. Pour soup mixture over all. Bake 40 minutes at 375 degrees. Yield: 8-10 servings

JOANN CHURCHILL, Lake View, IA Age 61

HAMBURGER-CABBAGE CROCKPOT CASSEROLE

1 medium onion, chopped
3 tablespoons butter
1 1/2 pounds ground beef
3/4 teaspoon salt
1/8 teaspoon pepper
6 cups coarsely shredded cabbage
1 cup uncooked regular rice
2 10 1/2-ounce cans tomato soup
1/2 soup can of water

Saute onion in butter. Add hamburger and heat through, but do not brown. Add salt and pepper to hamburger mixture. Spread 3 cups cabbage in bottom of crockpot. Cover with meat mixture. Pour rice on top of meat; top with balance of cabbage. Pour soup and water over top. Cover and set crockpot on high; cook for five hours. Yield: 6 servings

ELEANORE HORNING, Bismarck, ND Age 64

CORN PONE PIE

1 pound hamburger, browned and drained
1 medium bell pepper, diced
1 16-ounce can chili beans
1 8-ounce can kidney beans
1 can small red beans
2 cloves of garlic, crushed
1 medium onion, diced
1 15-ounce can tomato sauce
1 teaspoon salt

CORNBREAD

1 cup flour
1 cup cornmeal
2 to 4 tablespoons sugar
1/2 teaspoon salt
1/4 cup oil or shortening
1 cup milk
1 tablespoon baking powder
2 eggs

Preheat oven to 375 degrees. Combine hamburger, bell pepper, beans, garlic, onion, tomato sauce, and salt in a large baking dish. Mix cornbread ingredients in a medium bowl and pour over hamburger mixture. Bake 45 minutes or until cornbread is golden brown. Yield: 6-8 servings

LOUISE M. MILSTEAD, Albany, GA Age 71

HOBO HOT DISH

1 1/2 pounds ground beef (do not brown)
Salt and pepper to taste
2 tablespoons minced onion
6 raw potatoes, sliced
4 carrots, sliced
1 cup green beans, drained
1 cup mushroom soup
1 cup cheddar cheese soup

Grease a casserole or baking dish and layer beef, seasonings, and vegetables. Spread undiluted soup on top. Bake covered for 1 1/2 to 2 hours. Yield: 6 servings

MARY L. GUSTAFSON, Port Wing, WI Age 71

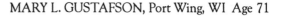

SYRIAN CABBAGE ROLLS

This recipe originated in the Middle East. For real authenticity,
substitute wild grape leaves which are sold in jars at specialty stores.

1 medium cabbage
1 pound ground beef
1 cup cooked rice
1 chopped onion
1 stick margarine
Salt and pepper to taste
1/2 pound pork steak or chops
Juice of 3 lemons
2 tablespoons chopped garlic

Remove core from cabbage; steam with a small amount of water in a
covered pan to wilt leaves. Cool; remove main vein from each leaf
and cut through leaf. Set aside. In a large mixing bowl, combine
ground beef, rice, onion, margarine, salt and pepper. Place mixture
along the vein side of leaf and roll up. Place pork steak or chops on
the bottom of a dutch oven or large kettle, Lay the cabbage rolls on
top; add lemon juice, garlic, and enough water to cover. Bring to a
boil on top of stove; turn down to medium heat. Cover and cook for
about an hour or until most of the water has evaporated. Arrange on a
platter to serve. Yield: 10 servings

MARGERY M. COMPTON, Homer, LA Age 67

My father came to America from Syria and settled in Homer, Louisiana, where he ran a grocery store. I suppose every immigrant from the little village of Dahr Safra who came through New Orleans found his way to our door for a good meal and a pillow for his head. More often than not, they were served these delicious cabbage rolls.

Margery Compton

SUPER SUPPER MEAT BALLS

1 pound hamburger
1 small onion
2 eggs
10 to 12 soda crackers, crumbled
1 tablespoon Miracle Whip
1 can chicken and rice soup
1 can chicken and stars soup
1/4 cup water

Preheat oven to 350 degrees. Mix all ingredients except soups in a
large bowl. Roll into one-inch balls. Brown on all sides in a skillet;
place browned meatballs in the bottom of a baking pan. Pour soups
over meatballs and add a small amount of water. Bake 1 hour. Yield:
6-8 servings

SALLY FOOTE, Lipton, IA Age 60

We love this over mashed potatoes. Add a green salad and hot rolls, and you have a real good meal.

-115-

Pot Luck

I am a founder and leader of the Christian Singles Group in my hometown. Once a month, the group holds a pot luck supper at church. The gentlemen particularly look forward to these occasions and the opportunity to sample so much home-cooked food. All members bring something different, but casseroles are the hands-down favorite. Casseroles are synonymous with pot luck suppers. They are easy to prepare, ideal for travel, taste even better after being reheated, and are a snap to serve.

Joan Brown

BEEF POTATO CASSEROLE

When I take this dish to a potluck, I always get requests to bring it again.

1 envelope dry onion soup mix
1 pound hamburger, browned and drained
1 cup milk
1/2 cup bread crumbs
1 teaspoon salt
4 cups thinly sliced potatoes
1 cup cubed cheese

Preheat oven to 350 degrees. In a large bowl, mix 3 tablespoons of the soup mix with the browned meat, milk, bread crumbs, and salt. Spread the mixture in a two-quart casserole dish. Mix the remaining soup mix with the potatoes and spread over the meat. Cover and bake 1 1/2 hours. Uncover and sprinkle with cheese. Return to oven for 15 minutes. Yield: 10-12 servings

JOAN BROWN, Watertown, SD Age 55

BEEF 'N NOODLES IN SOUR CREAM

1 cup chopped onion
2 tablespoons margarine
1 pound ground beef
3 cups noodles
3 cups tomato juice
2 teaspoons salt
Dash pepper
2 teaspoons Worcestershire sauce
1 cup sour cream

In a large skillet, cook onion in margarine until tender but not brown. Add meat and brown lightly. Layer noodles over meat. Combine remaining ingredients except sour cream; pour over noodles. Bring mixture to a boil, cover and simmer for 30 min. or until noodles are tender. Stir in sour cream and heat just to boiling. Yield: 6 servings

KAY WILES, Torrington, WY Age 59

BEEF & BEANS SUPREME

1 pound hamburger
1/2 pound bacon, diced
1 medium onion, chopped
1 can pork and beans
1 1-pound can great northern beans
1 can lima beans, drained
1 can kidney beans
1/3 cup brown sugar
1/4 cup barbecue sauce
1/4 cup catsup
1 teaspoon prepared mustard

Preheat oven to 350 degrees. Brown hamburger and drain. Brown bacon pieces till crisp; drain. Combine the meat and bacon with all remaining ingredients; stir well. Pour into a large baking dish and bake, covered, for 40-60 minutes. Remove lid the last 15 minutes. Yield: 6-8 servings

SHIRLEY LIGGETT, Hancock, MD Age 58

BEEF CRUST PIE

1 pound ground beef
1 cup soft bread crumbs
1/2 cup milk
1 tablespoon chopped onion
1 teaspoon Worcestershire sauce
Salt and pepper to taste
Mashed potatoes or vegetable filling of choice

Preheat oven to 350 degrees. Mix all ingredients except filling in a large bowl. Pat the mixture into a 9-inch pie pan. Press another pie pan on top. Bake 7 minutes; remove the upper pan and bake 3 more minutes or until beef is thoroughly cooked. Fill the hot meat crust with mashed potatoes, or a vegetable mixture of your choice. Return filled pie to oven and bake 20 minutes. Yield: 6 servings

HELEN MARONEY, Age 79

The Meat Man

I grew up during the Depression, but unlike city folks, we were never hungry. My father worked for an orchard farmer who grew apples, cherries, and peaches. A small plot of land for a vegetable garden, wood, milk, fresh eggs, maple syrup, all the fruit we wanted from the orchard, and the house we lived in were part of my father's wage. The only thing we had to buy was meat. Once a week, the travelling meat man came to the farm in his refrigerated truck. My sisters and I looked forward to his visit because he would treat us to a hot dog or a slice of bologna.

*Grace Amon,
Sodus, NY
Age 80*

MULLIGAN STEW

3 pounds hamburger
1 can beer (optional)
4 carrots, cut into small pieces
4 potatoes, cut in pieces
1/2 onion
6 stalks celery

Mix all ingredients and cook in a kettle or soup pot over medium heat for 2-3 hours. Yield: 8 servings

WILLIAM SCHAFFER, SR., Bradford, OH Age 62

SHIPWRECK STEW

1 large onion, chopped
1 pound hamburger meat
4 potatoes, sliced
1 can baked beans
1 head cabbage, sliced
1 can tomato soup

Preheat oven to 350 degrees. Brown beef and onions; drain. Place sliced potatoes on bottom of 13 x 9 casserole dish and layer with beef mixture, beans, and cabbage. Pour tomato soup over the top and bake for 1 hour. Yield: 6 servings

LEONA M. GRIFFITH, Lewistown, PA Age 75

IRISH STEW
Being Irish, I love it.

1 1/2 pounds beef or lamb, cut into cubes
1/2 cup flour
1 teaspoon salt
3 tablespoons shortening
1/2 cup diced carrots
1/2 cup diced turnips
1/2 cup sliced onion
1 1/2 cups diced potatoes
1 1/2 cups water

Dredge meat cubes in mixture of flour and salt. Brown in shortening in stew pot; add vegetables and water; cover and simmer 1 1/2 hours. Drain off liquid and thicken with 1 tablespoon each of flour and water for each cup of liquid. Blend and stir until thickened and add to meat. Yield: 4-6 servings

ANNE MARSHALL, Clayton, NY Age 82

STAY IN BED STEW

This is wonderful on a cold day. Just know when 5 hours are up, you have a delicious stew awaiting. Cornbread is great with a bowl.

2 pounds stew meat
2 large onions, chopped
1 can whole kernel corn, drained
1 can carrots, drained
1 can peas, drained
1 can lima beans, drained
6 potatoes, diced
1 bay leaf
1 can tomato soup
Enough water to cover vegetables

Preheat oven to 275 degrees. Put stew meat on bottom of oven-proof covered kettle or baking dish. Layer vegetables over meat and add tomato soup. Add enough water to cover meat and vegetables. Bake with lid on for approximately 5 hours. Once in oven, you never have to look at it or stir. Do not lift lid. Yield: 8 servings

FRANCES M. BRYANT, Copeville, TX Age 77

OVEN BEEF STEW

3/4 pound beef chuck, cut in small cubes
1 tablespoon all purpose flour
3/4 teaspoon salt
Dash pepper
1 tablespoon shortening
1 can tomato soup
1 soup can water
3/4 cup chopped onion
1/4 teaspoon dried basil, crushed
2 medium potatoes, pared and cubed
2 medium carrots, cut in 1" pieces
1/4 cup dry red wine (or water)

Preheat oven to 350 degrees. Dredge meat cubes in a mixture of flour, salt, and pepper. Brown meat in hot shortening in a small dutch oven; add soup, water, onion, and basil. Cover and bake about 1 hour. Add potatoes, carrots, and wine. Cover and bake 1 hour or until tender. Yield: 4 servings

KIM POPOLOSKI, Garoner, MA

I was a cook on a ranch for quite a few years and the "hands" needed good food and plenty of it. This casserole was a favorite served with a garden salad and bread sticks.

BEEF & NOODLE CASSEROLE

8 ounces noodles
1 pound ground beef
1/2 teaspoon garlic salt
2 14 1/2-ounce cans tomatoes, drained, reserve 1/4 cup liquid
3 tablespoons flour
1/4 cup minced onion
1 1/2 teaspoons salt
1/4 teaspoon pepper
1 teaspoon oregano
5 slices American cheese
2 tablespoons grated Parmesan cheese

Preheat oven to 375 degrees. Cook and drain noodles. Set aside. In a large skillet, brown ground beef with garlic salt. Drain excess fat. Mix reserved tomato liquid with flour; add to beef and stir thoroughly. Add tomatoes, onion, salt, pepper, and oregano to beef. Simmer 10 minutes. In a lightly greased casserole dish, alternate layers of meat and noodles. Top with cheese slices; sprinkle Parmesan on top. Bake 20-25 minutes. Yield: 6-8 servings

IRENE BEAMAN, Lewellen, NE Age 68

BEEF-CABBAGE CASSEROLE

1 small head cabbage
1 pound ground beef
1 small onion, minced
1/3 cup uncooked rice
Salt and pepper to taste
1 cup undiluted tomato soup
1 soup can water
1 small can tomato sauce

Chop cabbage in large pieces and place in the bottom of a greased baking dish. In a medium skillet, brown meat and onions; pour off excess fat and add rice, salt and pepper. Pour meat mixture over cabbage. Mix soup, water, and tomato sauce in a small bowl. Pour over meat. Bake 1 hour. Yield: 4-6 servings

BETTY M. HERRING, St. Henry, OH Age 73

A STROGANOFF CASSEROLE

1 cup chopped onions
Oil for sauteing
1 pound round steak cut in strips, or ground round beef
2 cups uncooked bow tie macaroni
2 teaspoons Worcestershire sauce
1/2 cup celery tops finely chopped
2 1/2 cup tomato juice
Salt and pepper to taste
1/2 pint "lite" sour cream

Preheat oven to 350 degrees. In a medium skillet, simmer onions in a little oil until transparent; add and brown the steak strips or ground beef. In a large casserole dish, mix onions, beef, uncooked macaroni, Worcestershire sauce, celery, and tomato juice. Cover and bake 45 minutes. Remove from oven; add salt and pepper and fold in sour cream. Serve immediately. Yield: 4 servings

EDITH F. HOUK, Lakeland, FL Age 65

MOCK CHOP SUEY

1 pound ground beef
Water for simmering vegetables
1 1/2 cups chopped onion
1 1/2 cups chopped celery
1 can cream of mushroom soup
1 small can mushrooms-optional
1 can chow mein noodles
Salt and pepper
Soy sauce to taste

Preheat oven to 350 degrees. Brown ground beef in a skillet; drain and remove to a casserole dish. Using the same skillet and a small amount of water, cook onions and celery. Mix all ingredients in the casserole, reserving 1/2 chow mein noodles. Bake 45 minutes; sprinkle remaining noodles on top, return to oven for 15 minutes. Yield: 4 servings

ARLINE DORRLER, Stevens Point, WI Age 64

Corned Beef & Cabbage, or Not?

Being of Irish descent, my husband was a basic meat and potatoes man. His absolute favorite was a boiled dinner of corned beef and veg-etables. That's why as a young newlywed wife (of French heritage) I was surprised when he took to tadials. This is a French-style homemade noodle. It's made with a dozen eggs and cut by hand. He loved it, but never as much as his corned beef and cabbage.

Alice M. Handley, Malone, NY Age 64

CORNED BEEF AND NOODLE CASSEROLE

1 8-ounce package egg noodles
1 can cream of chicken soup
1 cup milk
1/4 pound American cheese, finely cut
1 12-ounce can corned beef, broken up
1/2 cup chopped onions
3/4 cup buttered crumbs

Cook noodles according to package directions; drain. Combine soup, milk, cheese, corned beef, and onions. Alternate layers of noodles and corned beef mixture in a greased 2-quart casserole dish. Sprinkle top with bread crumbs; cover and refrigerate for 2 hours. Preheat oven to 375 degrees. Bake uncovered until heated through. Yield: 6-8 servings

MARTHA SHAW, Clarksville, IA Age 60

RED FLANNEL HASH
A great way to use left-overs.

3 cups cooked corned beef, cubed
3 cups cold cooked potatoes, cubed
Salt and pepper to taste
3 tablespoons minced onion
1 green pepper, chopped (optional)
3/4 cup chopped cooked beets
1/4-1/2 cup milk

For best results, corned beef and potato cubes should be about the same size. Combine all ingredients but milk in a large bowl. Moisten mixture with a little milk. Spread mixture evenly in a lightly greased hot skillet. Brown on one side over low heat. Fold over omelet-style. May also be baked at 350 degrees in a greased casserole for 30 minutes or until brown. Yield: 6 servings

DORIS BROWN, Age 75

DIJON REUBEN

1/2 cup chopped onion
1/4 cup butter or margarine
1 8-ounce container sauerkraut, drained
1 teaspoon sweet pickle relish
1/2 cup prepared Dijon mustard
3/4 cup sour cream
1 teaspoon caraway seed
8 sheets phyllo dough
1-2 pounds thinly sliced corned beef
1/4 pound sliced Swiss cheese

Preheat oven to 375 degrees. In a skillet, saute onions in 1 teaspoon butter until tender. Stir in saurkraut, relish, 1/4 cup mustard, sour cream, and caraway seed. Melt remaining butter. Stack phyllo sheets, brushing with butter between each layer. Top with layers of corned beef, cheese, and kraut mixture to within 1" of edge. Roll from long edge, jelly roll fashion, tucking ends and brushing with butter. Place seam-side down on greased baking sheet. Cut 12 slits on top of roll, 1/2 inch deep. Bake 30-35 minutes or till browned. Yield: 6 servings

EUNICE WILLIAMS, Coldwater, MI Age 63

REUBEN CASSEROLE
Can be made up early in the day and cooked later.

1 1-pound can sauerkraut, drained
8 ounces sour cream
1 12-ounce can corned beef
2 cups shredded swiss cheese
4-6 slices of rye bread, cubed or crumbled
1/2 cup melted butter

Preheat oven to 350 degrees. Blend sauerkraut and sour cream in a medium mixing bowl. Spread in a greased 9 x 13 pan. Crumble corned beef and sprinkle over kraut. Spread shredded cheese over beef; spread bread crumbs, drizzle with melted butter. Bake 30 to 40 minutes. Yield: 8 servings

LAURA OLDSON, Cambridge, OH

CARIBBEAN HAM STACKS

1 pound ground fully-cooked ham
1/4 cup pickle relish
1 teaspoon mustard
2 cups mashed, cooked sweet potato
1 egg, lightly beaten
1/3 teaspoon grated orange peel
1/2 teaspoon salt
1/8 teaspoon pepper
1 20-ounce can pineapple slices
8 bacon strips, halved lengthwise

Rules of Thumb:

Before roasting ham, make a slit in the rind on the underside. The rind will pull away as the ham bakes and can be easily removed.

Wrap smoked hams and bacon in a cloth that has been saturated in vinegar and squeezed until just moist. Wrap again in wax paper and store in the refrigerator.

Preheat oven to 350 degrees. Combine the ham, relish and mustard in a large bowl. Shape 1/3 cupfuls into eight patties--about the same size as pineapple rings. In a separate bowl, combine the sweet potatoes, egg, orange peel, salt, and pepper. Shape 1/4 cupfuls into eight patties the size of pineapple rings. On a lightly greased baking sheet, stack as follows: 2 strips of bacon, 1 pineapple slice, 1 ham pattie, 1 sweet potato pattie, and one pineapple slice. Fold bacon ends up and over the top slice of pineapple and secure with wooden toothpicks. Bake 50 minutes or until bacon is crisp. Yield: 8 patties

PATSY BESSILL, Salt Lake City, UT Age 67

HAM LOAF

1 pound ground smoked ham
2 eggs, beaten
3 cups wheat or corn flake cereal
1 cup milk
1 teaspoon salt
Dash of pepper

Preheat oven to 350 degrees. In a large mixing bowl, thoroughly blend all ingredients. Pack into a greased 9 x 5 loaf pan. Bake 1 1/2 hours. Unmold onto serving plate. Yield 8 servings

VARIATIONS
Line loaf pan with pineapple slices; pack ham loaf; pour 1/2 cup pineapple juice over meat. Cover with a paste of 2 teaspoons brown sugar and 2 teaspoons mustard before baking.

Add 4 tablespoons peanut butter to basic recipe.

KAY BOLEY, Kingsport, TN

POTATO & HAM CASSEROLE

6 to 8 potatoes
1 or 2 onions
2 cups chopped ham
1 can cream of mushroom soup
2 cups milk
Salt and pepper to taste

Preheat oven to 400 degrees. Peel and thinly slice potatoes and onions. Layer in casserole dish as follows: potatoes, onion, ham. Mix soup and milk in a small bowl and pour over top. Cover and bake 1 hour. Yield: 6 servings

AILEEN C. REED, Lancaster, PA Age 59

CHURCH SUPPER
MACARONI & CHEESE WITH HAM

32 ounces macaroni
1/2 teaspoon vegetable oil
1/2 cup onions
2 1/2 teaspoons butter
1/2 can plus 2 tablespoons celery soup
3/4 cup milk
2 pounds American cheese
2 pounds diced ham

Preheat oven to 350 degrees. Cook macaroni according to package directions and drain well. In a large skillet, saute onions in butter until tender. Combine soup and milk, add to cooked onions. Add cheese, stir until melted. Mix in diced ham and cooked macaroni. Stir well to combine; pour into greased pan(s). Bake about 30 minutes. Yield: 25 servings

VIRGINIA PAYTON, Covington, IN Age 72

Rule of Thumb:

Inexpensive foil baking dishes available in the grocery store make it easy to bake and take large casseroles. And they're reusable.

ROAST PORK CASSEROLE

Pork end-of-loin or spare ribs
1 8-ounce container sauerkraut, drained and squeezed dry
1 medium onion, chopped
1 apple, chopped
1-2 tablespoons cooking oil
2 chicken bouillon cubes
Boiling water to cover pork
Salt to taste
1 medium raw potato, grated

Place pork and sauerkraut in a large kettle or dutch oven. In a small skillet, saute onion and apple in oil. Add onion-apple mixture and bouillon cubes to pork; cover with water and salt to taste. Simmer for 1 1/2 hours. Grate potato; add to pot (with a little more water if needed) and cook another 1/2 hour. Yield: 6-8 servings

ROY A. WILEY, Cape Vincent, NY Age 72

CHEESE-TOPPED PORK CHOPS

6 pork chops
1 package frozen shredded potatoes
1/2 cup chopped onions
1 teaspoon salt
1/4 teaspoon pepper
1 can mushroom soup
1 cup grated cheddar cheese

Preheat oven to 350 degrees. In a large skillet, brown pork chops on both sides. In a separate pan, cook potatoes in boiling water for 15 minutes; drain. Spoon potatoes into a lightly greased 13 x 9 casserole. Add half the onions and season with salt and pepper. Arrange pork chops over potatoes, then sprinkle with remining onion. Spread soup evenly over top. Bake 30 minutes; sprinkle cheese over top and bake an additional 30 minutes. Yield: 6 servings

JAMES T. YATES, Springfield, KY Age 72

PORK-STEAK SKILLET SUPPER

4 pork steaks
1 tablespoon cooking oil
1 medium onion, chopped
2 stalks celery, chopped
4 cloves garlic
4 potatoes, sliced or cubed
4 carrots, sliced
1 pint broth or water
Salt and pepper to taste
Italian seasoning to taste (optional)

In a large skillet, brown pork in cooking oil; drain. Add remaining ingredients and simmer about 45 minutes. Yield: 4 servings

JUDITH LEE MILLER, Niagara Falls, NY

PORK CHOP-POTATO CASSEROLE

I am a mother of eight. This is a good, simple, easy to prepare meal. When my husband retired, I went to work. My Green Thumb job has been a "wife saver."

6 pork chops
2 tablespoons cooking oil
1 envelope dry onion soup mix
1 can cream of mushroom soup
5 cups raw diced potatoes
1 can green beans, drained
Salt and pepper to taste

Preheat oven to 350 degrees. In a skillet, brown pork chops in oil; remove to greased 9 x 13 inch baking dish. Combine soup mix, mushroom soup, potatoes, and green beans in a large mixing bowl. Season to taste. Place mixture on top of pork chops; cover with foil. Bake 1 1/2 hours. Yield: 6 servings

BARBARA JOHNSON, Sacred Heart, MN Age 62

A Quart of Cream

My parents had a dairy farm in Greensburg, Kansas. Growing up, my two older brothers and I did not place too much value on currency because we saw how our parents bartered for most of the things our family needed. My mother exchanged a crate of eggs for flour, sugar, and coffee. And for a quart of cream, I received a piano lesson. Every Christmas Eve, my parents gave my eldest brother two dozen eggs; my second brother received a quart of cream; a pound of butter was placed in my hand. My parents then asked us to choose someone from our church to bestow these gifts on. Mom and Dad also wanted us to know the joy of giving.

Rhuy Ellen Lewis, Dodge City, KS Age 76

-127-

BAKED PORK CHOPS

1 medium onion sliced
1/2 cup chopped celery
2 tablespoons oil
Salt and pepper to taste
4 pork chops
1 cup water
2 tablespoons brown sugar
1 6-ounce can tomato sauce
1 cup regular rice, uncooked

In a skillet, cook onions and celery in oil. Sprinkle salt and pepper
on pork chops; add to pan and brown on both sides. Remove from
pan and add water, sugar, and 1/2 tomato sauce; stir. Add rice and
stir. Return chops to pan; cover and simmer 30 to 35 minutes. Pour
in remaining tomato sauce and cook 15 to 20 minutes longer. Yield:
4 servings

BURNICE LUTRELL, Hampton, AR Age 75

ORANGE PORK CHOPS ON RICE

6 3/4"-thick pork chops
Salt and pepper to taste
1 1/3 cups uncooked packaged rice
1 cup orange juice
1 10 1/2-ounce can condensed chicken with rice soup

Preheat oven to 350 degrees. In a skillet, brown pork chops on both
sides. Season with salt and pepper. Place rice in a 12 x 71/2" baking
dish; pour orange juice over rice. Arrange pork chops on rice; pour
chicken soup over all. Cover and bake 45 minutes. Uncover and bake
10 minutes. Yield: 6 servings

DONALD LOWMAN, Yellville, AR Age 65

PORK CHOPS AND ONION GRAVY

4 pork chops
1 tablespoon cooking oil
1 can French onion soup
1 8-ounce container sour cream or yogurt
2 cups cooked rice

Trim fat from pork chops and brown in oil in a medium skillet; drain. Add onion soup and simmer until chops are very tender. (May need to add a little water.) When chops are cooked, add sour cream (or yogurt for low-fat option). Serve over cooked rice. Yield: 4 servings

MAX HAMM, Maynard, AR Age 69

PORK CHOPS AND DRESSING
This is my family's favorite meal.

4 pork chops
1 tablespoon cooking oil
3 to 5 slices bread
1 small onion, chopped
2 eggs, beaten
1 teaspoon sage
1/4 cup butter
1 1/2 cups water
1 can cream of mushroom soup
2/3 cup milk

Preheat oven to 350 degrees. In a skillet, brown pork chops in cooking oil. Melt butter in water in a small saucepan. Break bread into small pieces in a mixing bowl; add onion, eggs, and sage. Melt butter and combine with water; add to dry dressing mixture. Place chops in a 9 x 13 baking pan. Cover with dressing. Mix soup and milk; pour over chops and dressing. Bake for 30 minutes. Yield: 4 servings

DELORES DOALEY, Hantington, NE Age 69

The Woodsman's Revenge

My grandmother-in-law told me about a notorious woodsman who was just about the biggest practical joker in Arkansas. When he heard that she had gotten rid of her wood stove for a modern butane gas stove, he paid a visit one Sunday morning. To show he had no hard feelings, he handed her a generous portion of boar meat. She put the meat in her new stove to roast. As soon as the family walked into the house after church, they smelled something horrible. The woodsman had given Grandmother the meat of a boar that had not been "fixed." For some reason, meat from unneutered boars releases an extremely offensive odor when it is cooked. He certainly made his point!

Mary Sue Whitehead, Dandridge, TN

Hurricane Bar-B-Q

My mother used to buy "freezer orders" of meat-- 125 pounds of roasts, hamburger, and steaks which would become part of our family menu for several months. A new order had just arrived and been packed into our freezer right before Hurricane Donna blew through. After three days without power, Mother worried that the meat would defrost and go bad so she began cooking it on our outdoor grill. There was so much to cook, however, that we borrowed extra grills from neighbors and invited them to eat with us. We kids loved the impromptu block party, but my Mother saw meat that should have lasted through Christmas literally going up in smoke!

Helen Pendergrass

BARBECUED SPARERIBS

1 celery stalk
1 small carrot
1/2 onion
4-5 pounds spareribs

MARINADE

1/2 cup pineapple juice
2 cups chicken stock
1 cup soy sauce
3/4 cup catsup
1/2 cup sherry
2 teaspoons sugar
1/2 teaspoon fresh ginger, finely minced
1/2 teaspoon garlic, minced
1/2 teaspoon ground pepper

GLAZE

1/4 cup reserved marinade
2/3 cup honey
2 teaspoons soy sauce
1 teaspoon ground pepper
1 teaspoon ground ginger

Fill stockpot 2/3 full of water. Add celery, carrot, and onion; bring to a boil over high heat. Add ribs, reduce heat and simmer about 1 hour. Drain ribs well and let cool. Combine marinade ingredients in a shallow pan, reserving 1/4 cup for glaze. Add ribs and marinate in refrigerator for 24 hours, turning occasionally. Preheat oven to 375 degrees. Remove ribs from marinade and arrange on a baking sheet. Combine glaze ingredients in a small bowl; brush onto ribs and bake. Brush additional glaze onto ribs every 10 minutes; bake until edges are crispy. Yield: 4-6 servings

SHARON HUTCHINS, Boonesville, KY

ROAST PORK TETRAZZINI

1/4 pound noodles
2 cups beef broth
1/2 pound cheddar cheese, grated
1 large onion, finely chopped
1/4 cup diced green pepper
1/8 teaspoon paprika
1/8 teaspoon curry powder
Pepper to taste
2 cans cream of mushroom soup
3 to 4 cups diced roast pork

Preheat oven to 350 degrees. In a dutch oven or kettle, cook noodles in broth until done. Add cheddar cheese and stir to blend. Add onion, green pepper, paprika, curry powder, and pepper. Add undiluted cream of mushroom soup and meat; stir thoroughly to coat. Pour into a greased shallow baking pan. Bake about 30 minutes. Yield: 8-10 servings

THELMA R. CURRENCE, Eldon, MO Age 73

SAUSAGE-ZUCCHINI ITALIANO

1 pound bulk pork sausage
1 cup chopped onion
1 green pepper, chopped
1 clove garlic, minced
1 16-ounce can tomatoes
1 8-ounce can tomato sauce
1 1//4 teaspoons salt
1 teaspoon oregano
1/4 teaspoon pepper
1 1/4 pounds zucchini, sliced
1 cup wide noodles
1 cup water
1 cup shredded cheddar cheese

Brown sausage in a large skillet. When it begins to brown, add onion, green pepper, and garlic. Saute until meat is well cooked. Drain off excess fat and stir in tomatoes, tomato sauce, salt, oregano, pepper, zucchini, uncooked noodles, and water. Bring to a boil and reduce heat; cover and simmer 15 minutes. Top with cheese and cook until cheese melts. Yield: 8-10 servings

MILDRED LUCILLE MICHAEL, Indianola, IA Age 66

The Best Meal I Ever Had

I got married when I was twenty, and for the first three years we lived with my in-laws. 1943 was one of the best years of my life. That was the year my husband and I had finally saved enough money to build a house of our own. Back then it wasn't uncommon to build your own house with help from your neighbors. When it was finally finished, my humble home of two rooms seemed like a palace to me. I can still vividly recall our very first meal--fried potatoes, pork sausage, and biscuits. It was the best meal I ever had!

Ruby Boyd, Tracy City, TN Age 75

TOUCHDOWN TREAT

We prepare this dish in advance of sporting events and then reheat it in the microwave after the "game."

1/2 package small shell macaroni
1 pound seasoned sausage
1 package frozen mixed vegetables
1 can cream of chicken soup
1/2 cup milk
1/2 cup grated cheddar cheese
French fried onion rings

Preheat oven to 350 degrees. Boil and drain macaroni according to package instructions. In a large skillet, fry sausage until red disappears, drain off excess fat. Add frozen vegetables, soup, milk, cheese, and macaroni, stirring to combine. Place mixture in a greased casserole and cover the top with onion rings. Bake 30 minutes. Yield: 6-8 servings

LUCILLE M. NOBILING, Carroll, IA

HUNGARIAN PIGS IN BLANKETS

1 head cabbage
1 1/2 pounds ground pork (or 1/2 beef,1/2 pork)
1 onion, chopped
1/2 cup cooked rice
Dash of pepper, salt, and paprika
1 quart whole canned tomatoes or tomato juice

Preheat oven to 325 degrees. Boil cabbage in salted water. Cover and let stand until cabbage is soft. Mix remaining ingredients, except tomatoes, and roll up in cabbage leaves. Place in baking dish and top with tomatoes or tomato juice. Add water to cover, cover casserole, and cook about an hour until done. Yield: 4 servings

MRS. MELVIN DESJARLAIS, Doggett, MI Age 72

PAN FRIED CHICKEN

1/2 cup plain cornmeal
1 teaspoon salt
1/2 teaspoon black pepper
1 teaspoon paprika
1 teaspoon poultry seasoning
1/2 teaspoon garlic salt
1 egg, slightly beaten
1 tablespoon milk
2 1/2 to 3 pounds frying chicken
1 3/4 cups cooking oil

Combine cornmeal, salt, pepper, paprika, poultry seasoning, and garlic salt in a paper bag or plastic bag. Combine egg and milk in a medium bowl. Dip chicken pieces in egg mixture, then shake in cornmeal mixture. Heat cooking oil in a skillet over medium heat. Brown chicken on all sides. Reduce heat and cook, tightly covered, until meatiest pieces are tender--about 30 minutes. Remove cover and cook 10 minutes to crisp chicken. Yield: 6 servings

WILLIE H. JENNINGS, Jackson, TN Age 75

CHICKEN AND PEACHES

This is a good recipe for dieters.

2 teaspoons vegetable oil
12 ounces boned, skinless chicken
Dash each of salt, cinnamon, and cloves
1/3 cup apple juice
2 medium peaches or 1 can "lite" sliced peaches
2 teaspoons cornstarch
Mint leaves for garnish

Heat oil in skillet; add chicken and saute until lightly browned. Add salt, cinnamon, cloves, and apple juice to chicken. Cover and cook 20 minutes over low heat until chicken is tender. Slice peaches and add to chicken, stirring contantly. Slowly add cornstarch and cook until thickened. Garnish with mint leaves. Yield: 2-3 servings

MARGARET C. WOOD, Kingston, NY Age 65

Spring Chicken

When I was growing up on a farm in Missouri, spring meant chicken season. My mother raised chickens and as soon as they were old enough, our family had fresh young spring chicken for breakfast, lunch, and supper. While this seems like a lot, if we didn't eat the chickens while they were young, the meat would get tough because we didn't have the luxury of a freezer back then. We didn't mind, though. Mother's fried chicken was the best in the world.

*Cleva Kerr,
Carlisle, Iowa
Age 70*

Grandma's House

Every summer I spent a couple of weeks at my grandmother's house in Pennsylvania. It was a magical place with ducks, geese, chickens, and a one-eyed rooster that chased me whenever I went into the yard. I remember the wonderful smells in her house-- bread baking, saurkraut curing in a crock, and herbs drying in the basement. Each year we went into the mountains and picked huckleberries which my grandmother kept in a big bowl. Every time I walked through the kitchen, I grabbed a handful. I also remember that those huckleberries usually resulted in at least one stomach ache!

Richard Cooper, Newton, NJ

CHICKEN STIR-FRY

1 pound boneless chicken breast
2 tablespoons oil
3/4 cup chopped onion
1 garlic clove, minced
1 carrot, cut in strips
1/2 teaspoon ginger
1 green pepper, cut in strips
1 8-ounce can pineapple chunks, drained
10 3/4-ounce can chicken broth
3 tablespoons brown sugar
1/4 cup soy sauce
2 tablespoons sherry (optional)
3 tablespoons vinegar
2 cups instant rice

Slice chicken into thin strips. Heat wok or large frying pan with a tight-fitting lid. Add oil and chicken and saute until done. Add onion and garlic. Saute until onions become transluscent. Add carrots and cook until soft. Add all remaining ingredients except rice to chicken. Bring to a boil; add rice. When mixture comes to second boil, remove from heat and cover. Let stand for 10-12 minutes or until rice is soft. Fluff with fork and serve. Yield: 2-4 servings

NONA CHRISTENSEN, Verillion, SD Age 61

MEXICAN CHICKEN

3-4 pound cooking hen
1 bag taco chips
1 can cream of chicken, celery, or mushroom soup (your choice)
1 large can tomatoes, with liquid
1 large can whole kernel corn, with liquid
2 cups shredded cheddar cheese

Boil hen until done, reserve about 1 cup of broth; pick meat off bone. Preheat oven to 350 degrees. In a mixing bowl, soak taco chips in chicken broth, then crush. Place a layer of taco chips in bottom of a large casserole dish. Arrange chicken pieces over taco chips. Mix soup, tomatoes, and corn in a large bowl. Pour over chicken and bake 20 minutes. Top with shredded cheese and return to oven to melt. Yield: 6-8 servings

FRANCES CHAILLAND, Kennett, MO Age 76

GREEN CHILE PEPPER CHICKEN

1 chicken--about 3 1/2 pounds
Water to cover chicken
1 stalk celery, cut into pieces
1 carrot, peeled and cut into pieces
1 medium onion, chopped
Cornstarch to thicken broth
1 4-ounce can chopped green chiles
4 cups cooked regular or instant rice

Cut chicken into pieces; place in a stew pot and cover with water.
Add celery, carrot and onion and cook until chicken is tender.
Remove chicken and vegetables. Strain broth and thicken with corn
starch (1 tablespoon to 1 cup liquid) Add chiles to sauce, add
chicken and vegetables. Reheat chicken in sauce. Serve chicken over
rice. Yield: 6-8 servings

DORIS E. BAKER, Grandview, TX Age 72

CHERRY CHICKEN

This is a very attractive dish that I serve for holiday meals.

3 tablespoons margarine
1/4 cup all purpose flour
1/2 teaspoon salt
1/4 teaspoon pepper
1/4 teaspoon paprika
2-2 1/2 pounds cut up chicken
1/4 teaspoon ground nutmeg
1/4 teaspoon ground allspice
1 teaspoon salt
1/4 teaspoon ground cloves
1/4 cup packed brown sugar
1 21-ounce can cherry pie filling
1/2 cup dry white wine (or substitute lemon-lime beverage)

Preheat oven to 375 degrees. Melt margarine in bottom of a
12 x 7 1/2" baking dish. Mix flour, salt, pepper, and paprika in a large
bowl. Coat chicken and place in baking dish. Bake 40 minutes,
turning once after 20 minutes. In a large saucepan, heat spices, brown
sugar, cherry filling, and wine. Pour over chicken. Continue baking for
30 minutes or until chicken is done. Skim off excess fat before serving.
Yield: 4 servings

RUTH POWERS, Taylor, NE Age 68

International Delights

Before I was born, my father moved the family from the South to the less segregated state of Pennsylvania. I remember growing up happily in a colorful international neighborhood. Our closest neighbors were the Italian Diazo family who lived across from us, and the Mexican Hernandez family who lived down the street. Every Thursday, Mama Diazo sent her two sons over with a big pot of freshly-made spaghetti and meat sauce. In return, I carried a huge platter of fried chicken to them on Saturdays. And not to forget Mrs. Hernandez, she made the best flap-jacks and egg rolls--and she always had plenty to share with the Baxter family.

Solomon Baxter, Reading, PA

CHICKEN FAST & FANCY

8 large chicken breast halves, skinned and boned
8 slices Swiss cheese
1 1/4 cups fresh mushrooms, sliced
1 can cream of mushroom soup
1/4 cup dry white wine
2 cups herbed stuffing mix
1/4 cup melted butter

Preheat oven to 350 degrees. Place chicken in a single layer in a buttered baking pan. Top each piece with cheese and sprinkle with mushrooms. Combine soup and wine in a small bowl and pour over chicken. Sprinkle with stuffing mix and drizzle with butter. Bake uncovered until chicken is cooked through, about 35 minutes. Yield: 8 servings

ANN LIVERS, Loogootee, IN Age 81

MARINATED CHICKEN BREASTS

8 boneless chicken breasts
1/4 cup margarine
1/4 cup shortening
Cornflake crumbs

MARINADE

1 8-ounce carton sour cream
2 tablespoons lemon juice
2 teaspoons Worcestershire sauce
1/2 teaspoon salt
1/4 tablespooon garlic salt
1/4 tablespoon pepper
2 teaspoons celery salt

Place chicken in a shallow dish. Mix ingredients for marinade; pour over chicken and let stand at least 8 hours, turning occasionally. When ready to cook, preheat oven to 350 degrees. Melt margarine and shortening in a medium saucepan; roll chicken in melted mixture and then cornflake crumbs. Place in a large baking dish; cook uncovered for 45 minutes. Freezes well. Yield: 6-8 servings

CLEMELL LYLES, Monticello, AR Age 66

PAN-FRIED NOODLES WITH SHREDDED CHICKEN

For added flavor, serve stir fry noodles with vinegar or hot chili oil as condiments.

    1 pound Chinese noodles
    2 tablespoons oriental sesame seed oil
    1 chicken breast, cooked and shredded (about 1 cup)
    4 tablespoons stir fry sauce
    2 tablespoons garlic and ginger stir fry oil
    1 slice ginger root
    3 cups shredded Chinese cabbage
    3/4 cup scallions, cut into 2" lengths
    1/2 cup black mushrooms, soaked, stemmed, and shredded
    1/3 cup chicken broth

Cook noodles according to package directions; do not overcook. Drain, rinse, and toss with 2 tablespoons oriental sesame seed oil; set aside. Mix chicken with stir fry sauce; heat 2 tablespoons oil in wok or large frying pan over high heat. Add chicken and ginger slice; stir fry for 30 seconds. Add cabbage, scallions, and mushrooms; continue cooking until cabbage is wilted. Add chicken broth and cook covered for 15 to 20 minutes. Add cooked noodles, tossing until they are well-mixed and heated. Serve on a large platter. Yield: 4 servings

BETTIE ARMONTROUT, Pryor, OK Age 67

PARMESAN CHICKEN

    1/2 cup melted margarine
    2 teaspoons prepared Dijon mustard
    1 teaspoon Worcestershire sauce
    1/2 teaspoon salt
    1 cup dry bread crumbs
    1/2 cup grated Parmesan cheese
    6 to 8 boneless, skinless chicken breast halves

Preheat oven to 350 degrees. In a pie plate, combine margarine, mustard, Worcestershire, and salt. In a plastic bag, combine crumbs and Parmesan cheese. Dip chicken in margarine mixture, then shake in crumb mixture. Place in lightly greased 13 x 9 baking pan. Bake 40-45 minutes or until juices run clear. Drizzle with any remaining margarine mixture. Yield: 6-8 servings

JOYCE BRIDGES, Montevallo, AL Age 59

CASHEW CHICKEN

4 chicken breasts
4 tablespoons soy sauce
2 tablespoons sugar
4 eggs, beaten
1/2 cup water, 1/4 cup water
Corn starch
Oil for frying
3/4 cup cashews, chopped
chopped green onions/cashews
Cooked rice

SAUCE

4 cups water
4 chicken bouillon cubes
1/2 cup chopped celery
1/4 cup soy sauce

Cut chicken in 1/2 inch cubes. Mix soy sauce and sugar; marinate chicken for at least 1 hour. In a medium bowl, mix beaten eggs and 1/2 cup water. Dip chicken in egg mixture. Roll in corn starch; deep fry in skillet or fryer until tender. Place in oven-proof casserole dish. Sprinkle with cashews and 1/4 cup water. Heat in 250 degree oven for 15 minutes. Garnish with green onions and chopped cashews if desired. To prepare sauce, combine water, bouillon, celery, and soy sauce in a large saucepan. Cook over low heat until celery is tender, thicken with corn starch. Serve chicken over cooked rice; pour sauce over all. Yield: 6 servings

MARY NEWTON, Wheatland, MO Age 74

POPPY SEED CHICKEN

6 chicken breasts, cooked (pick off bone in small pieces)
2 cans cream of chicken soup
2 6-ounce cartons sour cream
2 tablespoons poppy seeds
3 stacks Ritz or other crackers, crushed
1 1/2 stick margarine, melted

Preheat oven to 350 degrees. In a large bowl, mix soup, sour cream, and poppy seeds. Layer ingredients in a baking dish as follows: crushed crackers, chicken, soup mixture, crackers. Pour melted butter over top; bake 1 hour. Yield: 6 servings

JO MAC AYDELOTT, Avery, TX Age 64

A+ CHICKEN FOR A BUSY DAY

This recipe can be prepared the night before and popped into the oven the next day. It a great "working mom or wife" recipe.

> 2-3 pounds chicken parts
> 1/4 cup cooking oil
> 1 cup regular rice
> 1 package dry onion soup mix
> 1 can cream of mushroom soup
> 1 can cream of chicken soup
> 1 soup can water

Preheat oven to 350 degrees. In a large bowl, roll pieces of cut up chicken in cooking oil. Place in 13 x 9 baking dish; sprinkle with rice and dry soup mix. Mix canned soups and water in a bowl; spread evenly over chicken. Cover completely with foil and bake 1 1/2 hours. Yield: 4-6 servings

MILDRED TAYLOR, Denton, TX Age 77

SMOTHERED CHICKEN

> 6 thin slices packaged sliced beef
> 1/2 pound uncooked bacon
> 6 boneless chicken breasts
> 1 8-ounce container sour cream
> 1 cup cream of mushroom soup
> Sliced almonds
> Cooked rice

Preheat oven to 350 degrees. Line the bottom of a casserole dish with single slices of beef. Place a slice of bacon on each piece of chicken. Place chicken on top of beef slices. In a medium bowl, mix soup, sour cream, and 1 soup can of water. Add sliced almonds. Pour mixture over chicken; cover dish with foil and bake 2 hours. Serve with rice. Yield: 6 servings

JOYCE W. TAYLOR, Aiken, SC Age 60

Tastes Like Chicken!

We used to say times were so bad during the Depression, all we had to eat were fried rabbit tracks and wind pudding! Back then, rabbit hunting was both recreation and necessity. A young jackrabbit is delicious, and there is no cost except for a few .22 shells. It was common for young fellas to go hunting and bring the fresh rabbits home for Mom to cook up. One rabbit is about the same size as a chicken. . .and yes, it kind of tastes like one too.

Cy Carpenter, Minneapolis, MN

-139-

MRS. McCANN'S
CHICKEN WITH RICE

This is one of my favorite recipes to serve to company. I still love to have people over for dinners, although it takes me a little longer to get going.

1 1/2 cups brown rice
1 cut up chicken, or 3 pounds breasts or thighs
1 package dry onion soup mix
2 1/2 cups of water
1 can of mushroom soup

Preheat oven to 350 degrees. Sprinkle uncooked rice evenly in the bottom of a 9 x 12 baking dish. Place chicken over rice and sprinkle with onion soup mix; add water. Bake uncovered 50 minutes. Remove from oven, spread undiluted mushroom soup over top. Cover with foil and bake another 50 minutes. Yield: 6-8 servings

ELIZABETH V. SUTLIFF, Independence, OR Age 83

CHICKEN IN WINE SAUCE

1/2 garlic bulb
2 tablespoons salt
1 teaspoon oregano leaves
1 teaspoon black pepper
1 chicken cut in four pieces
2 slices of bacon
Paprika
1 tomato, diced
2 green peppers, diced
1 onion, diced
1 stick margarine, sliced into pats
1 cup white wine
3 ounces beer

Preheat oven to 350 degrees. In a small bowl, crush and mix garlic, salt, oregano, and black pepper. Cut chicken in four pieces, rinse and score lightly, coat with spice mixture. Place chicken in a baking dish; dust with paprika. Lay bacon slices on top of chicken; add diced vegetables, margarine pats, wine, and beer. Roast uncovered for 1 1/2 hours. Yield: 4 servings

LUIS VARGAS, Adjuntas, Puerto Rico Age 63

QUICK CHICKEN BROCCOLI DIVAN

1 pound fresh broccoli, cut into spears (or 1 package frozen
    spears, cut and drained)
1 1/2 cups cubed cooked chicken or turkey
1 can cream of broccoli soup
1/3 cup milk
1/2 cup shredded cheddar cheese
1 tablespoon butter, melted
2 tablespoons dry bread crumbs

Preheat oven to 450 degrees. Arrange broccoli in a 9 inch pie plate or
shallow casserole. Top with chicken. Combine soup and milk in a
small bowl and pour over chicken. Sprinkle with cheese. Combine
butter and bread crumbs and sprinkle over cheese. Bake 15 minutes
or until hot. Yield: 4 servings

CORA WESTMORELAND, Bryans Road, MD Age 57

CHICKEN SPAGHETTI

1 cup chopped celery
1 medium onion chopped
1 8-ounce can mushrooms
3 tablespoons margarine or butter
1 large chicken cut up and boiled or cooked in a pressure pan
1 8-ounce can chopped green chilies
1 8-ounce package. spaghetti
1 cup grated cheese of choice

This recipe serves my family well; When we have get-togethers, it's always on request. I work at CCTV Channel 9 and have met many wonderful people, it's so good to be back in the work force.

Boil or cook chicken in a pressure cooker. Cool, and remove meat
from bones. Strain and reserve the broth. Preheat oven to 375
degrees. In a small skillet, saute celery, onion, and mushrooms in
margarine until soft. Bring broth to a boil in a kettle or soup pot; add
spaghetti and cook until done (this is the secret to the spaghetti).
Combine all ingredients in a 13 x 9 pan. Sprinkle with cheese. Bake
until cheese is melted and casserole bubbles. Yield: 12-14 servings

LOUISE ATHEY, St. Helens, OR Age 81

CHICKEN & YELLOW RICE CASSEROLE

5 chicken breasts
1-ounce package yellow rice
1 medium onion, chopped
1 tablespoon margarine
1 1/2 cups chicken broth

Preheat oven to 350 degrees. Boil chicken breasts in a kettle until cooked through; reserve 1 1/2 cups broth. Debone chicken. Mix all ingredients in a 13 x 9 casserole dish; cover tightly; and bake for 30 minutes. Yield 4-6 servings

JEAN STARKEY, Pisgah, AL Age 55

ROAST CHICKEN AND SHRIMP

1 large head elephant garlic
2 teaspoons olive or salad oil, plus 1 tablespoon
3 1/2 pounds chicken parts, skin removed
1 tablespoon fresh rosemary, finely chopped
1 1/2 teaspoons salt
2 teaspoons lemon juice
1/2 teaspoon black pepper
1 pound large fresh shrimp
Fresh rosemary sprigs for garnish

Rule of Thumb:

If you cook the shrimp in the shell it retains more of the shrimp flavor and makes the dish look even prettier. If you prefer, shell and devein shrimp before adding them to the roasting pan.

Preheat oven to 450. Separate garlic into cloves, removing any loose papery skin, but do not peel. Toss garlic cloves with 2 tsp. olive or salad oil in a large roasting pan. Cover roasting pan with foil and roast garlic 15 minutes. In a large bowl, mix rosemary, salt, lemon juice, pepper, and 1 tablespoon oil; add chicken and toss until well coated. Place chicken in the roasting pan with the garlic. Bake 15 minutes, uncovered, basting chicken one or twice with drippings. While chicken is roasting, cut along the back of each shrimp with kitchen shears, exposing the vein, but keeping the shell intact. Rinse each shrimp under running cold water to remove vein. Pat shrimp dry with paper towel. Add shrimp to chicken drippings and cook an additional 15 minutes. Remove cover and roast 10 minutes. Yield: 6 servings

MARY A. SMITH, Jackson, MI Age 78

CHICKEN-WHITE BEAN CHILI

4 boneless chicken breasts
1 tablespoon vegetable oil
1 onion, chopped
2 cloves garlic, minced
1 can mild or medium salsa
3 cans small white beans
3 tablespoons mesquite or similiar flavoring
1/3 cup chopped cilantro
Grated Monterey Jack cheese

Heat oil in a dutch oven; add chicken and saute over medium heat until meat is no longer pink. Add the onion and garlic and saute until onion is transparent and chicken is lightly browned. Remove chicken, cut into cubes, and return to pan. Reduce heat to low; add salsa, white beans, mesquite flavoring, and cilantro. Simmer 5-10 minutes, stirring occasionally. Sprinkle cheese on top. Yield: 6-8 servings

MARJORIE GUENTHER, Marion, OH Age 68

CHICKEN POT PIE

This recipe freezes well; top with biscuits when ready to bake. I also use homemade baking powder biscuits for the crust. This is good to take to potlucks.

1 stewing hen
3-4 medium potatoes, peeled and diced
2 medium carrots, grated
Salt and pepper to taste
2 cans cream of chicken soup
2-3 cups milk
1 can refrigerator biscuits

Place cut-up chicken in a large kettle, cover with water, and cook until tender. Remove from liquid and allow to cool. Pick meat off bones. In a large saucepan, cook potatoes and carrots until tender; drain. Combine soup with milk in a large bowl; add meat and cooked vegetables, stirring well to coat. Divide mixture between two 2-quart casserole dishes. Preheat oven to 350 degrees. Roll biscuits to 1/2" thickness and top casseroles. Bake for 1 hour. Yield: 10-12 servings.

ROBBIE YAEBER, Deep River, IA Age 58

Catsup Sandwiches

I grew up with nine siblings and there were times when my parents could barely make ends meet. I can remember coming home to catsup sandwiches and thinking how good they were. Hunger is the best appetizer, and going hungry once in a while can be a good thing. It makes us think twice about taking things for granted.

Richard Dandurand, Jackson, MI

The Thanksgiving We Didn't Eat Turkey

Once, right before Thanksgiving, my parents piled all eight kids into the car and headed to Ichabod's Turkey Farm to select a fresh turkey for our holiday meal. The turkeys flapped around and jumped on the car. As the oldest girl my sister had the honor of choosing the bird. She selected the largest one which was then dressed for us to take home. Mother prepared the traditional feast and brought the star of the meal to the table for my father to carve. "Who wants a drumstick," he asked. No answer. "Wings?" No answer. "White meat? Dark meat?" We realized that we couldn't eat a turkey we had even briefly known personally.

Peggy Auker, Cheyenne, WY

SUCCULENT TENDER TURKEY

The veggies help to retain moisture in the turkey, while their flavors permeate the turkey.

Turkey, any size
Crisco savory seasoning vegetable oil
Whole carrots
Celery stalks
Scallions (preferred) or onions
1/2 stick margarine
2 1/2 cups water
2 tablespoons Old Bay seasoning, plus 1 tablespoon
1 tablespoon seasoning salt

Thaw, wash, and dry turkey. Remove contents from turkey's cavity. Lightly coat turkey with Crisco classic herb savory seasonings vegetable oil. Stuff turkey cavity with washed whole carrots, celery stalks, scallions, and margarine. Make a bed for the turkey by lining a roaster with carrots and celery stalks; place turkey on top. Mix water and 2 tablespoons Old Bay seasoning in a small bowl. Pour into roaster over vegetables. Sprinkle 1 tablespoon Old Bay and 1 table-spoon of seasoned salt over turkey. Roast at 325 degrees according to size. Optional: place in cooking bag and cook per instructions according to size. When turkey is done, remove vegetables from cavity and stuff with favorite stuffing.

JUANITA BRANCH, Norlina, NC Age 62

THANKSGIVING TURKEY STUFFING

12 slices bread
1 stick melted margarine or butter
1/2 cup chopped walnuts
1 1/2 cup chopped celery
1 large onion, chopped
1/2 cup chopped green olives
8 ounces fresh or canned mushrooms
3/4 cup raisins
3 cups milk
Salt and pepper to taste

Crumble bread into small pieces in a large mixing bowl; add all other ingredients. Refrigerate until ready to put stuffing into turkey cavity and neck. Cook turkey as directed. Yield: 15-20 servings

CHRISTINE KULAS, Fort Pierce, FL Age 55

TURKEY MEAT LOAF

*Serve with steamed broccoli and cauliflower for a healthy meal.
Inexpensive, healthy, quick and easy. With a molded salad, dessert.
and beverage, it is fit for serving company.*

1 pound ground turkey
1/4 teaspoon salt
2 eggs, lightly beaten
1/4 teaspoon pepper
1 cup canned or frozen green peas
3/4 cup tomato sauce
18 saltine crackers, crumbled
1/4 cup uncooked oatmeal
1/3 cup canned or frozen corn
1/2 cup chopped onion
1 tablespoon Worcestershire sauce
1 clove garlic, minced

Preheat oven to 350 degrees. Spray 9 x 5 loaf pan with non-stick
spray. Mix all ingredients thoroughly in large bowl. Pat into loaf
shape; place in pan and bake for one hour. Unmold onto serving
platter. Yield: 8 servings

LEOLA C. BURNS, Strong, AR Age 72

TEXAS BAKED TURKEY

1 box Uncle Ben's wild rice w/herbs, cooked
1 can cream of mushroom soup
1 can french style green beans, drained
1 can sliced water chestnuts, drained
1 medium red onion, chopped
1 can cream of celery soup
1 cup mayonaise
1 package slivered almonds
2 cups cooked turkey

Preheat oven to 350 degrees. Mix all ingredients together in a large
bowl. Use as much meat as desired. Pour into a 9 x 13 baking dish.
Bake uncovered for 1 hour. Best if cooked a day ahead and reheated.
May be reheated in microwave. Yield: 12 servings

MARIE S. DEAN, Farmerville, LA Age 83

Company for Dinner

One Thanksgiving we enjoyed a delicious holiday meal. After dinner, we cleaned up and put the turkey bones outside in the trash. Later we heard a commotion and looked outside to investigate; someone or something had gotten into the trash. As we looked more closely, we discovered a raccoon lying flat on its back--it was sleeping off the effects of its second-hand traditional turkey dinner!

Charles Toftoy, Arlington, VA

This is a tasty recipe that goes well at covered dish gatherings. It also freezes well. I have been a widow for 20 years. My pleasures in life are family, church, arts and crafts, cooking, and my Green Thumb job.

-145-

BAYOU FRIED CATFISH

6 catfish fillets, 5-6 ounces each
3/4 cup yellow cornmeal
3/4 cup white flour (all purpose)
1 cup vegetable oil

SEASONING MIX

Rules of Thumb:

For fresher flavor, defrost frozen fish in milk.

To serve fish, place on a preheated platter. Garnish, and serve immediately. Fish becomes soggy when it stands.

1 teaspoon salt
2 teaspoons paprika
1 1/2 teaspoons onion powder
1 1/2 teaspoons dried sweet basil leaves
1 teaspoon dried thyme leaves
3/4 teaspoon dried oregano leaves
1 teaspoon black pepper
1/2 teaspoon white pepper

Thoroughtly combine the seasoning mix ingredients in a small bowl. Sprinkle the catfish fillets with 2 teaspoons of seasoning mix and rub it in well with hands. In a shallow pan, combine the cornmeal, flour, and 2 teaspoons plus 1 tablespoon of the seasoning mix. Heat oil in a large skillet over high heat. While the oil is heating dredge 3 fillets at a time in the cornmeal mixture, pressing the fish into the mixture to make it stick. When the oil is very hot, add the fillets to the skillet and fry, turning 4-5 times until the fish is brown and very crispy on both sides. Remove and drain on paper towels. Dredge the remaining fish in the cornmeal mixture. Let the oil get very hot again and repeat the procedure. Serve immediately. Yield: 6 servings

ANN LIVERS, Loogootee, IN Age 81

BAKED FISH

1 to 1 1/2 pounds haddock, halibut, or orange roughy
1 can cream of celery soup
1 1/2 tablespoons dried onion flakes
1 teaspoon pepper
1 can French fried onions

Preheat oven to 350 degrees. Rinse fish and pat dry. Place in oblong baking dish. Mix soup, onion, and pepper together and pour over fish. Top with french fried onions. Cover tightly. Bake for 1 hour. Yield: 4-6 servings

ARLENE WHEELER, Linesville, PA Age 55

GULF FISH MOLD

1 tablespoon gelatin
1/4 cup cold water
2 egg yolks, slightly beaten
1 scant teaspoon salt and white pepper
1 teaspoon prepared mustard
1/2 tablespoon melted butter
3/4 cup cold milk
2 tablespoons lemon juice or mild vinegar
2 cups canned salmon, drained
2 cups canned tuna fish, well drained
2 cups crabmeat, drained and boned
Few drops of Worcestershire

CUCUMBER SAUCE

2 cups heavy cream
Salt and pepper
mild vinegar or lemon juice
1/2 medium cucumber, chopped

Soften the gelatin in the cold water. Combine egg yolks, salt, pepper, and mustard in a double boiler. Add the butter, milk, lemon juice or vinegar, and cook; stirring constantly until mixture thickens. Cool until mixture is almost set; fold in the fish and Worcestershire sauce. Turn into a wet mold and chill. To make cucumber sauce: Beat cream until stiff; season with salt and pepper, and vinegar or lemon juice. Fold in chopped cucumber. To serve, fill the center of the mold with cucumber sauce. Garnish with sliced cucumbers and ripe olives. Yield: 4-6 servings

MARGARET P. HINTON, Zephyrhills, FL Age 66

-147-

Legend has it that Minnesota's Boy River got its name when an Indian woman cried out, "Boy, river! Boy, river!" In her limited English, she was trying to convey that her son was drowning and needed help. My father took us fishing on this infamous river often. I always felt proud to take home the bullheads and sunfish that I had caught. My mother fried, baked, and boiled the fish, but we loved it best when she made her delicious fish . soup.

*Irene Godfrey
Boy River, MN
Age 79*

TOMATO-VEGGIE FISH BAKE

1 pound fish fillets
4 teaspoons olive oil
1//3 cup chopped carrots
1/3 cup chopped celery
1/3 cup chopped onion
1 clove garlic
1 large ripe tomato, chopped
1 tablespoon chopped parsley
1/2 teaspoon lemon zest

Preheat oven to 350 degrees. Arrange fish in single layer in shallow baking dish. Heat oil in a skillet over medium heat. Add carrots, celery, onion, and garlic. Cook stirring, as for stir fry, 3-5 minutes. Remove from heat, stir in tomato, parsley, and grated lemon. Spoon vegetable mixture over fish. Bake until fork tender, about 15 minutes. Yield: 4 servings

DELORES L. DOOLEY, Elcho, WI Age 70

SALMON SOUFFLE

3 tablespoons butter
3 tablespoons flour
1 cup milk
1/2 teaspoon salt
1/2 teaspoon paprika
1 teaspoon lemon juice
1 tablespoon minced parsley
1/2 teaspoon celery salt
3/4 cup grated cheddar cheese
1 cup salmon, flaked
4 eggs, separated

Preheat oven to 375 degrees. Melt butter in a medium saucepan; blend in flour. Add milk and cook until thick, stirring constantly. Remove from heat, season with salt, paprika, lemon juice, parsley, and celery salt. Add cheese, salmon, and beaten egg yolks. Fold in stiffly beaten egg whites. Pour into a casserole and bake 40 to 45 minutes or until a pointed knife comes out clean. Yield: 6-8 servings

KATHLEEN GERBER, Bloomsburg, PA Age 79

SALMON CROQUETS

1 tall can salmon, drained and deboned
1/2 cup flour
1 cup cornmeal
1 teaspoon baking powder
1 egg, beaten
1/2 cup milk

Mix all ingredients together in a large bowl. Drop by teaspoonsful into deep hot oil in a skillet or fryer. Cook until golden brown; they cook fast. Serve while hot for best flavor. Yield: 4-6 servings

JANICE ROBERTS, Bennington, OK Age 63

TUNA BAKE

1 can tuna, drained and flaked
1 medium onion, chopped
1 1/4 cups grated cheddar cheese
1 can cream of mushroom soup, undiluted
1 10-ounce bag potato chips
1 can asparagus with juice

Preheat oven to 350 degrees. Butter a 2-quart baking dish. Place 1/3 of tuna in bottom, top with 1/4 of potato chips, followed by 1/3 of onions, 1/3 of cheese, and 1/3 of asparagus. Repeat 2 more times. Top final asparagus layer with mushroom soup and cover with crushed chips. Bake 45 minutes. Yield 4-6 servings

KATHRYN KNAPP, Lancaster, OH Age 59

TEXAS TUNA CASSEROLE

2 cans tuna in water, drained
2 cans tomatoes, including liquid
2 cans cream of chicken soup
2 cans cream of mushroom soup
1 large onion, chopped
2 12-ounce packages shredded cheese, reserve 1 cup
1/2 jar jalapeno peppers (optional)
1 36-count package corn tortillas

Preheat oven to 350 degrees. Mix all ingredients except tortillas in a large bowl. Overlap tortillas in the bottom of a large baking pan. Cover with tuna mixture; sprinkle reserved cheese on top. Bake 45 minutes, or microwave on high for 20 minutes. May be served hot or cold. Yield: 12-14 servings

WILLIAM C. PRICE, Abilene, TX Age 58

SHRIMP-STUFFED PEPPERS FOR TWO

2 medium-sized green peppers, cored and seeded
1 4 1/2 ounce can shrimp, drained and rinsed
1/4 cup cooked rice
1/3 cup mayonnaise
1 tablespoon chopped onion
2 drops hot sauce
1/4 cup cracker crumbs
1 tablespoon margarine or butter, melted

Cook green peppers in boiling salted water for 5 minutes; drain. Set aside two shrimp. Combine rice, remaining shrimp, mayonnaise, onion, and hot sauce; mix well. Spoon into peppers; place in a loaf pan. Combine cracker crumbs and butter; mix well. Sprinkle on peppers; bake uncovered for 30 minutes. Garnish with reserved shrimp. Yield 2 servings

PEGGY PAPPAS, Age 74

SHRIMP DELIGHT STIR-FRY

1 2-pound package boiled shrimp
2 green bell peppers, cut in strips
2 medium onions, cut in strips
4 cups cooked rice

SAUCE

6 tablespoons butter
Garlic salt to taste
1 cup Kraft sweet and sour mix

Prepare a medium skillet with non-stick cooking spray. Stir-fry the shrimp, peppers, and onions for 3 minutes. Combine sauce ingredients in a small saucepan and bring to a boil. Put rice on serving dish, top with stir-fry mixture, and spoon sauce over all. Yield: 4 servings

BARBARA EDEFEN, Chiefland, FL Age 55

SEAFOOD NEWBURG

SAUCE
   4 tablespoons butter
   3 tablespoons flour
   2 1/2 cups milk

   1/2 pound fresh lobster
   1/2 pound shrimp
   1/2 pound crabmeat
   3 eggs, beaten
   2 tablespoons sherry
   Salt to taste
   Paprika for garnish

Melt butter in a medium saucepan over medium heat; add flour, and milk. Stir frequently to make a smooth cream sauce. Add lobster, shrimp, and crabmeat, then egg, sherry, and salt. Stir over medium heat until thoroughly heated. Spoon into serving dishes; dust with paprika. Yield: 4 servings

RACHEL W. HALE, Dallas, PA

WILD RICE AND OYSTERS

   1/2 cup wild rice
   2 cups bread crumbs
   1/2 cup melted margarine or butter, 2 tablespoons
   1 cup oysters, reserve liquid
   Canned chicken broth

Preheat oven to 350 degrees. Steam wild rice according to package directions. Combine bread crumbs with melted butter in a small bowl. In a buttered baking dish, arrange in layers: half of the crumbs, half the rice and all the oysters. Pat the oysters wth 2 tablespoons butter and top with the remaining rice. Add enough chicken broth to the reserved oyster liquid to make 1 1/2 cups; pour over the oyster mixture. Sprinkle remaining buttered crumbs over the top. Cover with foil and bake 30 minutes. Remove foil and bake 15 minutes or until crumbs are golden. Yield 4 servings

ARDYS J. ZIMMERMAN, Montevidio, MN Age 68

Vegetables & Side Dishes

VEGETABLES & SIDE DISHES

CONTENTS

ASPARAGUS ALMOND CASSEROLE

2 cans cut asparagus
1 1/2 cups grated sharp cheese
2 cups medium thin white sauce
1/2 cup slivered almonds
Cracker crumbs
Butter

WHITE SAUCE

3 tablespoons butter
3 tablespoons flour
1 teaspoon salt
1/8 teaspoon pepper
2 cups milk

Preheat oven to 350 degrees. To prepare white sauce, melt butter over low heat: add flour, salt, and pepper. Stir until well blended. Very gradually add milk. Stir constantly until thick and creamy. If too thick, add a little more milk. Place a layer of drained asparagus in casserole. Cover with half the cheese, then half the sauce, then half of the almonds. Repeat and sprinkle with cracker crumbs and dots of butter. Bake for 20-25 minutes. Yield: 6 servings

PAT HODGE, Dandridge, TN

BROCCOLI AND BEAN CASSEROLE

2 10-ounce packages chopped frozen broccoli
2 packages large lima beans
1 can mushroom soup
1 8-ounce container sour cream
1 can sliced water chestnuts
1 envelope dry onion soup mix
1 stick butter or maragine, melted
4 cups crispy rice cereal

Preheat oven to 350 degrees. Mix broccoli, limas, soup, sour cream, water chestnuts, and dry soup mix in a large bowl. Pour into a 9 x 13 inch casserole dish. Mix butter with cereal and pour over vegetables. Bake one hour. Yield: 8 servings

BETTY DOWNEY, Monticello, IL

BROCCOLI RICE CASSEROLE

1 small onion, chopped
1/2 cup chopped celery
1 10-ounce package frozen chopped broccoli
1 tablespoon butter or margarine
1 jar processed cheese spread
1 can mushroom soup, undiluted
1 5-ounce can evaporated milk
3 cups cooked rice

Preheat oven to 325 degrees. In a large skillet over medium heat, saute onion, celery, and broccoli in butter for 3 to 5 minutes. Add cheese, soup, and milk and stir until smooth. Place rice in a greased 8-inch square baking dish. Pour cheese mixture over; do not stir. Bake uncovered for 25-30 minutes or until hot and bubbly. Yield: 8-10 servings

PAULINE SMITH, Ochlocknee, GA Age 74

Rule of Thumb:

When cooking cabbage, place a piece of bread on top before putting on the lid. There will be no tell-tale odor.

BAKED CREAMED CABBAGE

1 medium cabbage, finely shredded
1/2 cup boiling salted water
3 tablespoons margarine
1/2 teaspoon salt
3 tablespoons flour
1 1/2 cup milk
1/4 cup bread crumbs
1/2 cup grated cheese (your choice)

Preheat the oven to 350 degrees. Simmer the cabbage in water in a large saucepan for 9 minutes. Remove from heat, drain well, and place cabbage in a 13 x 9" casserole dish. In a small saucepan, melt margarine. Add flour and salt, and stir until the mixture is smooth. Gradually add the milk and continue stirring until the sauce thickens. Pour the sauce over the cabbage, sprinkle with bread crumbs and cheese. Bake until bubbly and lightly browned. Yield 6 servings

KATHRYN M. DOMINY, Cochran, GA Age 56

CABBAGE-TOMATO CASSEROLE

This is one of my favorite ways to serve cabbage.

    5 cups cabbage, coarsely shredded
    1 cup drained canned tomatoes, or
        2 1/2 cups fresh peeled, cut-up tomatoes
    1/2 cup tomato juice
    1/4 cup chopped onion
    1/2 cup crushed saltine crackers
    1 1/2 teaspoons salt
    1/8 teaspoon pepper
    1/2 cup grated American cheese

Preheat oven to 350 degrees. Steam the cabbage in a covered saucepan with a small amount of water until it becomes tender-crisp
(almost done). Drain if necessary. Arrange cabbage, tomatoes, and
tomato juice in layers in a buttered 1-quart casserole. Top with
chopped onion and cracker crumbs. Season with salt and pepper;
cover and bake for 30 minutes. Remove cover and bake 10 minutes
longer. Top with cheese and bake uncovered about 5 minutes until
cheese is melted and bubbly. Yield: 6 servings

BLANCHE A. SLAUGHTER, Darwin, MN Age 58

FRIED CABBAGE AND RICE

    1 medium head cabbage
    Vegetable oil for skillet
    1/2 cup chopped onions
    1/2 cup chopped green pepper
    Dash of thyme
    1/2 cup cooked rice

Cut up the cabbage and place in a skillet with a small amount of oil.
Add onions, green pepper, and a dash of thyme. Add the rice to the
vegetable mixture and fry until tender. Yield: 4-6 servings

DOROTHY RALEY, Lebanon, KY Age 67

CARROT MEDLEY

1 pound carrots, cut diagonally
1 medium green pepper, chopped
1/3 cup pineapple juice
1 tablespoon cornstarch
1/2 teaspoon salt
2 tablespoons sugar
2 tablespoons soy sauce
1 8-ounce can pineapple chunks

In a large saucepan, cook carrots 15 minutes. Add green pepper and cook an additional 3 minutes. Drain and set aside. Mix pineapple juice with cornstarch, salt, sugar, and soy sauce. Cook and stir until bubbly. Add pineapple, carrots, and peppers to sauce and heat through. Yield: 6 servings

WILMA M. NICKELS, Marshfield, MO Age 57

WESTERN CARROT BURGERS

4 cups corn flake cereal
1 1/2 cups carrots, cooked and mashed
1 egg, beaten
1 tablespoon finely chopped green onion
1/4 cup finely chopped celery
2 teaspoons salt
Pepper to taste

Crush corn flakes into fine crumbs. In a medium bowl, mix half the crumbs with carrots, egg, onion, celery, salt, and pepper. Shape into patties and dip in remaining crumbs. Fry in shallow hot oil until brown on both sides. Yield: 8 patties

ELSIE CLEVELAND, Greeley, CO Age 70

EASY CHILE RELLENOS

My daughter won 1st prize at county level and 2nd place at state level in a dairy recipe competition with this recipe.

6 eggs, separated
1 tablespoon flour
1/4 teaspoon salt
1 4-ounce can green chiles, drained, diced and seeded
1/2 pound grated Monterey Jack or cheddar cheese
1/2 cup sour cream
1/4-1/2 cup salsa
Garnish: ripe olives, parsley

Preheat oven to 325 degrees. Beat egg whites until soft peaks form. In a separate bowl, beat yolks slightly with a fork, add flour, and salt; mix until smooth. Fold in whites until well blended. Turn half the mixture into a well greased 12 x 8 baking dish. Cover with chiles and cheese. Top with remaining egg mixture. Bake 25 minutes. In a small bowl, mix sour cream and salsa. Top each serving with a dollop of sour cream mixture; garnish with ripe olive slices and parsley. Yield: 6-8 servings

DIANE CHAPMAN, Magnolia, AR Age 58

CORN PATTIES

2 eggs, separated
1/2 teaspoon salt
Dash pepper
1 1/2 cups cooked fresh corn (cut off cob)
2 teaspoons cream
1 teaspoon butter
2 tablespoons flour

Beat egg yolks in a small mixing bowl. Add salt, pepper, corn, cream, butter, and flour. Beat egg whites until stiff; fold into corn mixture. Drop batter by teaspoon onto a hot, greased griddle. Cook until brown on each side. Serve hot. Yield: 24 fritters

ALICE CAMPBELL, Age 82

Good Neighbors

Early American rural communities depended on a good corn harvest. Neighbors in those farming communities put corn cobs or dried corn on their doors as a symbol of luck for the harvest. Hanging corn on the door has since become a tradition to signify the coming of fall--the harvest season.

Rule of Thumb:

Use a damp paper towel to remove silk from fresh corn. Wipe down from top to effectively remove all silk.

CORN CASSEROLE

Nebraskans are known as "corn huskers," hence the corn casserole.

2 eggs, slightly beaten
1 8 1/2-ounce package corn muffin mix
1 can cream styled corn
1 can whole kernel corn
1 cup sour cream
1/2 cup shredded Swiss cheese

Preheat oven to 350 degrees. Mix all ingredients, except the cheese. Place in an 8" square baking pan. Bake 30-35 minutes. Remove from oven and top with cheese. Bake 10 to 15 additional minutes. Yield: 12-14 servings

DARLENE REGNOLDSON, Eagle, NE Age 8?

DRIED SWEET CORN

Mom used to make this on top of the old cookstove. We children ate it like candy!

1 cup cream or evaporated milk
1 cup sugar
1/4 cup salt
8 pints corn, cut off cob

In a large kettle, combine the milk, sugar, and salt. Blanch the corn in this liquid and then place it in a dehydrator. If you don't have a dehydrator, spread the corn in thin layers on cookie sheets and place in the oven at 250 to 300 degrees. Stir occasionally. It will take several days to dry, but it is well worth the time. When dry, store the corn in jars. It also freezes well. To use, cover a small amount of corn with warm water and simmer until cooked. Yield: 16 cups

MARY CALENDINE, Hiddinite, NC Age 76

STEWED CUCUMBERS

The amount of flour and milk is up to the individual according to how thick you like your gravy.

3 large cucumbers
1 teaspoon salt
Water
Flour (to thicken)
Evaporated milk
3-4 tablespoons margarine

Peel cucumbers and cut in medium-sized pieces. Place in a medium bowl, sprinkle with salt, cover, and put in refrigerator for about 1/2 hour. Put cucumbers in a saucepan with just enough water to cook. When tender, remove from heat and sprinkle with flour; add milk and margarine. Heat and stir. Yield: 2-4 servings

HILDEGARD McDOWELL, Franklin, KY Age 74

EGGPLANT PARMESAN

1 large eggplant
1 can mushroom soup
1/4 can water
1 1/2 cups Italian bread crumbs
Parmesan cheese

Preheat oven to 350 degrees. Peel eggplant and slice 1/4" thick. Cut into even chunks. Blanch in boiling water for 2 minutes and drain. Mix soup and water together. Line a 6 x 9" oven dish with bread crumbs, layer eggplant, soup, bread crumbs, and cheese. Repeat until dish is full. Bake for 1 hour. Yield: 4-6 servings

VIOLA E. ENGEL, Mount Dora, FL Age 67

BAKED BEANS

1 medium can pork & beans
1/2 cup catsup
1 tablespoon prepared mustard
1 tablespoon Worchestershire sauce
1/2 cup brown sugar
1/4 cup onions, chopped fine
1/4 cup molasses
10 strips bacon, cooked crisp and crumbled

Preheat oven to 350 degrees. Mix all ingredients except bacon in a
large casserole. Crumble bacon over the top and bake 1 hour. Yield:
6-8 servings

EDNA ROGERS, Warsaw, WI Age 60

GARLIC GREEN BEANS

2 pounds fresh green beans
1 cup water
1/2 cup sliced green onions
4 cloves garlic, crushed
1/4 cup plus 2 tablespoons margarine
1/2 cup chopped fresh parsley
3 tablespoons lemon juice
Slivered almonds
1/4 teaspoon salt
1/4 teaspoon pepper

Place green beans and water in a large dutch over. Bring to a boil,
cover, reduce heat and simmer 6 to 8 minutes or until crisp-tender.
Drain and set aside. Cook green onions and garlic in butter over
medium heat for 3 minutes. Stir in parsley, lemon juice, and almonds. Add salt and pepper. Yield: 8-10 servings

SHEILA EARP, North Carolina

SWEET AND SOUR GREEN BEANS

2 cans green beans, drained
3/4 cup sugar
1/2 cup white vinegar
1 large onion, diced
1 1/2 cups water

Mix all ingredients in a large saucepan; cook about 1 hour Yield: 6-8 servings

CECILE S. LOVELL, Aberdeen, MS Age 70

QUICK AND EASY CREAMED MACARONI

2 cups macaroni
1/2 cup sugar
2 teaspoons butter or maragine
1/2 cup milk

Cook macaroni 6 to 8 minutes and drain. Stir in sugar, butter, and milk. Yield: 4-6 servings

EMMA LOU HANCOCK, Marion, IN Age 57

IMPERIAL MACARONI AND CHEESE

1 cup uncooked macaroni
1/2 cup soft bread crumbs
1/4 cup melted butter
1/4 cup diced red pepper
1/4 cup diced green pepper
1 1/2 teaspoon chopped onion
1/2 teaspoon salt
1 cup sharp cheese, cut fine
1 1/2 cups scalded milk
3 eggs, separated
1/2 teaspoon salt

Preheat oven to 350 degrees. Cook and drain macaroni. Mix bread crumbs, butter, green and red peppers, onion, salt, and cheese in a large bowl. Add milk and beaten egg yolks. Beat egg whites to form stiff peaks. Add macaroni and egg whites. Pour into buttered 1 1/2-quart casserole. Place casserole dish in pan of hot water and bake for one hour. Yield: 6 servings

JANE F. KENYON, Lyndonville, NY Age 77

And She Forgot the Meat

My mother led a hard life--when Father passed away she worked as a cleaning lady at St. Paul's postal office to provide for her five children. Money was always tight and we didn't have meat too often, which reminds me of this particular story. My grandparents, who were farmers, paid us a visit and brought gifts of food from their farm. My mother prepared a feast and we sat down to a hearty meal of soup, potatoes, corn, salad, vegetables, bread, and pie. It was after supper, when she was cleaning up, that she realized that she forgot the meat--it was in the warming oven. We had meat so seldom we didn't even miss it!

Mabel McDowell, Hendricks, MN Age 67

Cooking Boo-Boos

Peanut Potatoes
I've never been much of a cook, but my three-year-old grand daughter recently told me that she didn't like the peanuts in the mashed potatoes I had served her. Unfortunately, those weren't peanuts--they were lumps!

Anne Hutchison
Mountain Grove, MO

This is a Zucchini
I make a wonderful zucchini bread. One time, however, I confused zucchini and cucumbers. The finished loaves looked beautiful, but they tasted awful; people would take a bite and discreetly get rid of it. Before making the recipe recently, a friend held up a green vegetable in each hand. Now, Suzanne," she said, "this is a cucumber and this is a zucchini."

Suzanne Sigfried

MIXED VEGETABLE CASSEROLE

1 pound mixed vegetables, frozen or canned
1 6-ounce can water chestnuts, chopped
2 cups grated cheddar cheese
1 onion, chopped
1 cup mayonnaise
3/4 cup melted margarine
2 1/2 cups crushed crackers

Preheat oven to 350 degrees. Prepare frozen vegetables according to package directions; drain. (If using canned vegetables, drain before using.) Mix vegetables, water chestnuts, cheese, onion, and mayonnaise. Spread in 9 x 13 casserole. Combine melted margarine and crushed crackers. Spread over vegetables. Bake 35 to 40 minutes. Yield: 8-10 servings

JUANITA COLLINS, Hugo, OK Age 71

MARINATED MIXED VEGETABLES

1 can French green beans
2 cans corn
1 small can English peas
1/4 cup celery, chopped
1/4 cup bell pepper, chopped
1/4 cup onions, chopped
1 small jar pimentos and liquid

SAUCE
2/3 cup sugar
1/3 cup oil
1/2 teaspoon salt
1/2 teaspoon pepper
1/2 cup white vinegar

Drain canned vegetables and pour into a large bowl. Add celery, bell pepper, onion, and pimentos with juice. Combine sugar, oil, salt, pepper, and vinegar in a saucepan and bring to a boil. Simmer until sugar is dissolved. Let cool and pour over vegetables. Cover and let set 8 hours in the refrigerator. Stir well before serving. Yield: 8 servings

EUNICE McCLAIN, Laurie, MS Age 68

CREAMED PEAS AND POTATOES

Fresh garden peas and new potatoes make this recipe extra special.

    6 medium potatoes
    1 1/2 cups fresh or frozen peas
    Salt and sugar to taste
    2 tablespoons cornstarch
    1-3 teaspoons milk or water
    Butter (to taste)

Peel and cube 6 medium potatoes. Place potatoes in a large saucepan, cover with water, and cook until soft. In a separate pan, heat peas in a small amount of water; add both peas and cooking water to potatoes. Heat until flavors blend; season to taste. Mix the cornstarch in small amount of milk or water. Add to peas and potatoes. Add butter to taste. Yield: 6 servings

MILDRED H. CANNON, Mt. Ayr, IA

FRESH PEAS

    Boiling salted water (1" deep in pan)
    2 pounds fresh peas, shelled just before cooking
    2-4 tablespoons margarine or butter
    Herbs of choice (basil, mint, thyme, tarragon)

Add peas to boiling salted water. Bring to a second boil over high heat; cover; reduce to simmer and cook until tender, 15-20 minutes. Toss with butter and herbs. Yield: 6-8 servings

J. ORTWIG, Age 68

STUFFED LONG PEPPERS

Hot or sweet!

    8 peppers
    1 cup seasoned bread crumbs
    1 egg, beaten
    1 tablespoon garlic powder
    Salt and pepper

Cut tops off peppers. Combine bread crumbs, egg, garlic, salt, and pepper in a medium bowl. Add enough water to moisten. Stuff the peppers with mixture. If frying, put open side against the side of frying pan. If baking, spray pan, add peppers and bake for 30 minutes at 350 degrees. Yield: 8 servings

JOSEPHINE GRAVANTI, Niagara Falls, NY Age 72

SCALLOPED PINEAPPLE

4 cups cubed bread (may use dried bread)
3 eggs, beaten
1/2 cup margarine
1 1/2 cups sugar
1 cup chunk pineapple, partly drained

Preheat oven to 350 degrees. Mix all ingredients in a large bowl and place in a greased casserole dish. (If using dry bread, use all the pineapple juice.) Bake 25-30 minutes. Serve warm or cool.

HELEN WITTRUP, Turtle Lake, ND Age 68

PINEAPPLE CASSEROLE

2 20-ounce cans crushed pineapple, drained
1/3 cup sugar
3 tablespoons flour
1 cup shredded cheddar cheese
1 stick margarine
1 sleeve Ritz crackers

Preheat oven to 350 degrees. Place drained pineapple in casserole dish. Mix together sugar, flour, and cheese. Spread over the pineapple. Melt margarine and mix with crushed crackers. Pour topping over the casserole and bake 30 minutes. Yield: 6 servings

PAULINE BRADY, Gallatin, TN Age 70

PINTO BEANS
This is a delicious side dish and a terrific addition to chili.

1 cup pinto beans, washed
1 teaspoon salt, or salt to taste
1 tablespoon sugar
1/2 cup vegetable oil, or ham hock
4 cups water

Wash beans thoroughly. Put in water to soak 8 hours or overnight. After soaking, combine beans, salt, sugar, oil, and water in a medium saucepan. Bring to a boil over medium heat, reduce heat and simmer 4 hours. Yield: 4 servings

BERTHA L. ILES, Post, TX Age 77

MASHED POTATO CASSEROLE

It's the favorite mashed potato dish in my family.

8 medium potatoes, cooked and mashed
1 8-ounce package cream cheese
1/2-1 1/2 cups sour cream
Dot of butter or margarine
Salt or seasoned salt to taste
Pepper to taste

Preheat oven to 350 degrees, and butter a 9 x 13 casserole dish. In a large bowl, combine cooked and mashed potatoes with cream cheese, sour cream, butter, and seasonings. Beat with electric mixer until the mixture is smooth and creamy. Pour into casserole dish and bake 20 minutes. Make ahead for holiday or company dinners; if frozen, thaw prior to baking. Yield: 8 servings

VIRGINIA MOORE, Coffeyville, KS Age 76

POTATO DUMPLINGS

This was my grandma's recipe brought from Germany.

6 medium-sized potatoes
2 eggs
3/4 cup flour
1/2 cup bread crumbs
1 teaspoon salt

TOPPING

1/4 cup butter
1/2 cup bread crumbs
1/4 teaspoon nutmeg or mace

Boil potatoes in jackets. Peel and put through a ricer. Mix riced potatoes, eggs, flour, bread crumbs, and salt; roll into balls. If too wet, mix in more bread crumbs. Drop into boiling water. When dumplings surface, boil 3 minutes. Drain and place in serving dish. For topping, melt butter in a small skillet; add crumbs and nutmeg. Brown topping slightly and pour over potatoes. Yield: 6-8 servings

LAURA BIESEMEIER, Chamois, MO Age 76

Wood Stove Romance

During cold winter months, the best place to be was near an old-fashioned wood stove. When I was dating my husband, we spent many cozy Sundays near the wood stove, making and eating torites. Torites are thinly-sliced potatoes that are browned on the stove-top griddle. It is then seasoned with butter, salt, and pepper. The secret is in the griddle-- it makes the potato slices nice and crispy.

Veronica Miller, Churubusco, NY Age 58

-167-

Gnocchi Before Cornbread

My American name is Ann, but my Italian name is Anna Rosa Colosimo. Both of my parents immigrated from Italy and I was born in Minnesota. Because of financial uncertainties, however, my parents decided that my mother should return to Italy with the children until things were more stable. Do you know the heel part of Italy? The small town of Petrona there is where I spent most of my childhood. Before I ate pork with beans and cornbread in America, I grew up on pasta fogieli (pasta with beans), gnocchi (potato dumplings), and roasted Italian chestnuts.

Ann Livers

POTATO GNOCCHI

2 medium potatoes
1 tablespoon butter or margarine
1/2 teaspoon salt
1 egg yolk
1 to 1 1/2 cups all purpose flour

Cover potatoes with boiling water in a covered saucepan; cook 25 to 30 minutes or until tender; drain and peel. In mixer bowl, beat hot potatoes, butter, and salt until smooth. Add egg yolk and 1/4 cup flour; beat until smooth. By hand, stir in enough remaining flour to make a moderately stiff dough. Turn out onto floured surface. Knead for 4 to 5 minutes. With generously floured hands, shape dough into balls, using 1 tablespoon dough for each ball. Crease center of ball with handle of wooden spoon. Cook, several at a time, in large amount of boiling salted water for 8 to 10 minutes. Remove; drain on paper toweling. Serve immediately with desired sauce, pesto, or butter and cheese. Yield: 4 servings

ANN LIVERS, Loogootee, IN Age 81

GRECIAN-FETA POTATO SALAD

3 cups cooked, diced potatoes
1/2 cup chopped celery
1 tablespoon chopped green pepper
2 tablespoons minced onion
2 tablespoons chopped pickle
1 cup mayonnaise
Salt and pepper to taste
2 tablespoons lemon juice
1 cup feta cheese, crumbled

Combine potatoes, celery, green pepper, onion, and pickle; chill. Blend mayonnaise, seasonings, and lemon juice. Combine with potato mixture, add feta cheese. Toss. Yield: 6 servings

CAROL ANN RUTCHA, Citrus Springs, FL Age 61

CHEESY POTATO CASSEROLE

1 2-pound bag frozen hash browns
1/2 cup melted butter or margarine
1 can cream of chicken soup
1/4 teaspoon pepper
1/2 cup chopped onion
1 teaspoon salt
1 pint sour cream
2 cups grated cheddar cheese

TOPPING

2 cups crushed corn flakes
1/2 cup melted butter or margarine

Preheat oven to 350 degrees. Thaw potatoes. Mix all ingredients in a large bowl and turn into a 13 x 9 baking dish. Mix topping and cover potato mixture. Bake 1 hour. Yield: 10-12 servings

JEAN BURKE, Atlantic Beach, FL Age 57

MEXICAN FIESTA RICE
This may be eaten warm or cold.

1 large green bell pepper, diced
1 large sweet onion, diced
Vegetable oil for frying
Chili powder to taste
Salt and pepper to taste
1 can whole kernel corn, drained
1 can stewed tomatoes, cut up
1 1/4 cup boiling water
3 beef bouillon cubes
1 1/4 cups minute rice, uncooked

Fry peppers and onions in oil in a large skillet. Stir in chili powder, salt, pepper, and corn. Add the tomatoes and simmer 5 minutes. Boil water and dissolve bouillon cubes. Add to mixture in skillet and boil. Add the uncooked rice and stir until all rice is moistened. Cover and let stand for 5 minutes. Fluff with fork. Yield: 8 servings

NORMA McCALVANO, Niagara Falls, NY Age 68

YELLOW RICE-CORN CASSEROLE

1 8-ounce bag spicy yellow rice
1 16-ounce can corn (cream or whole)
1 8-ounce can cream of chicken soup
2 tablespoons mild salsa
1 cup shredded cheese
Additional shredded cheese for topping

Preheat oven to 300 degrees. Cook yellow rice according to package directions. Add corn, soup, salsa, and cheese. Mix well and transfer to 9 x 13 baking dish; place in oven for 10 minutes. Sprinkle additional cheese over top and bake 5 minutes or until top is brown. Yield: 12 servings

MAXINE JOHNSON, Leighton, AL Age 58

CHINESE-STYLE FRIED RICE

1 egg, slightly beaten
3 tablespoons butter
1/3 cup onions, shredded
1 1/2 cups cooked rice
1/2 cup water
3 tablespoons soy sauce

In a 10-inch skillet, cook egg in butter. Add shredded onion and rice. Saute, stirring over medium heat until mixture is lightly browned. Mix water with soy sauce and stir into the rice. Yield: 4 servings

SHIRLEY BIGGS, North Adams, MA Age 64

BROWNED RICE

1 cup long grain rice
1 stick butter or margarine
1 cup beef broth
1 cup clear onion soup
1 4-ounce can chopped mushrooms

Brown rice in butter, stirring constantly. Mix rice, broth, onion soup, and mushrooms in a two-quart casserole with cover. Bake at 350 uncovered for 30 minutes. Fork up rice, cover and bake 30 more minutes. Yield: 8 servings

MARGARET MOTT, Georgia

SPINACH PUFF

Frozen broccoli or frozen corn may also be used for this recipe.

2 10-ounce packages frozen chopped spinach
1 cup Bisquick
1 cup milk
2 eggs
1/2 teaspoon salt
1 cup shredded cheddar cheese

Preheat oven to 325 degrees. Butter a 5 1/2-cup souffle dish or 1 1/2-quart casserole. Cook spinach as directed on package and drain. Beat baking mix, milk, eggs, and salt with hand beater until smooth.Stir in spinach and cheese. Pour into souffle dish. Bake until knife inserted halfway between center and edge comes out clean, about 1 hour. Serve immediately. Yield: 6 servings

MARIE TOOMEY, Greensburg, PA Age 68

SWEET AND SAUERKRAUT

1 quart sauerkraut
1 pound bacon, cut up in small pieces
3/4 -1 pound brown sugar

Preheat oven to 350 degrees. Drain the sauerkraut, and put it in a flat pan, approximately 8 x 10. Cover with bits of bacon. Cover mixture with brown sugar. Bake 45-60 minutes until brown. Yield: 10 servings

I work at the high school in Tryon, Nebraska, and I love the young people and staff.

BUFORD SCHMIDT, Tryon, NE Age 74

SPAGHETTI SQUASH

Rule of Thumb:

When squash is not available you may substitute most any pasta.

1 medium spaghetti squash, 3-4 lbs.
1 medium onion
1 clove garlic
1 teaspoon parsley flakes
2 tablespoons cooking oil or olive oil
1 cup spinach or Swiss chard, chopped
1 teaspoon Italian spices
1 1/2 teaspoons salt
Pepper to taste
1/2 cup grated Parmesan cheese
3 eggs beaten
1 cup fine bread crumbs

Preheat oven to 350 degrees. Cut the spaghetti squash in half and scrape out the seeds. Place the squash, skin side up, in a large saucepan; cover with water and bring to a boil. Lower the heat, cover, and simmer for 20 minutes or until soft. Scoop out the center with a fork and set the spagetti-like strands aside; reserve shells. In a large skillet, saute onion, garlic, and parsley. Toss spinach or chard into squash, and add mixture to onions; saute a few minutes. Add spices and Parmesan cheese. Mix well. Add eggs and bread crumbs. Spoon into squash shells. Top with bread crumbs. Bake for 45 minutes in glass casserole dish. Yield: 4 servings

MARY J. DUSSAULT, Erwin, SD Age 56

SQUASH CASSEROLE

2 pounds yellow squash
1 medium onion
1/2 stick butter
Dash salt
Dash pepper
Dash celery salt
1/2 cup milk
1 cup grated cheese
1/2 cup cracker crumbs

Preheat the oven to 375 degrees. In a large saucepan, cook the squash until tender; drain well. Slightly mash the squash, and add salt, pepper, and celery salt to taste. Mix in the beaten eggs, onions, and cheese. Pour into a 1 1/2 quart casserole dish. Top with cracker crumbs and bake for 40 minutes until lightly browned. Yield: 8 servings

LOU F. COX, West Point, MS Age 74

SWEET POTATO CASSEROLE

3 cups mashed sweet potatoes
1/2 teaspoon salt
2 slightly beaten eggs
1/3 stick margarine
1/4 cup water
1/4 cup evaporated milk
1 teaspoon vanilla
1/2 cup pecan pieces

TOPPING

1 cup granulated sugar
1 cup light brown sugar
1/3 cup flour
1/3 stick margarine

Preheat oven to 350 degrees. Mix all ingredients except pecans in a large bowl; pour into a 9 x 12 casserole dish. Combine topping ingredients and crumble over potatoes. Cover top with broken pecans and bake 25 minutes. Yield: 10-12 servings

MARJORIE G. POPE, Millen, GA Age 66

GREEN TOMATO CASSEROLE

8 medium green tomatoes, sliced
1/4 cup lemon juice
1 1/2 teaspoon salt
1/2 teaspoon pepper
3 tablespoons chives, chopped
7 cups toasted bread crumbs
1/4 cup butter
1/3 cup grated Parmesan cheese

Preheat oven to 400 degrees. Layer the sliced tomatoes in a 9 x 13 baking dish. Sprinkle each layer with a little lemon juice, salt, pepper, chives, and bread crumbs; dot with butter. Top with cheese and bake 45 minutes. Yield: 6 servings

IRMA H. ADAMS, Nettleton, MS Age 73

Christmas Tomatoes

We had a wonderful garden patch when I was growing up. I always hated for summer to end because that meant the end of fresh vegetables. I especially loved the vine ripened red tomatoes. Come late August, we would save the "last of the pickings." This was when we picked the last green tomatoes and wrapped them in newspapers. We put them in the fruit cellar where it was cool and dark. By Christmas time, they were ready to eat!

Leona M. Griffith, Lewistown, PA Age 76

YAM PUFFS

2 cups cooked, mashed yams
1 large banana
1 1/2 tablespoons butter, melted
1 egg
1 1/2 teaspoons salt
Several tablespoons milk

Preheat oven to 500 degrees. In a medium mixing bowl, mash yams and banana together. Add butter, egg, and salt; blend . Add enough milk to make the mixture fluffy. Drop batter in mounds 1 to 2 inches apart on a greased cookie sheet. Bake 12 minutes until heated through and slightly brown. Yield: 6 servings

LILLIAN B. BRUZOUSKI, Urbana, OH Age 72

APPLES & YAMS

1 cup sugar
3 teaspoons cornstarch
1 teaspoon salt
1 stick margarine
2 cups water
5 yams, cut up
6 apples, sliced thick

Preheat oven to 350 degrees. In a small bowl, mix sugar, cornstarch, and salt; set aside. Bring margarine and water to a boil and add sugar mixture. Cook over medium heat until thick. Layer yams, apples, and sauce in a 1 1/2-quart casserole dish. Bake 45 minutes. Yield: 6 servings

FANNIE KELLY, Dade City, FL Age 73

FRIED YAMS
My mother's recipe.

5 yams
1/4 cup butter
4 tablespoons brown sugar
Salt (optional)
3/4 cup milk

Peel and slice yams. Melt butter in a large skillet and fry yams over medium heat. When almost done, add brown sugar, salt, and milk. Simmer over low heat until milk is absorbed. Serve hot. Yield: 4 servings

A. BRADY, Cedar City, UT Age 75

VEGETABLE ACCOMPANIMENTS
Many, many Green Thumbs in the Kitchen contributors grew up on, owned, or worked on farms and had easy access to fresh vegetables. They suggest several ways to add to the enjoyment of fresh, frozen, or canned vegetables:

DRESSED-UP BUTTERS
Lemon butter: add 2 teaspoons lemon juice and 1 teaspoon grated lemon peel to 1/4 cup melted butter or margarine.

Garlic butter: add 1 small garlic bud, peeled and cut in 2 (remove before serving) to 1/4 cup melted butter or margarine.

Cheese butter: 2 tablespoons grated Swiss or Parmesan cheese to 1/4 cup melted butter or margarine.

BUTTERED CRUMBS
Melt 2 tablespoons butter; add 1 cup of fine dry bread crumbs and stir until lightly browned.

STUFFING FOR ONIONS, ZUCCHINI, OR TOMATOES
Mix 1 1/2 cups soft bread crumbs, 3/4 cup grated Parmesan cheese, 3 tablespoons minced parsely, 1/4 cup hot bouillon, salt and pepper to taste.

Desserts

DESSERTS

CONTENTS

OATMEAL CAKE

1 1/3 cups boiling water
1 cup quick oats
1 cup brown sugar
1 cup granulated sugar
1 stick margarine
1/2 teaspoon cinnamon
1 1/3 cups flour
2 eggs
1 teaspoon baking soda
1/2 teaspoon salt

TOPPING

1 stick margarine
1 1/2 cups brown sugar
1/4 cup cream
1 cup coconut, divided
1 teaspoon vanilla

This tastes like a good coconut cake. My cousin gave me the recipe more than 25 years ago and it has been a favorite with my family ever since. The cake actually gets better after a day or so; it stays very moist. I work in the gift shop at Natural Tunnel State Park in Duffield, Virginia.

Preheat oven to 350 degrees. Pour boiling water over oatmeal and let stand 20 minutes. In a large bowl, combine remaining ingredients and beat until smooth. Add oatmeal and blend well. Pour mixture into a 9 x 13 pan and bake about 35 minutes. To prepare topping, combine margarine, sugar, and cream in a small saucepan. Cook over low heat to dissolve sugar. Remove from heat, add vanilla and 2/3 cup coconut. Pour over top of cake. Sprinkle with remaining coconut. Yield 12 servings

GENEVA R. BLAIR, Clinchport, VA Age 68

BLACKBERRY GRUNT CAKE

1 egg
1/2 cup sugar
1 tablespoon shortening
1 cup milk
2 teaspoons baking powder
1/2 teaspoon salt
2 cups flour
2-3 cups blackberries

This Pennsylvania Dutch recipe is especially good with milk and sugar poured over it. I am assigned to the Accord Corporation in Belmont, NY, where I work with battered women who are victims of domestic violence.

Preheat oven to 350 degrees. Mix all ingredients except berries in a large bowl. Fold in blackberries. Pour into a greased and floured 8 x 8 pan. Bake 40 minutes. Yield: 4 servings

MARLYN A. SHARP, Bolivar, NY Age 62

BEET CAKE

3/4 cup corn oil
1 1/2 cups white sugar
3 eggs, separated
3 teaspoons lukewarm water
1 teaspoon vanilla
2 cups sifted all purpose flour
3 teaspoons baking powder
1 1/2 teaspoons salt
1 teaspoon cinnamon
1 cup beets, grated
1 cup carrots, grated
1/2 cup pecans, chopped
1/2 cup dates, chopped

Preheat oven to 325 degrees. Grease and flour a 10" tube pan. In a large bowl, combine oil, sugar, and egg yolks and beat well. Add the water and vanilla, blending well. Sift the flour with baking powder, salt, and cinnamon. Blend dry ingredients into the batter. Add beets, carrots, pecans, and dates to the mixture. Beat egg whites until stiff and fold into batter. Pour into prepared pan. Bake about 1 1/2 hours. Yield: 12 servings

MILDRED M. ZIEGLER, Traverse City, MI Age 87

APPLE DESSERT CAKE

My husband and I, and our 18 children, lived on a farm with lots of apple trees. Everyone enjoyed this recipe back then. My 46 grandchildren enjoy it now.

1 cup brown sugar
1/4 cup vegetable shortening
1 egg
1 teaspoon soda in 1 teaspoon hot water
Dash cinnamon
Pinch of salt
Dash of nutmeg
1 cup flour
2 cups raw apples, peeled and chopped
1/4 cup nuts
1/2 teaspoon cinnamon
1/2 teaspoon nutmeg

Preheat oven to 350 degrees. In a large bowl, cream sugar and shortening; add egg, soda and dry ingredients. Add chopped apples and mix well. Pour into a greased and floured 9 x 13 pan. Sprinkle nuts, cinnamon, and nutmeg on top. Bake in cake pan for 30-40 minutes. Yield: 10 servings

AGNES BOT, Marshall, MN Age 76

POPPY SEED CAKE

1/2 cup poppy seeds
1 cup milk
3/4 cup butter or margarine
1 1/2 cups sugar
2 cups sifted flour
1 1/2 teaspoons baking powder
4 egg whites, beaten
1 teaspoon vanilla

Soak poppy seeds in milk at least 2 hours. Preheat oven to 350 degrees. In a large bowl, cream butter and sugar. Add the poppy seed/milk mixture. Sift the flour and baking powder together and add to batter. Beat vanilla with egg whites, fold into mixture. Bake in a 9 x 13 pan or two 8" layer pans for 30 minutes. Cake is done when tester comes out clean. Yield: 24 servings

SUMMER ICING

2 pounds powdered sugar
1/4 cup dry Dream Whip
1/3 cup cornstarch
1 1/2 cups Crisco
2/3 cup water or milk
Vanilla or other flavoring, optional

In a large bowl, mix sugar, Dream Whip, and cornstarch with an electric mixer on low speed. Add Crisco followed by water or milk--use a few extra drops of liquid if frosting is too thick. Vanilla or other flavoring may be added if desired. Beat with mixer until mixture is fluffy.

HELEN JOCHIM, David City, NE Age 72

This is a Czecho-slovakian favorite. Tradition says you can tell a Czech by the poppy seed in his teeth. I was referred to Green Thumb when my husband passed away two weeks after our 51st wedding anniversary. I am an assistant activity director at St. Joseph Nursing Home. I still love to dance the polka and waltz.

The Nereledge Inn

Between 1957 and 1977, my husband and I operated a small inn--the Nereledge Inn--in North Conway, New Hampshire. You can still visit the Inn, but it is now a bed and breakfast. The charming farmhouse had 11 bedrooms for rent and accommodated up to 30 people. We attracted skiers during the winter, but come summer, young families and retired couples spent their vacations with us. I did all the cooking. We served a full breakfast--none of this continental breakfast nonsense--and a lovely dinner. This cake was frequently requested for dessert and snack. It is truly a favorite with our family, especially our sons.

Janet Greene

NERELEDGE INN SHEET CAKE

1 cup water
2 tablespoons unsweetened cocoa
2 sticks margarine
2 cups sugar
2 cups flour
1/2 teaspoon salt
1 teaspoon baking soda
2 eggs, slightly beaten
1/2 cup sour cream

FROSTING

1 stick margarine
4 tablespoons unsweetened cocoa
6 tablespoons milk
1 box confectioner's sugar
1/2 teaspoon vanilla

Preheat oven to 400 degrees. In a small saucepan, mix water with cocoa and margarine; heat just to a boil. In a large bowl, mix sugar, flour, salt, and soda. Add cocoa mixture. Add eggs and sour cream, mixing well. Pour batter into a greased jellyroll pan. Bake 12-15 minutes. Cool. To prepare frosting, bring margarine, cocoa, and milk to a boil, stirring constantly. Remove from heat. Add 1 box confectioner's sugar and 1/2 teaspoon vanilla. Spread on cake. Yield: 24 servings.

JANET GREENE, Brownfield, ME Age 72

A CREAM CAKE

1 box yellow cake mix
1 egg
1 stick margarine
3 eggs
1 pound powdered sugar
1 8-ounce package cream cheese, softened

Preheat oven to 325 degrees. Mix cake mix, eggs, powdered sugar, and cream cheese in a large bowl. Pour into a 9 x 13" pan and pat evenly. In a separate bowl, mix the eggs, powdered sugar, and cream cheese. Pour over cake mixture and bake 30-35 minutes. Yield: 10 servings

MYRTLE HONAKEU, Galion, OH Age 60

PUMPKIN PIE CAKE

1 large can pumpkin pie filling
4 eggs
1 13-ounce can evaporated milk
1 1/2 cups sugar
2 teaspoons cinnamon
1 teaspoon ginger
1/2 teaspoon nutmeg
1 box yellow or white cake mix
1 stick margarine, melted
Chopped nuts, optional

Preheat oven to 350 degrees. Mix pumpkin, eggs, milk, sugar, and spices in a large bowl. Pour into a 9 x 13 ungreased pan. Sprinkle the cake mix on top. Sprinkle with nuts, if desired. Bake until tester comes out clean (but not more than an hour). Yield: 12-18 servings

ALICE MASKER, Waverly, IA Age 73

The manager of my housing project told me about Green Thumb. Green Thumb gave me a chance when no one else did. I have no intention of retiring yet. I am a clerical aide at the Department of Human Services in Waverly, Iowa. I really enjoy going out and meeting the public. Green Thumb keeps me busy, and keeps me independent.

Alice Masker

GREEN TOMATO CAKE
Tastes like really good spice cake.

3 cups flour
2 cups sugar
2 teaspoons baking soda
1 teaspoon cloves
1 teaspoon cinnamon
1/2 teaspoon salt
3 eggs
2 teaspoons vanilla
1 1/2 cups applesauce
3 cups grated green tomatoes

Preheat oven to 350 degrees. Mix flour, sugar, baking soda, cloves, cinnamon, and salt in a large bowl. Add the eggs, vanilla, applesauce, and tomatoes; stir to combine. Pour into a greased and floured 9 x 13 pan. Bake 45 to 60 minutes. Yield: 12-18 servings

FROSTING
1/2 stick margarine
8 ounces cream cheese
1 teaspoon vanilla
1 1/2 cups powdered sugar

Cream margarine, cream cheese, and vanilla. Beat in powdered sugar. Spread on cooled cake.

KATHY GREEN, Norwall, OH

My mother made this kind of cake every Saturday for dessert at Sunday dinner during the years of the Depression. It seems we always had company for dinner on Sunday. She had a large garden with not just vegetables, but blackberries and grapes that grew on the fence. She used the fruit to make jam and jelly for her jam cakes.

JAM CAKE

1/2 cup shortening
1 cup sugar
1 teaspoon vanilla
2 eggs
2 1/4 cups flour
1/2 teaspoon salt
3 teaspoons baking powder
3/4 cup milk
Jam or jelly

Preheat oven to 350 degrees. In a large bowl, cream the shortening, sugar, and vanilla until light and fluffy. Add eggs and beat thoroughly. Sift flour, salt, and baking powder together, and add alternately with the milk to the shortening mixture. Bake in two 8-inch round cake pans lined with waxed paper for about 30 minutes. When cool, add your favorite jam or jelly on top and between the layers. Yield: 8 servings

CHRISTINE LARMORE, Sebring, FL

COCONUT POUND CAKE

This is a good and beautiful cake and serves a lot of people.

1 cup Crisco
1 stick of margarine
3 cups sugar
6 eggs, separated
3 cups flour
1 cup milk
1 tablespoon vanilla
1 tablespoon almond extract
1 tablespoon coconut flavoring
1 3 1/2-ounce can coconut

Preheat oven to 325 degrees. Cream Crisco and margarine in a large bowl. Add sugar and beat well. Add egg yolks, one at a time, and beat well after each. Alternately add flour and milk, beginning and ending with flour. Add flavorings; fold in stiffly beaten egg whites and coconut. Bake in a bundt pan 2 or more hours. Yield: 18-24 slices

EVELYN WHITLEY, Meridian, TX Age 82

BLACK BOTTOM
CREAM CHEESE BARS
Blue ribbon winner at the Fair.

CRUST

1 cup flour
1/4 cup firmly packed brown sugar
1/2 cup butter or margarine, softened
2/3 cup semi-sweet chocolate chips, melted

FILLING

1/2 cup granulated sugar
1/2 cup firmly packed brown sugar
1/3 cup butter or margarine, softened
1 8-ounce package cream cheese
1 cup flour
1/2 teaspoon baking powder
1/4 teaspoon salt
1 tablespoon rum or 1/4 teaspoon rum extract
1 tablespoon vanilla

GLAZE

1/4 cup semi-sweet chocolate chips
1 tablespoon rum or 1/4 teaspoon rum extract
1-2 teaspoons water

Preheat oven to 325 degrees. In a large bowl, combine flour, brown sugar, butter, and chocolate chips; mix well. Press mixture in bottom of ungreased 9-inch square pan or 11 x 7-inch pan. In separate bowl, beat sugar, brown sugar, butter, and cream cheese until smooth. Add flour, baking powder, salt, rum, and vanilla; blend well. Spread over crust. Bake for 38-43 minutes, or until edges are light golden brown and set. Cool 30 minutes. In a small saucepan over low heat, melt chocolate, rum, and water, stirring constantly until smooth. Drizzle over warm bars. Refrigerate at least one hour before serving. Cut into bars; store in refrigerator. Yield: 36 bars

ANNE PERHAM, Neptune Beach, FL Age 65

63 Ribbons for Baking

Every fall I look forward to the Greater Jacksonville Agricultural Fair which is held in October. In the past 10 years I have entered the baking contest and have won a total of 63 ribbons. The baking contest is extremely competitive and the rules are stiff. The recipes have to be original and made from scratch. No pies and cakes--you must submit breads, rolls, doughnuts, muffins, brownies, and cookies. I am already experimenting to get ready for the next Fair.

Anne Perham

UNSINKABLE CHEESE CAKE

1 1/2 pounds cream cheese, softened
14 ounces sweetened condensed milk
4 eggs, separated
1 cup sour cream
1 tablespoon powdered sugar
1 teaspoon vanilla
1 teaspoon orange rind
1 teaspoon lemon rind
1/2 teaspoon salt
Crushed graham crackers for crust

Preheat oven to 275 degrees. Beat cream cheese and milk together in a large bowl. Increase mixer speed and add 4 egg yolks, one at a time, beating well after each addition until mixture is very smooth. Lower mixer speed and add sour cream, sugar, vanilla, orange and lemon rinds. Beat egg whites with salt until stiff and fold into cheese mixture. Line bottom of springform pan with crushed graham crackers and pour cheese mixture into pan. Bake for one hour. Turn off the oven and do not open the door for one hour. Let the cake cook completely inside the oven. Do not try to release the cake until the pan is cool. Yield: 12 servings

ANNA M. BLACKSTOCK, Jonesburg, MO Age 72

CHESS PIE

My mother-in-law made this recipe by the pinch and dab method, and I worked the amounts by trial. The pie traces its roots to her family in the Deep South of the 19th century.

3 eggs
1 1/2 cups sugar
2 sticks butter or margarine, melted
1/2 teaspoon vanilla
1/2 teaspoon almond flavoring
1/2 cup cornmeal
9" unbaked pie shell

Preheat oven to 400 degrees. In a medium bowl, beat eggs. Mix in sugar until smooth. Beat in melted butter. Add vanilla, almond flavoring, and cornmeal. Pour into pie shell and bake at 400 degrees for 15 minutes. Reduce heat to 350 degrees and bake at least 30 minutes, or until the upper crust formed by the cornmeal is brown. Yield: 6-8 servings

ALICE ARMSTRONG, Windsor, MO Age 72

CARAMEL DUMPLINGS

1 1/4 cups granulated sugar, divided
2 1/2 cups hot water
5 tablespoons butter, divided
1 teaspoon vanilla
1/2 cup milk
2 teaspoons baking powder
1/2 teaspoon salt
1 cup flour
Whipped topping or milk, optional

Preheat oven to 350 degrees. In a heavy pan or skillet over low heat, caramelize 1/2 cup sugar stirring until brown (do not over-brown). Add hot water and stir until mixture is smooth. Add 1/2 cup sugar, 2 tablespoons butter, and vanilla; bring to a low boil. In a medium mixing bowl, cream together 1/4 cup sugar and 3 tablespoons butter. Add milk, baking powder, salt, and flour. Beat mixture until fluffy; drop by teaspoonsful into boiling syrup. If using a cast iron skillet, place skillet in oven and bake dumplings 15 minutes or until tester comes out clean (do not overbake). If you don't have a cast iron skillet, remove boiling syrup to an ovenproof baking dish and follow above instructions. Serve warm or cold; top with whipped topping or milk. Yield: 8-10 servings

SHIRLEY SMALL, Lancaster, MO Age 69

GINGERSNAP DESSERT

1/2 pound gingersnaps
1 stick butter
1/2 box powdered sugar
3 egg yolks
1 can crushed pineapple, drained
2 bananas, diced
1/2 pint cream, whipped and sweetened

Butter a 9 x 13" baking dish. Crumble the gingersnaps and divide in half. Spread half in bottom of pan. Cream the butter, powdered sugar, and egg yolks in a medium mixing bowl and spread over crumbs. Mix pineapple and bananas in a small bowl. Spread over creamed mixture; top with whipped cream; sprinkle with remaining crumbs. Yield: 15 servings

MAHALA M. AINSWORTH, Lockport, NY Age 77

I love to cook, and Green Thumb worked with me to determine the most suitable community service assignment and identified employment, training, and service objectives. I was assigned to the Schuyler County Jail as a cook. I was doing something I loved and getting paid for it too. I pride myself on my economical and honest-to-goodness home-cooking, and I was able to save them a lot of money. I planned menus, ordered, and cooked the food for up to 12 inmates. I moved off the program and now work in a cafe where several of my recipes are part of the menu.

Shirley Small

RAISIN PIE

I won a blue ribbon and $250 for this pie in a raisin pie contest.

2 cups seeded raisins
2 cups boiling water
1/2 cup sugar
2 tablespoons flour
1/2 cup nuts
2 teaspoons lemon rind
3 tablespoons lemon juice
Double pie crust
Cinnamon and sugar, optional

Rule of Thumb:

Mrs. Bier suggests microwaving any fruit pie to cook the filling before placing the pie in a conventional oven to brown the crust. This prevents boil-over of the filling which burns on the crust and makes a mess in the oven.

In a medium saucepan, cook raisins in boiling water until tender (about 5 minutes). Stir in sugar and flour; cook over low heat, stirring constantly until mixture comes to a boil. Remove from heat; stir in nuts, lemon rind, and lemon juice. Place bottom crust in a non-metal pie pan; pour in cooled raisin mixture and cover with top crust. Cut a circle in the center of the crust and slit crust with a knife in several places to allow steam to escape. Sprinkle cinnamon and sugar around center vent hole. If desired, decorate with piecrust leaves. Bake pie in microwave on high 10 minutes. Preheat oven to 425 degrees. Remove pie from microwave to conventional oven and bake 15 minutes until crust is lightly browned. Pie is best served slightly warm. Yield: 6-8 servings

MARTHA BIER, Madera, CA Age 77

RAZORBACK SWEET POTATO PIE

1 3/4 cups cooked, mashed sweet potatoes
1 teaspoon salt
1 1/2 cups milk
3 eggs
1 cup sugar
1 teaspoon cinnamon
1/2 teaspoon nutmeg
1/2 teaspoon ginger
1 tablespoon melted butter or margarine
9-inch unbaked pie shell

Preheat oven to 425 degrees. Cook potatoes in jackets in water and salt until soft. Peel and mash. In a large bowl, beat milk, eggs, sugar, spices, and butter into potatoes, and pour into pie shell. Bake 40-50 minutes. The pie is done when a knife inserted near the center comes out clean. Yield: 6-8 servings

NANCY FITTS, Green Thumb Arkansas State Office

FRESH STRAWBERRY PIE

When I am invited to visit, friends always ask for my strawberry pie.

1 cup sugar
1 cup water
2 1/2 tablespoons cornstarch
2 tablespoons light corn syrup
1 4-ounce package strawberry jello
2 pints fresh strawberries, washed and halved
1 9-inch graham cracker crust
Whipped topping, optional

Mix sugar, water, cornstarch, and syrup. Cook until thick and clear in appearance. Add half of the dry jello to syrup mixture and stir. Place strawberries in graham cracker pie crust. Pour filling over strawberres. Chill and serve with whipped topping. Yield: 8 servings

LUCILLE U. DERBONNE, Oakdale, LA Age 74

BLUE RIBBON CUSTARD PIE

I won a blue ribbon on this pie at the Iowa State Fair. It is creamy smooth and uses ordinary ingredients found in every home.

4 eggs, slightly beaten
1/4 teaspoon salt
1/2 cup sugar
3 cups milk, scalded
1 teaspoon vanilla
1 unbaked 9" pie shell
Ground nutmeg

Preheat oven to 450 degrees. Mix eggs, salt, and sugar in a medium bowl. Slowly stir in milk and vanilla. Pour into pie shell, and sprinkle with nutmeg. Bake for 10 minutes. Reduce heat to 325 degrees and bake 30 to 40 minutes, or until knife inserted half way between center and edge of pie comes out clean. Cool on rack. Store in refrigerator. Yield: 6-8 servings

DELORIS GOOD, Ogden, IA Age 67

Hudspeth's Store

My grandparents who raised me were farmers, and I worked hard on their farm from morning until suppertime. I did all of my chores and never complained when they sent me on errands, especially if it was to Hudspeth's Grocery. My grandfather would say, "Jimmy, run along to Hudspeth's, and if there's change left over (and there usually was), treat yourself to some sweets." Back then, candies were displayed in big glass jars. It drove old Hudspeth crazy when kids took forever to pick what they wanted. I, however, didn't have this problem--as soon as I walked into the store, I immediately pointed to the jar that contained the best milk chocolate chunks in the world.

Jim Baker, St. Joe, AR Age 61

CHOCOLATE PIE

2 cups milk
1 1/2 cups sugar, 1/4 cup sugar
1/2 cup flour
3 eggs, separated
1 tablespoon vanilla
2 tablespoons cocoa
1 tablespoon butter
1 baked pie shell
1 tablespoon marshmallow creme

Preheat oven to 350 degrees. Combine milk, 1 1/2 cups sugar, flour, egg yolks, vanilla, and cocoa in a large saucepan. Cook over medium heat until thick, about 6 to 7 minutes. Stir in butter, and pour into pie shell. Beat egg whites until stiff, beat in marshmallow, then 1/4 cup sugar. Spread over pie and bake until brown. Yield: 6-8 servings

MATTIE ALLEN, McKenzie, TN Age 69

BUTTERSCOTCH PIE

I have been using this recipe since 1941. It is the most requested one that I bake.

3/4 cup brown sugar
5 tablespoons flour
1/2 teaspoon salt
2 cups milk
3 egg yolks beaten
2 tablespoons butter
1 teaspoon vanilla

MERINGUE

3 egg whites stiffly beaten
3 tablespoons sugar
1 tablespoon powdered sugar
Dash salt
1 teaspoon vanilla

Preheat oven to 425 degrees. Combine the first seven ingredients in the top of a double boiler and cook over medium heat until thick. Pour the mixture into a 9" baked pie shell. Beat the egg whites until stiff, then add sugars, salt, and vanilla and beat well. Spread the meringue over the pie, sealing at the edge of the pastry. Bake 5 to 7 minutes or until lightly browned. Yield: 8-10 servings

NINA STEPHENSON, Sulpher Springs, TX Age 75

MINCE MEAT PIE

My husband and I are of German descent and we both enjoy this recipe very much.

1/2 to 1 pound ground pork
1 teaspoon salt
1 cup water
3 cups chopped tart apples, unpeeled
1 cup raisins
1 orange, and half the rind
1 lemon, and half the rind
1 cup brown sugar
1/4 cup corn syrup
1 teaspoon cloves
1 teaspoon cinnamon
1 double pie crust

Preheat oven to 425 degrees. In a heavy pan, cook ground pork with salt on low heat just until brown. Combine water, apples, raisins, orange, lemon, and rinds, and grind small amounts at a time in a blender or food processor. Add blended fruit to meat and cook about 40 minutes on low heat. Mixture needs to be stirred often. Pour mixture into a prepared pie shell and cover with the top crust. Bake 15 minutes at 425 degrees; reduce heat to 350 degrees and bake for an additional 45 minutes. Refrigerate or freeze any remaining filling for another day. Yield: 6-8 servings

VELMA BUTT, Dows, IA Age 61

LEMON-KIWI PIE

1 14-ounce can sweetened condensed milk
1 6-ounce can frozen lemonade, thawed
1 8-ounce container frozen non-dairy whipped topping (3 1/2 cups)
1 9" baked pie shell
2 kiwi fruits peeled and sliced

In a large mixing bowl, combine condensed milk and thawed lemonade concentrate; blend well. Fold in whipped topping and pour into the prepared pie shell. Arrange kiwi slices evenly on top of pie. Cover and refrigerate 4 hours until set. Yield: 6-8 servings

MABEL M. McDOWELL, Hendricks, MN Age 68

APPLE BETTY PIE

4 cups sliced and pared tart apples
1/4 cup orange juice

TOPPING
1 cup sugar
3/4 cup flour
1/2 teaspoon cinnamon
1/4 teaspoon nutmeg
Dash of salt
1/2 cup butter or margarine
Vanilla ice cream, optional

Preheat oven to 375 degrees. Mound apples in a buttered 9-inch pie plate and sprinkle with orange juice. In a small bowl, combine sugar, flour, cinnamon, nutmeg, and salt. Cut in butter until mixture is crumbly, and place it over the apples. Bake for 45 minutes until apples are done and topping is crisp and brown. Serve warm with vanilla ice cream. Yield: 6-8 servings

BETTY FACE, Medina, NY

PINK LEMONADE PIE
This is a light refreshing dessert that is also low in cholesterol. It's best made the day before you plan to serve it.

1 cup evaporated skim milk
1 envelope unflavored gelatin
1 6-ounce can frozen pink lemonade, thawed
3/4 cup sugar
1 9" pie shell, baked

Chill the evaporated milk in the freezer until ice crystals began to form around the edges. In a medium saucepan, soften the gelatin in water (per package directions). Add the lemonade and stir over low heat until the gelatin dissolves. Add sugar, stirring until dissolved but not thickened. Transfer the chilled evaporated milk to a large chilled bowl and beat at high speed until stiff. Fold in the cooled gelatin mixture. Pour into the baked pie shell and chill until firm, about 3 to 4 hours. Yield: 6-8 servings

BLANCHE A. SLAUGHTER, Darwin, MN Age 58

CARAMEL POPCORN

You'll probably have to double or triple this recipe.

6 cups popped popcorn
1 stick butter
1 cup brown sugar
1/3 cup light corn syrup
1/2 teaspoon vanilla
1/4 teaspoon baking soda

Preheat oven to 200 degrees. Spread popcorn on a cookie sheet or roasting pan. Melt butter in a medium saucepan; stir in brown sugar syrup, and vanilla. Cook mixture over low heat for about six minutes, stirring constantly. Add baking soda, and cook for one additional minute. Mixture will bubble up and change from dark brown to a golden color. Pour over the popcorn, covering the entire pan. Bake for one hour, stirring every 15 minutes. Yield: 4-6 servings

SONDRA MOORE, Richmond, IN Age 61

OLD-FASHIONED TAFFY

Our family made this candy way back in the 1930's.

1 cup brown sugar, packed
1/4 cup light corn syrup
1/3 cup water
1 tablespoon butter
1/8 teaspoon salt
3/4 teaspoon vanilla

In a heavy saucepan, boil all ingredients, except vanilla, until it forms a hard ball in cold water, or reaches the soft crack stage (275 degrees on a candy thermometer). Remove from heat and add the vanilla; pour into a well greased pan. When cool enough to handle, pull and twist until golden. Cut into pieces with scissors and wrap individually in waxed paper or plastic wrap. Yield: 6 servings

ALFRED ZAHN, Odessa, MN Age 75

Sweetened with Sorghum

During the Depression sugar was scarce, but my family was lucky. My parents had a sugar cane farm and we grew up with foods sweetened with sorghum--the syrup from the sugar cane. Making this syrup was a family affair. First we stripped the leaves from the cane; the naked cane was then put through a press. A horse pulled this press around and around tirelessly for hours as the candy cane juice was squeezed out. Next we boiled the juice till it turned into a thick syrup--the longer you boiled, the thicker and sweeter it got. The end result was sorghum. To reward us for all this hard work, my mother let us invite friends over for taffy pulls.

Geraldine Thornhill, Butler, MO Age 67

This was the only kind of candy we had at Christmas while growing up during the Thirties. Everyone helped shell the peanuts that my mother raised.

PEANUT BRITTLE

1 cup sugar
1/2 cup light corn syrup
Dash of salt
1 to 1 1/2 cups shelled peanuts
1 tablespoon butter or margarine
1 1/2 teaspoons baking soda
1 teaspoon vanilla

Preheat oven to 350 degrees. Combine sugar, corn syrup and salt in a 3-quart casserole. Stir in peanuts. Put in oven until brown, stirring at least twice. Add butter, baking soda, and vanilla. Stir until light and foamy. Quickly spread on greased baking sheet. Spread as thin as possible for brittle candy. Cool and break into pieces. Yield: varies

CHRISTINE LARMORE, Sebring, FL

WEST COAST FUDGE

1 8-ounce package chocolate chips
1 stick margarine
2 cups powdered sugar
1 egg
1 teaspoon vanilla
1 cup chopped nuts

In a medium saucepan, melt chocolate chips and margarine over low heat. Add powdered sugar, egg, vanilla, and nuts. Mix well and pour into a greased 8 x 8 x 2" pan. Refrigerate. Yield: 32 pieces

MILDRED GOINS, Vinita, OK Age 76

WHITE FUDGE

3 cups granulated sugar
1 stick margarine
1 large can evaporated milk
2 tablespoons peanut butter
1 7-ounce jar marshmallow cream
1 cup nuts, chopped

Combine sugar, margarine, and milk in a large saucepan. Bring to a boil, stirring constantly until mixture reaches the soft ball stage. Remove from heat and add remaining ingredients. Beat well and pour onto a 9 x 12 cookie sheet. Cool and place in refrigerator to set. Cut and store in an air-tight container. Yield: about 48 pieces

LAURA HURT, Urichsville, OH Age 87

RUM BALLS

2 cups crushed vanilla wafers
1/4 cup rum or orange juice
1 cup chopped nuts
2 tablespoons cocoa
2 tablespoons honey or corn syrup
Sifted confectioners sugar

Mix crushed cookies, rum, nuts, cocoa, and honey in a medium bowl. Blend well and shape into small balls. Roll in sifted confectioners sugar. Store in an airtight container. It may be necessary to re-roll in sugar after storing. Yield: 4 dozen

ANNE PERHAM, Neptune Beach, FL Age 65

HAWAIIAN DELIGHT

This recipe has been in our family for 60 years.
It is very rich and very good.

1 cup granulated sugar
1/2 cup packed brown sugar
1/4 cup cream or evaporated milk
1/2 cup crushed pineapple
1/2 cup butter or margarine
1/2 teaspoon vanilla
1/2 cup chopped nutmeats or coconut

In a heavy saucepan, cook sugars, cream, and pineapple to soft ball stage (235 degrees). Remove from heat, add butter and beat until creamy. Add vanilla and nutmeats or coconut, and stir well. Drop from spoon onto waxed paper. Yield: 25 pieces

CORA JEAN OLSON, Lewistown, MT Age 74

NEVER-FAIL DIVINITY

2/3 cup water
3 cups sugar
1/4 teaspoon salt
2 pints marshmallow creme
1 teaspoon vanilla
3 cups finely chopped pecans

Bring water, sugar, and salt to a boil in a medium saucepan, and cook to the soft ball stage (235 degrees). In a large bowl, beat marshmallow creme and the cooked mixture until it forms peaks. Add vanilla and pecans. Drop by teaspoonful onto waxed paper. Yield: 4-6 dozen

WILDA GRANT, San Angelo, TX Age 62

Cement Frosting

I'll tell you about the most embarrassing thing that ever happened to me. When I was engaged to my husband, I wanted to impress my future in-laws. I was famous for my chocolate cake with chocolate frosting, so I decided to play hostess and serve them this cake. I had everything prepared and things were going smoothly until I tried to cut the cake. The darn knife wouldn't go through the frosting! The frosting was hard as cement, and I thought it was the end of the world when the platter actually cracked. I lost the platter but gained a new set of parents-- they thought it was funny and approved of me anyway.

Mabel McDowell, Hendricks, MN Age 67

Sweet on Each Other

Back when I was a young lady, things were certainly different as far as dating was concerned. We didn't call it dating, we called it courting. We didn't have boyfriends, we had beaus. We didn't like or love one another, we were "sweet on each other." And when a beau paid a visit, we were never allowed to be alone--we were always chaperoned by family. Refreshment was iced tea or lemonade, but if my beau happened to be a particularly nice fellow, Mother served ice cream.

A. Brady, Cedar City, UT Age 74

DIPPED CHOCOLATES

1 stick margarine
1 can sweetened condensed milk
2 pounds powdered sugar
1 14-ounce package coconut
3 cups pecans (chopped)
1 12-ounce package semi-sweet chocolate
3/4 bar paraffin wax

In a heavy saucepan, melt margarine, add milk and powdered sugar. Mix well; add coconut and pecans. Mix well with hands and roll into balls; chill in refrigerator. Melt chocolate and paraffin in the top of a double boiler. Use a toothpick or long fork to dip balls into chocolate. Lay on wax paper to set. Remember to keep chocolate hot while dipping. Yield: varies

JANICE ROBERTS, Bennington, OK Age 63

CANDY BOX BON-BONS
Have fun experimenting with the candy "dough."

1/2 stick butter or margarine
3/4 cup sweetened condensed milk
6 cups sifted confectioners sugar
1 teaspoon vanilla, coconut, peanut butter, maple, or other flavoring

COATING
10-12 ounce bag chocolate chips
3-4 drops salad oil

Melt butter in top of a double boiler; stir in condensed milk and sugar to make a firm dough. Add flavoring(s) and chill or freeze. When firm, dough can be formed into balls or rolled out and cut with cookie cutters. Melt chips in a heavy saucepan; add oil to melted chocolate. Put candy on a long-handled fork and dip into chocolate sauce. Let set on waxed paper, store in refrigerator. May be decorated with nut halves, coconut, or frosting. If desired, add chopped nuts, candied or dried fruit, or peanut butter to the dough. Yield: varies

NANCY D. COLVIN, South Butler, NY

ENGLISH TRIFLE

1 package lady fingers or sponge cake
1 package frozen strawberries
2-3 tablespoons sherry (optional)
1 package vanilla pudding (not instant)
1 package strawberry jello
1 pint whipping cream
Garnish: whole almonds, maraschino cherries

Arrange lady fingers or sponge cake slices in bottom of glass serving dish. Spoon strawberries and sherry over (don't let it get soggy). Refrigerate until set. Prepare pudding according to package directions; cool; spoon over strawberries. Refrigerate until set. Prepare jello and refrigerate. Beat set jello and layer over pudding. Top with whipped cream and decorate with almonds and cherries. Yield: 8 servings

FAY MARTIN, Clovis, NM Age 72

I came to the States as a War Bride in 1945 and have never returned to England. My formative years were really here in America, the country I have grown to love. But as my husband says, you can take me out of England, but never the English out of me. Hence, lots of English cooking like this trifle.

EGG CUSTARD

3 eggs
3 tablespoons self-rising flour
1 cup sugar
2 tablespoons butter, melted
1 large can evaporated milk
1 teaspoon nutmeg
1 teaspoon vanilla

Preheat oven to 325 degrees. In a large mixing bowl, beat all ingredients together. Pour into a greased and floured 9" pie pan. Bake 30 to 35 minutes. Yield: 8 servings

EVELYN VANCE, Bristol, VA Age 72

CARAMEL SYRUP

3/4 cup sugar
1/2 cup hot water

In a heavy saucepan over low heat, melt sugar, stirring until brown. Add hot water; cook and stir until all lumps are dissolved. Drizzle over custard.

The Four-H Club

When I was a schoolgirl, Minnesota's Swift County Agents formed what was called the Four-H Club for young students. The four H's stood for Head, Hand, Heart, and Health. We had a pledge that went something like this: "I pledge my head to clearer thinking, my hand to service, my heart to greater loyalty, and my health to better living." One year I was the Four-H Club's muffin champion. I won a baking set!

Blanche Slaughter, Darwin, MN Age 58

DATE PUDDING

1 1/2 cups brown sugar
1 1/2 cups flour
1 1/2 cups chopped dates
1 1/2 teaspoons baking powder
1/2 teaspoon salt
3/4 cup milk

TOPPING

1/2 cup brown sugar
1 1/8 cups white sugar
2 1/4 cups boiling water
1 1/2 tablespoons butter
1 1/2 cups chopped nuts
Whipped cream, optional

Preheat oven to 350 degrees. Mix together brown sugar, flour, dates, baking powder, salt, and milk in a medium bowl and pour into a greased 9 x 13 pan. Mix brown and white sugars, water, butter, and nuts in a medium bowl and pour over the first mixture. Bake 30 minutes. Top cooled dessert with whipped cream. Yield: 8 servings.

MARY K. HART

RICE PUDDING

1 1/2 cups cooked rice
1/4 cup raisins
2 eggs
1 1/2 cups milk
1/2 cup sugar
1/2 teaspoon ground nutmeg

Preheat oven to 350 degrees. Place rice and raisins in a greased one-quart casserole. In a small mixing bowl, beat eggs, milk, sugar and nutmeg. Pour over rice and bake uncovered for 45 minutes. Cool and top with your favorite homemade or commercial lemon sauce. Yield: 4-6 servings

HELEN A. ROSE, Cameron, TX Age 67

VANILLA PUDDING

Layer this "scratch" pudding with vanilla wafers and sliced bananas.

4 cups milk
1 1/2 cups sugar
1/2 teaspoon salt
1/2 cup flour
2 tablespoons cornstarch
2 eggs, well beaten
2 teaspoons vanilla
2 tablespoons butter or margarine

Scald milk in the top of a double boiler. Sift sugar, salt, flour, and cornstarch together and add gradually to milk. Cook until the mixture begins to thicken. Add eggs and cook until thick. Stir in butter and vanilla. Yield: 8 servings

DAVIE GIPSON, McLean, TX Age 65

PERSIMMON PUDDING

It's not fall in Indiana until you have persimmon pudding.

2 scant cups sugar
2 scant cups flour
1 teaspoon baking powder
1/2 teaspoon baking soda
Pinch of salt
1/2 teaspoon cinnamon
2 cups milk, divided
2 eggs
2 cups persimmon pulp
1 stick melted margarine

Preheat oven to 350 degrees. Mix sugar, flour, baking powder, baking soda, salt, and cinnamon in a large bowl. Add 1 cup milk and beat; add eggs and beat. Add 1 cup milk and beat. Add persimmon pulp and beat very well. Add margarine and beat. Pour into 9 x 13 pan and bake for 45-50 minutes. Yield: 10-12 servings

PAULA A. BLEWETT, Nashville, IN

CORNFLAKE PUDDING

If you like banana pudding, you'll like this.

2 cups sugar
2 1/2 cups milk
4 tablespoons flour
3 eggs, slightly beaten
4 tablespoons butter or margarine
1 teaspoon vanilla
1 1/2-2 cups cornflakes

TOPPING

2 eggs beaten stiff
3 tablespoons sugar
1/4 teaspoon vanilla

Preheat oven to 400 degrees. In a medium saucepan, combine sugar, milk, flour, and eggs, and cook on medium until heated through. Add butter and cook until slightly thickened. Add vanilla and cornflakes. Spoon into a 13 x 9 glass baking dish. To prepare topping, add sugar and vanilla to beaten eggs and place over pudding mixture. Bake until brown. Yield: 12 servings

RUBY HARRIS, Dobson, NC Age 66

KREM (GRAPE JUICE PUDDING)

This is a Scandanavian treat.

3 tablespoons sugar
3 tablespoons cornstarch
3 tablespoons cold water
2 cups grape juice (if using frozen grape juice,
    add only one can of water to reconstitute)
Cream or whipped cream

In a small bowl, mix sugar and cornstarch with water and stir until smooth. Heat grape juice in a medium saucepan and slowly add the cornstarch mixture. Cook over low heat, stirring constantly, until mixture is clear. Cool 8 hours. Serve with cream or whipped cream. Yield: 4 servings

BLANCHE A. SLAUGHTER, Darwin, MN Age 58

FRUITS OF SUMMER PIZZA

1 roll commercial refrigerator sugar cookie dough
1 12-ounce package cream cheese
1/2 cup sugar
1 tablespoon vanilla
Cherry pie filling
Fruits in season, sliced (i.e., strawberries, kiwi, blueberries, bananas), reserve any juice for glaze

Slice cookie dough in 1/4 inch thick slices. Place on a greased pizza pan, sides touching, and bake as directed. While crust is baking, combine filling ingredients. Frost cooled cookie dough crust with filling edge to edge. Cover with foil and refrigerate overnight. To finish, begin with one kind of fruit and place it all around the crust. Work inward, alternating rows of fruit. Glaze with cherry pie filling. Yield: 8-10 servings

TOSSIE B. IVIE, Corsicana, TX Age 77

APPLE PIZZA

1 roll commercial refrigerator sugar cookie dough
1/2 cup golden raisins
2 tablespoons butter or margarine
2 1/2 tablespoons corn syrup
1 cup brown sugar
1/4 cup water
1 teaspoon lemon juice
1 1/2 teaspoons cinnamon
1/2 teaspoon ground nutmeg
1 cup pecans, finely chopped
1 1/3 pounds apples, peeled and chopped
1 cup powdered sugar
1 8-ounce package cream cheese, softened
1 cup cheddar cheese, shredded

Preheat oven to 325 degrees. Oil pizza pan and pat sugar cookie dough to fit; flute edges slightly. Bake 12-15 minutes. Combine raisins, butter, corn syrup, brown sugar, water, lemon juice, cinnamon, nutmeg, and nuts in a large saucepan; stir until sugar starts to melt. Add the apples and simmer until they are slightly tender and sauce is thick. Cool. Mix powdered sugar and cream cheese until smooth. Spread on top of cookie dough. Spread cooled apples on top of cream cheese. Sprinkle with cheddar cheese. Yield: 14-16 servings

LENA L. TRAGESSER, Tipton, IN Age 78

Johnnycakes for Dessert

Before fancy packaged pancakes were sold in supermarkets, there were johnnycakes. This was a flat griddlecake made with cornmeal, eggs, salt, and milk. With a family of thirteen to feed, my mother rarely had time to bake sweet goodies. That is why my siblings and I loved johnnycakes. No matter how hard times were, my mother always had sweet golden honey to pour over these pancakes. They were so good for breakfast, but even better for dessert!

Carrie Knutson, Jamestown, ND Age 73

Ice Cream for a Princess

We were poor and our house was a humble one, but we lived in a picturesque valley and a cheerful babbling brook ran in front of our house. Every year on my birthday, my parents treated me like a princess. My father climbed the mountain and filled a big bucket with icicles that fell from the cliffs. He cracked the icicles and put them into a wooden washtub followed by a metal bucket with a handcranker that was filled with cream, eggs, sugar, and vanilla. The final step was to hand crank the mixture until it thickened into ice cream. By the time my father proudly scooped out the ice cream, my mother was ready to slice her freshly-baked yellow cake with chocolate frosting. Truly a treat for a princess!

Eula Mae Combs, Beattyville, KY Age 68

ICE CREAM PIZZA

This creation took first place in a pizza competition.

CRUST

> 1 cup flour
> 1/2 teaspoon cream of tartar
> 1/4 teaspoon baking soda
> 1/4 teaspoon salt
> 1/4 cup oil
> 1 egg
> 1/2 teaspoon vanilla
> 1/3 cup sugar

Mix flour, cream of tartar, baking soda, salt, oil, egg, vanilla, and sugar in a large bowl. Chill dough. Spread on bottom and sides of a greased pizza pan. Bake at 375 degrees for 15 minutes until crust pulls away from pan.

TOPPING

> 1 cup strawberry jam
> 1 quart softened ice cream
> Chocolate chips, M&Ms, red hots, coconut, pecan halves

Spread the jam over the cooled crust and cover with the ice cream. Sprinkle with desired toppings. Freeze 8 hours before cutting. Yield: 8-10 servings

VIANNA BAGWELL, Covington, OH Age 72

BUTTERMILK SHERBET

> 2 cups buttermilk
> 1 1/2 cups sugar
> Pinch salt
> 1 teaspoon vanilla
> 1 can crushed pineapple and juice
> 1 egg white, beaten

In a large bowl, mix buttermilk, sugar, salt, and vanilla. Add pineapple and juice, and freeze until mixture is mushy. Beat well and fold in beaten egg white. Refreeze until ready to serve. Yield: 6-8 servings

BETTE F. MAYS, Jeffersonville, KY Age 59

MOCHA-FUDGE ICE CREAM PIE

You can use low-fat ice cream and this is still delicious.

1 cup cookie crumbs (macaroons, butter cookies, or chocolate
    wafers--I use Pecan Sandies)
2 tablespoons melted butter
1 quart chocolate ice cream, slightly softened
1/2 cup or more chocolate sauce, divided
1 quart coffee ice cream, slightly softened
4 ounces chocolate-covered toffee bars, coarsely crushed

Preheat oven to 350 degrees. Mix cookie crumbs and butter. Press
lightly into bottom of a 9" springform pan. Bake 8-10 minutes or until
light brown. Cool. Spread chocolate ice cream in an even layer over
the cooled crust; drizzle evenly with 1/4 cup chocolate sauce. Freeze
until firm. Top with an even layer of coffee ice cream (or scoop small
balls of ice cream and arrange over the surface. Sprinkle evenly with
crushed candy and drizzle remaining sauce over the top. Cover with
plastic wrap and freeze until firm. Remove from freezer a few minutes
before serving to make slicing easier.

RUTH ANN WEFALD, Manhattan, KS

CANDY CANE ICE CREAM PIE

1 quart peppermint ice cream, softened
1 prepared 9" chocolate cookie or pastry crust
1/2 pint fudge sauce (hot)
3 egg whites
1/2 teaspoon vanilla
1/4 teaspoon cream of tartar
6 tablespoons sugar
1/4 cup crushed candy canes

Spread half of softened ice cream in pie shell. Cover with half of fudge
sauce and cover with remaining ice cream. Add remaining fudge
sauce; cover with plastic wrap and freeze overnight or until firm. Just
before serving, preheat oven to 400 degrees. In a medium mixing
bowl, beat the egg whites, vanilla, and cream of tartar until peaks
form. Gradually beat in sugar. When peaks are stiff, stir in 3 tablespoons of crushed peppermint candy. Spread meringue over pie,
sealing to edges. Sprinkle remaining candy over the top. Bake until
meringue is golden. Yield: 8 servings

MRS. LLOYD WALK, Falls Creek, PA Age 58

The Patient Baker

My mother was the world's best baker, she really was. Her specialty was angel food cake. My father always said that you could measure a baker by her angel food because it was a difficult cake to bake. For those of you who make this cake from a mix, I have news for you--it is a totally different story to make it from scratch and make it without the luxury of an electric beater! My mother patiently beat the whites of 12 eggs until stiff peaks formed. The finished product was a light, airy sponge-type cake with orange-colored buttercream frosting. It was almost too elegant to eat, but eat it we always did.

Shirley Reineke, Huron, SD Age 72

FUDGY BROWNIES

4 eggs
2 cups sugar
1 cup margarine
4 squares unsweetened chocolate
2 cups flour
1 cup chopped nuts
2 teaspoons vanilla

Preheat oven to 350 degrees. In a large bowl, beat eggs, add sugar, creaming well. Melt margarine and chocolate together in a small saucepan over low heat. Combine mixtures, beating thoroughly. Mix in flour, nuts, and vanilla. Bake in greased jelly roll pan for 20 minutes. Yield: 16-20 brownies

KAY WILES, Torrington, WY Age 59

GERMAN CHOCOLATE SQUARES

I am the state director of Pennsylvania's Green Thumb program, and I live right in the heart of the Pennsylvania Dutch/Amish community. This is a popular recipe that combines the rich Amish baking tradition with the influence of Hershey, PA.

60 caramels
1/2 cup evaporated milk plus 1/3 cup
1 box German chocolate cake mix
3/4 cup butter, melted
1 cup chopped nuts
1 cup semi-sweet chocolate chips

Preheat oven to 350 degrees. Grease and flour a 13 x 9 pan. In a heavy saucepan, combine caramels and 1/2 cup milk. Cook over low heat, stirring constantly until melted. Set aside. In a large bowl, combine cake mix, butter, 1/3 cup milk, and nuts. Pat half of dough into pan, save rest for topping. Bake for 8 minutes. Sprinkle chocolate chips over crust. Spread caramel mixture over chips. Crumble remaining dough over caramel layer. Return to oven and bake 18-20 minutes. Cool slightly. Refrigerate 30 minutes to set caramel layer. Yield: 18-20 servings

ELIZABETH S. FRY, Reinholds, PA

GINGERBREAD

1/2 cup shortening
1/2 cup sugar
2 eggs
1 cup molasses
2 3/4 cups sifted flour
1 teaspoon soda
1/2 teaspoon salt
1 1/2 teaspoon ginger
3/4 teaspoon cinnamon
3/4 teaspoon cloves
1 cup hot water

Preheat oven to 375 degrees. Cream shortening and sugar in a large bowl. Add eggs, beating well. Blend molasses into mixture. Sift flour, soda, salt, and spices together. Add flour mix and hot water alternately, beginning and ending with flour. Beat one minute, then pour batter into greased 9 x 13 pan. Bake 40 minutes. Yield: About 24 servings

KAY WILES, Torrington, WY Age 59

GRAHAM CRACKER ROLL

1 pound graham cracker crumbs
1 pound marshmallows, cut into pieces
1 pound chopped dates
1 cup chopped nuts
2 cups evaporated milk or heavy cream
Whipped cream or topping, optional

Combine crumbs, marshmallows, dates, nuts, and milk in a large bowl. Mix thoroughly with a spoon or clean hands. Pat mixture into one large or two small rounded loaves; wrap in waxed paper and refrigerate at least 12 hours. Slice and serve with whipped cream or topping.

SISTER ADELINA ST. HILAIRE, Hudson, NY Age 74

I come from a family of nine children. Ever since I can remember, this graham cracker roll was served to family and guests at holiday time. Since we lost our parents and four of the family members, I continue the custom and deliver the treat to my sister and three brothers. Christmas and New Year's wouldn't feel right without it.

*That
Pie Plant*

*A neighbor
stopped by one
afternoon and my
mother offered
him a slice of her
rhubarb pie. He
accepted
gratefully because
he was getting
mighty tired of
that "pie plant"
his wife was
cooking. Little did
he know, rhubarb
was that pie
plant!*

*Joe Rankin,
Rall, TX*

APPLE CRISP

3 tablespoons butter
1 cup sugar
1 egg
1 cup flour
1/2 teaspoon baking soda
1/2 teaspoon salt
1/2 teaspoon baking powder
1/2 teaspoon cinnamon or nutmeg
2 cups peeled, diced apples
1 cup chopped nuts
1/2 cup raisins, optional
Whipped cream or ice cream, optional

Preheat oven to 325 degrees. Cream butter and sugar in a large bowl; add egg and beat well. Add flour, soda, salt, baking powder, and cinnamon or nutmeg and mix thoroughly. Add apples, nuts, and raisins. Pour into a greased and floured 9 x 13 pan. Bake for 1 1/2 hours, or until tester comes out clean. Cool and serve with whipped cream, ice cream, or other topping. Yield: 12-16 servings

WANDA M. RHODES, Hillsboro, OH Age 75

RHUBARB BUTTER CRUNCH

*I received my
GED through
Green Thumb last
year. It was very
rewarding as I had
only an 8th grade
education. I am
now learning to
work on comput-
ers. This recipe is
a family favorite
and easy to fix.*

3 cups diced fresh rhubarb
1 cup sugar
3 tablespoons flour
1 cup brown sugar
1 cup uncooked oatmeal
1 1/2 cup flour
2 sticks butter or margarine
Whipped cream, optional

Preheat oven to 375 degrees. Combine rhubarb, sugar, and flour in a large bowl. Place in greased 6 x 10 loaf pan. Mix remaining ingredients and sprinkle over rhubarb mixture. Bake 40 minutes. Serve with whipped cream. Yield: 8 servings

ANNA CHRISTOPHERSON, Vebarg, SD Age 75

CHERRY WINKS
THE $5,000 COOKY

Here's Ruth Derousseau's prize-winning recipe, reprinted with permission from Pillsbury, as shown on the back of a 1951 Kellogg's Corn Flake cereal box.

Junior winner in Pillsbury's BEST
2nd GRAND NATIONAL Recipe and Baking Contest

These Tasty, Crunchy Cookies Won Big Prize
for Rice Lake, Wis., Girl

Ruth Derousseau won $5,000 with her Cherry Winks cookies in Pillsbury's 2nd Grand National Contest. Kellogg's Corn Flakes give them crispness. Pecans and cherries add a flavor touch. Quick to prepare (mix them in 1 bowl). Let your family enjoy these wonderful cookies tonight.

2 1/4 cups sifted Pillsbury's Best Enriched Flour*
1 teaspoon double-acting baking powder
1/2 teaspoon baking soda
1/2 teaspoon salt
3/4 cup shortening
1 cup sugar
2 eggs
2 tablespoons milk
1 teaspoon vanilla
1 cup chopped pecans
1 cup chopped dates
1/2 cup chopped maraschino cherries
2 1/2 cups Kellogg's Corn Flakes

Sift together flour, baking powder, soda, and salt. Combine shortening and sugar; cream well. Blend in eggs; add milk and vanilla. Blend in sifted dry ingredients; mix well. Add pecans, dates, and cherries. Mix well. Shape into balls using a level tablespoon of dough for each cooky. Crush Corn Flakes. Roll each ball of dough in corn flakes. Place on greased baking sheet. Top each cooky with 1/4 maraschino cherry. Bake in moderate oven (375 degrees F.) 10 to 12 minutes. Do not stack or store until cold. Makes about 5 dozen cookies.

*If you use Pillsbury's Best Enriched Self-Rising Flour, omit baking powder and salt, decrease soda to 1/4 teaspoon.

FORGOTTEN COOKIES

2 egg whites
3/4 cup sugar
1 teaspoon vanilla
Pinch salt
1 cup chopped nuts
1 cup chocolate chips

Preheat oven to 350 degrees. Beat eggs whites with sugar until stiff. Fold in vanilla, salt, nuts, and chips. Drop by teaspoonsful on foil-covered cookie sheets. Place in preheated oven, and turn off heat. Leave cookies in oven overnight. <u>Do not open the oven until morning.</u> Substitute colored candies for chocolate chips to give cookies a different look and taste. Yield: 4-6 dozen

DIANE CHAPMAN, Magnolia, AR Age 58

ZUCCHINI COOKIES

These cookies are a favorite at the Bozeman Senior Center where I work and the retirement center where I live. They are in great demand, and everyone asks for the recipe.

P.S. A senior center co-worker says, "Frenchy works circles around most of us."

1 cup sugar
1 stick margarine
1 egg, beaten
1 cup grated zucchini
2 cups flour
1 teaspoon cinnamon
1/2 teaspoon ground cloves
1/2 teaspoon salt
1 teaspoon baking soda
1 cup chopped nuts
1 cup raisins

Preheat oven to 375 degrees. Cream sugar and margarine together in a large bowl. Add egg and zucchini, mix well. Sift dry ingredients together and blend into mixture. Stir in nuts and raisins. Chill dough two hours. Drop dough by rounded teaspoonsful onto a greased cookie sheet. Bake 12-15 minutes. Yield: 3 dozen

FRANCIS "FRENCHY" NORTHWAY, Bozeman, MT Age 91

GREEN THUMBPRINTS

1 cup butter
1/2 cup brown sugar
2 eggs
1/2 teaspoon vanilla flavoring
1/4 teaspoon salt
2 1/2 cup flour
1 1/2 cup finely chopped nuts
1/2 cup buttercream frosting, tinted green, jam or jelly

Preheat oven to 375 degrees. Cream butter and sugar in a medium bowl. Separate eggs and beat whites until fluffy. Set aside. Add yolks and vanilla into butter. Roll dough into 1-inch balls. Dip first in eggwhite, then in chopped nuts. Make thumbprint. Bake 12-15 minutes. Fill thumbprints with a small amount of jam or green frosting. Yield: 3 dozen

PHYLLIS MARR, Oregon City, OR

This is a favorite recipe because it gives us a chance to use some of our uniquely wonderful Oregon products. The chopped nuts of choice are filberts (hazelnuts). Oregon is the nation's largest grower of this nut.

RUM COFFEE COOKIES

1 cup packed brown sugar
1/2 cup margarine
2 eggs
1/2 teaspoon rum extract
1 teaspoon instant coffee
1 tablespoon boiling water
1 1/2 cups all purpose flour
1 1/2 teaspoon baking powder
1/4 teaspoon salt
1 cup pecans, finely chopped

Cream sugar and margarine in a large bowl. Add eggs and rum extract, beating well. Dissolve coffee crystals in boiling water and stir into creamed mixture. In a separate bowl, stir flour, baking powder, and salt together and add to creamed mixture, blending well. Chill dough several hours. Preheat oven to 350 degrees. Drop dough by spoonfuls onto nuts; roll to coat. Place on ungreased cookie sheet and bake 8-10 minutes.

GINA ROSPROY, Belleville, KS Age 71

My mother, my sisters and I used to gather in the kitchen to make these cookies. My favorite memories of my mother were these special times together.

Tomboy

*I was the only girl
in my family, and
more than
anything, I loved
being outdoors
helping my father
and three brothers
farm the land. I
felt kind of like
Laura Ingalls of
the Little House
on the Prairie
books. Laura, too,
was a tomboy who
preferred helping
her father instead
of doing house-
hold chores.
There was one
thing I didn't
mind being in the
kitchen for, and
that was baking
sugar cookies for
my father and
brothers.*

*Annita A. Heyer,
Green Ridge, MO
Age 67*

GRANDMA'S SOFT SUGAR COOKIES

1 cup margarine or butter
2 cups granulated sugar
1/2 teaspoon salt
1 teaspoon vanilla
1 teaspoon nutmeg
2 eggs plus enough milk to make 1 cup of liquid
1 teaspoon baking soda
1/2 cup milk
6 cups flour
2 teaspoons baking powder

Preheat oven to 350 degrees. In a large mixing bowl, cream margarine
and sugar; add salt, vanilla, and nutmeg. Add egg and milk mixture
and beat well. Dissolve baking soda in 1/2 cup milk; add to mixture
and beat well. Add baking powder and one cup of flour at a time. You
may use an electric mixer to beat ingredients up until adding the final
three cups of flour. Add the balance of the flour by hand since the
dough will be thick. Roll dough 1/4" thick; cut out and place on a
greased cookie sheet. Bake 8-15 minutes (depending on size of
cookie). Do not overbake. Yield: 6 dozen 2" cookies

JOYCE RAYMOND, Portville, NY

BUTTERFINGER COOKIES

1 cup margarine
2 cups all purpose flour
1/3 cup granulated sugar
1 teaspoon vanilla
2 cups pecans, finely chopped
Powdered sugar

Preheat oven to 300 degrees. Mix margarine, flour, sugar, vanilla, and
nuts in a large bowl. Roll into finger-shaped cookies and bake for 25
minutes. Let cool then roll in powdered sugar. Yield: about 2 dozen

JUANITA P. EVANS, Dublin, GA

RITZ CRACKER COOKIE

1 can sweetened condensed milk
1 cup cut-up dates
1/2 cup ground pecans
About 40 Ritz crackers

FROSTING

3 ounces cream cheese, softened
3/4 stick butter, softened
3 cups powdered sugar
1 teaspoon vanilla

In a medium bowl, combine milk, dates, and pecans. Stir constantly to form a paste. Spread about a teaspoon of the mixture on each cracker. Mix cream cheese, butter, sugar, and vanilla in a medium bowl. Top each cracker with frosting. Yield: 3 1/2 dozen

EDITH READ, Shelbyville, IL

PEANUT BUTTER CRACKLES

My mother found this recipe in the cooking section of the <u>Buffalo Evening News</u> in the 1920's. During the Depression, I always had "crackles," along with peanut butter and jelly sandwiches, in my school lunchbox.

1 3/4 cups flour
1 teaspoon baking soda
1/2 teaspoon salt
1/2 cup margarine
1/2 cup creamy or chunky peanut butter
1/2 cup sugar
1/2 cup brown sugar
1 egg
1 teaspoon vanilla
1/2 cup sugar
About 48 chocolate stars or kisses

Preheat oven to 375 degrees. Mix flour, baking soda, and salt in a medium bowl. In a separate larger bowl, stir margarine to soften, then mix in peanut butter until well blended. Add sugars and mix until creamy. Beat in egg and vanilla. Stir in flour mixture. Shape dough into 1-inch balls. Roll in sugar and place on ungreased baking sheet. Bake for 12 minutes, or until lightly browned. Remove from oven. Quickly press chocolate candy firmly into top of each cookie. Cookie will crack around edges. Yield: about 4 dozen 2" cookies

LILLIAN BRUTOUSKI, Urbana, OH Age 72

Christmas Nut Cookies

My father worked for a construction company, and he was frequently sent to different towns in Wisconsin on business. When he came home, he often had sacks of walnuts, hazelnuts, and butternuts that he bought from roadside stands. They were put away in the cellar, and come Christmas time, it was a tradition for the whole family to participate in making the holiday nut cookies. It was my father's job to shell the hard nuts, my mother made the cookie dough, and my sister and I decorated them. I can still hear my mother warning my father, "Don't eat all the nutmeats before the cookies get them."

Thelma Renderman, Fond du Lac, WI Age 73

Sauces, Pickles, Relishes, & Home Canning

SAUCES, PICKLES, RELISHES, & HOME CANNING

CONTENTS

FREEZER TOMATO SAUCE

Use in casseroles, sloppy joes, or any recipe that calls for tomato sauce.

20 large tomatoes, peeled and quartered
1/2 cup chopped parsley
3/4 teaspoon pepper
2 tablespoons salt
4 chopped onions
3 tablespoons sugar
4 grated carrots (optional)

Combine all ingredients in a large kettle and bring to boiling over medium heat, stirring often. Lower heat and simmer 30 minutes, or until mixture thickens. Cool slightly, then measure 2 cups at a time into a blender and puree until smooth. Pour into freezer containers, leaving 1/2 inch at the top. To use: Place frozen sauce in a pan. Cover and bring to bubbling over low heat. Yield: about 1 quart

JOAN BROWN, Watertown, SD Age 55

BARBEQUE SAUCE

From three + decades of year-round Florida cookouts.

1 quart catsup
1/4 cup plus 4 teaspoons Worcestershire sauce
1/3 bottle Tabasco sauce
1 tablespoon plus 1 teaspoon prepared mustard
1/4 cup plus 4 teaspoons white vinegar
5 ounces salad oil
3/8 cup plus 2 teaspoons sugar
1/2 tablespoon onion salt
1/2 tablespoon garlic salt
1/2 tablespoon basil
1/2 tablespoon Accent
1/4 cup molasses
1/2 teaspoon salt
1/2 teaspoon black pepper
1/2 teaspoon Kitchen Bouquet

Mix all ingredients together in a large saucepan. Bring to a boil over low heat and simmer for one hour. Place in jars or freezer bags; seal or freeze. Yield: about 1 quart

CONSTANCE HENDERSON, Berea, KY Age 67

They Lined Up at City Hall

My father was a farmer and a self-taught veterinarian. Cows with milk fever, mares going through difficult labor, castrations, vaccinations--my father was always there. One day he explained that he could no longer treat sick animals because the State required that only real veterinarians who had attended a special school and had a certificate could do so.. When our neighbors heard about this, they lined up at City Hall to give testimonials and references on my father's behalf. Not too long afterwards, he received a certificate and went on treating animals. That was what living in a rural farming community was all about.

Mae Rudroff,
Vienna, MO
Age 70

Secret Sauce

Back in the 1940's my father would barbeque every 4th of July. He cooked chickens, hogs, and goats. All the neighbors would come to our house to eat, and everyone would stay all day and have a great time. My daddy was the only one who knew how to make the barbeque sauce.

P.S. I did not eat the goat!

Joyce Oldman

DADDY'S BARBEQUE SAUCE

1/2 gallon tomato juice
2 cups catsup
2 cups vinegar
1/4 cup prepared mustard
1/2 cup Worcestershire sauce
1/2 cup cooking oil
1/4 cup brown sugar
1 tablespoon paprika
1 tablespoon hot sauce
2 tablespoons salt
1 tablespoon lemon juice
2 tablespoons black pepper
2 large onions, minced
2 hot peppers, minced
1/2 clove garlic, minced
1 tablespoon corn starch

Combine all ingredients except corn starch in a large kettle or dutch oven. Cook over medium heat for about 1 hour. Add corn starch to thicken. Yield: 5 pints

JOYCE OLDMAN, Harrisburg, AR Age 61

PESTO SAUCE

Delicious in sandwiches and salads or to top a baked potato.

2 cups lightly packed fresh basil leaves
1 cup (5 ounces) firmly packed grated Parmesan cheese
1/2 to 2/3 cup olive oil (must be olive oil)
2 cloves garlic

Whirl all ingredients in blender or food processor until smooth. Cover and chill up to five days or freeze in easy-to-use portions. Yield: 3-4 cups

MARGARET BREERS, Lakeport, CA Age 71

GREENS & REDEYE GRAVY

Best eaten with a slab of cornbread and a glass of buttermilk.

Bacon grease
Leftover bacon crumbs or pieces
Peck of curly leaf mustard or leaf lettuce
Boiled eggs
1 cup morning coffee

Heat bacon grease and bits until sizzling hot. Add the lettuce or mustard leaves intermittently as they wilt. During cooking time pour coffee over greens. Add sliced eggs over and around the finished product. Yield: up to 10 servings

LURINE DUDLEY, Muleshoe, TX Age 70

This dish was served in the 20's and 30's when high-cholesterol bacon was worked off in contamination-free fresh air while raising the ingredients and doing other farm chores!

ITALIAN SPAGHETTI SAUCE

1/2 cup diced onions
2 tablespoons olive oil or salad oil
1 pound ground beef
2 cloves garlic, minced
2 1-pound cans tomatoes
2 8-ounce cans tomato sauce
1 3-ounce can sliced mushrooms
1/4 cup chopped parsley
1 1/2 teaspoons oregano or sage
1 teaspoon salt
1/2 teaspoon monosodium glutomate
1/4 teaspoon thyme
1 bay leaf
1 cup water

In a dutch oven or kettle, cook onion in hot oil until golden. Add meat and garlic and brown lightly. Add remaining ingredients and simmer, uncovered, 2-2 1/2 hours. Remove bay leaf and serve on top of cooked spaghetti.Yield: 8 servings

JEANNE HENDON, Calvin, OK Age 65

I have a family of five, including three boys with big appetites. This was a favorite, served with a big green salad and french bread. I now have 9 grandchildren and am very active in church and community functions.

PASTA HOT SAUCE

This is a delicious meatless sauce for those watching their diets.

10 or more ripe tomatoes or 4 large cans tomatoes
2 green peppers, cut in strips
4 hot banana peppers, stripped
2 large onions, chopped
2 cans mushrooms (small bits and pieces)
Olive oil to measure 1/4" in pan
2 tablespoons oregano
20 fresh basil leaves or 2 tablespoons dried basil
1 bay leaf

Pour hot water over ripe tomatoes and remove skins. Place a colander in a deep pan; squeeze tomatoes and let drain (reserve juice). Pour oil into a large saucepan; saute onions until golden; add drained tomatoes, basil, and oregano. Simmer for 1 hour, stirring often so sauce doesn't burn the bottom of the pan. Add peppers, mushrooms, and bay leaf; simmer 1 hour. In a separate saucepan, simmer reserved tomato juice for 2 hours. Add to sauce for a nice red color. Sauce is now ready for any kind of pasta. Yield: 2 quarts

JOSEPHINE GRAVANTI, Niagara Falls, NY Age 72

NO-COOK HOLLANDAISE SAUCE

2 egg yolks
1 stick butter, melted
Juice from 1 lemon
Tabasco
Cayenne pepper
Paprika
Salt

In a small deep bowl, beat the egg yolks until thick and lemon colored. Add the melted butter, slowly at first. When you have used all of the melted butter, season to your own taste with lemon juice, Tabasco, cayenne pepper, paprika, and salt. Use immediately for best results. Store in refrigerator. May be reheated over hot, not boiling, water in the top of a double boiler. Yield: about 2 cups

SALLY BOOFER, Green Thumb National Office

SWEET AND SOUR SALAD DRESSING

1 1/4 cups white sugar
3-4 tablespoons brown sugar
1 heaping teaspoon prepared mustard
2 teaspoons salt
1/8 cup chopped onion
1 cup white vinegar
3 tablespoons water
2 teaspoons celery seed

Combine all ingredients and puree in a blender or food processor.
Yield: 1 1/2-2 cups

PAULINE CRUM, Caldwell, OH Age 73

FRENCH DRESSING

1 can tomato soup
1 cup vegetable oil
1 small onion, finely chopped
Juice of one lemon
1/2 cup sugar
1/2 cup vinegar
Dash of paprika
Pinch of salt

Combine all ingredients and puree in a blender or food processor.
Store in refrigerator. Yield: 2-3 cups

LaHOMA DAVIS, Pampa, TX Age 58

Walking the Fence Rows

Fence rows divided one farmer's land from another. These dividers weren't the steel or picket wood fences you see today. No, the fence rows of my childhood years were simply shrubs, bushes, and stones that lined the farm properties. And along these fence rows thimble berries, blackberries, yellow raspberries, and strawberries grew thick and wild. Walking the fence rows meant filling your pails to the brim with berries for Mom to preserve for the winter.

Katherine Gobeyn, Marion, NY Age 71

I remember taking my lunch to school every day as a child. If my mother had prepared deviled eggs using this dressing, it was a treat. So tasty! It gives that same extra flavor to potato salad.

POTATO SALAD MAYONNAISE

1/2 cup sugar
1 tablespoon flour
1/2 teaspoon salt
1 egg
1/2 cup vinegar
1/2 cup water

Combine sugar, flour, and salt in a small saucepan; add egg and mix well. Add vinegar and water. Cook mixture over medium heat, stirring constantly until it thickens. Remove from heat. Yield: about 1 1/2 cups

RHUY ELLEN LEWIS, Dodge City, KS Age 76

CUCUMBER KETCHUP

3 large cucumbers, peeled and chopped
2 large onions, peeled and chopped
1/2 cup salt
1 cup cider vinegar
1/4 cup white mustard seed
1 teaspoon black pepper

Mix cucumbers, onions, and salt. Pour into a sieve or colander and set in the sink to drain overnight. (A large amount of juice will drain.) Pour mash into a mixing bowl and cover with cider vinegar. Pour mixture into a blender and puree. Add mustard seed and pepper to puree. Pour into a large jar and seal tightly. May be used in three days. Keeps for years! Yield: about 1 quart

NEVA DARBY, Eldon, MO

Rule of Thumb:

Rice vinegar and chili garlic sauce are available in the oriental food section of the supermarket.

DRESSING FOR SLICED CUCUMBERS
Also good on spinach salad or other raw vegetables.

1 cup rice vinegar
1/4 cup oil (sesame oil is best)
1/2 teaspoon chili garlic sauce
1/3 cup sugar

In a jar, mix all ingredients together and shake vigorously. Yield: about 1 1/2 cups

OPAL ZOOK, Hillsboro, OR Age 60

GOOD GRAVY!

Green Thumbs in the Kitchen offer these gravy tips:

If you don't have enough juices to make gravy, add water or bouillon. Make a paste of water and flour in a jar and shake well. Gradually add to the drippings, stirring constantly to blend.

For extra flavor, add a bouillon cube to drippings. Adding potato water to drippings will also add flavor.

Add 1/2 cup sauteed sliced mushrooms per 1 cup gravy.

If gravy gets too thick after standing, add a small amount of hot water, return to heat and stir.

CRANBERRY SAUCE

1 12-ounce package (3 cups) fresh cranberries
2 cups sugar
1/2 cup apricot brandy

My family uses cranberry sauce on pork chops, ham, baked chicken, and turkey. I'm always asked to bring this to a pot luck; I also give it as a gift.

Preheat oven to 350 degrees. Combine ingredients in a large baking dish. Cover with lid or foil and bake one hour or until all berries have popped. Store in a tightly covered container in the refrigerator. Yield: about 4 cups

CARMEN NAPIER, Salina KS Age 68

CROCKPOT APPLE BUTTER

2 quarts unsweetened applesauce
3 1/2 cups granulated sugar
2/3 cup brown sugar
2 2/3 tablespoons vinegar
2 2/3 tablespoons lemon juice
1 teaspoon cinnamon
1 teaspoon allspice
1 teaspoon gound cloves

Combine all ingredients in a crockpot; cover and cook on high 2-3 hours, stirring occasionally. Remove lid, continue cooking until excess liquid cooks away (turn crockpot to low as necessary). Total cooking time will be 5-8 hours. Seal mixture in hot jars. Process in a hot water bath for 10 minutes. Yield: 6 pints

MARY L. TRAYLOR, Greensburg, IN Age 79

This recipe was given to me by an old lady I met who lived in the "head" of a holler in Morgan County, Kentucky. Homemade honey looks and tastes exactly like strained honey from the market, but once opened it doesn't turn to sugar like raw honey.

HONEY

45 white clover blossoms
45 red clover blossoms
35 rose petals
10 cups white sugar
2 cups water
1 teaspoon alum

Wash clover blossoms and rose petals. Place in a deep saucepan and add sugar, water, and alum. Bring to a boil, and stir constantly for three minutes. Strain twice: first through a sieve and again through cheesecloth. Pour into pint jars and seal. Yield: 6 pints

BETTE F. MAYS, Jeffersonville, KY Age 59

QUICK BUTTERSCOTCH SAUCE

1 cup brown sugar
1/2 cup corn syrup
1/4 cup butter, softened
1/2 cup cream

Combine all ingredients in a small saucepan. Cook over low heat, stirring to blend well, about 5 minutes. Serve warm. Yield: 2 cups

MARTHA SEXTON, Age 76

QUICK FUDGE SAUCE

2 1/4-pound semi-sweet chocolate bars
3 tablespoons cream
1 to 4 tablespoons water

In the microwave or top of a double boiler, melt chocolate. Stir in cream, one tablespoon at a time. Stir until smooth and glossy. Remove from heat. If too thick, thin with water. Yield: 1 1/2 cups

MARTHA SEXTON, Age 76

CHOCOLATE SUNDAE SAUCE

Reheats nicely in the microwave.

1 1/2 cups sugar
1 cup cocoa
1 1/4 cups hot water
Pinch of salt
2 teaspoons vanilla

Mix sugar, cocoa, hot water, and salt in a small saucepan. Cook over medium heat, stirring constantly, until mixture comes to a boil. Reduce heat and simmer 5 minutes. Remove from heat; add vanilla and mix well. Pour into a heat-resistant container and cool. Store in refrigerator. Yield: 15-20 servings

DOROTHY GILLEY, Knoblick, KY Age 67

LEMON SAUCE

Wonderful over fruit cake, plum pudding, gingerbread, mince or apple pie

1/2 cup sugar
1 tablespoon cornstarch
Dash of salt
Dash of nutmeg
1 cup boiling water
2 tablespoons butter or margerine
1 1/2 teaspoons lemon juice

Mix sugar, cornstarch, salt, and nutmeg in a medium saucepan. Gradually add boiling water and cook over low heat until thick and clear. Remove from heat, add butter or margerine and lemon juice. Mix. Serve warm or cool. Yield: 1 cup

LOUISE M. MILSTEAD, Albany, GA

Winter Strawberry Hills

My father farmed three acres of strawberry fields on the beautiful rolling hills of Missouri. During strawberry season, the hills were carpeted with fragrant ruby red berries. But for me, the winter months were the best time of all. I could barely wait for the hills to be covered with snow so that I could go sledding. I can still remember the thrill of taking my makeshift cardboard sled and riding down my father's winter strawberry fields.

Tamlin Turner, Owensville, MO Age 62

RED CUCUMBER APPLE RINGS

These rings are delicious as a relish or pickle.

> 1 peck cucumbers (turning yellow)
> 2 cups lime juice
> 8 1/2 quarts water

FIRST SYRUP

> 1 cup white vinegar
> 1 ounce red food coloring
> 1 tablespoon alum

SECOND SYRUP

> 1 package red hot candies
> 10 cups sugar
> 2 cups white vinegar
> 2 cups water
> 8 sticks cinnamon

Peel and seed cucumbers. Cut into 1/4 inch rings. Soak in lime water 24 hours; drain. Mix all ingredients to prepare first syrup and pour over cucumbers, adding enough water to cover cucumbers; simmer two hours. Drain and add second syrup. To prepare second syrup, melt red hots in water, mix all ingredients and heat. While hot, add to pickles and soak overnight. Next day, drain and reheat the syrup and pour back over pickles. Soak overnight. Repeat this for four consecutive days. Fifth day: Pack pickles in jars; heat syrup and pour over pickles. Seal. Yield: about 8 quarts

MABLE HOLCOMB, Paducah, TX Age 80

PICKLED BEETS

> 1 gallon small beets
> 3 1/2 cups vinegar
> 2 cups sugar
> 1 1/2 teaspoons salt
> 2 sticks cinnamon
> 1 tablespoon allspice
> 1 1/2 cups water

Wash beets and cover with boiling water in a kettle or dutch oven; cook until tender and drain. Remove skins and return to the kettle. Add vinegar, sugar, salt, spices, and water. Simmer 15 minutes. Pack beets into hot jars. Pour boiling liquid over beets. Process 30 minutes in boiling water bath. Yield: about 8 pints

KAY WILES, Torrington, WY

GREEN TOMATO SLICED CATSUP

2 gallons sliced green tomatoes
Salt to taste

SYRUP

3 pounds brown sugar
1 quart vinegar
Cinnamon bark to taste
Cloves to taste

Place salted, sliced tomatoes in a large bowl or crock. Let stand overnight. Squeeze out liquid; place in a large kettle and cover with cold water. Bring mixture to a boil and cook until tomatoes turn white. Drain. Combine vinegar, brown sugar, cinnamon bark, and cloves in the kettle over medium heat. Transfer tomatoes to the syrup and simmer 15-20 minutes. Yield: 4-6 pints

OPAL SCOTT, Manchester, OH Age 78

BREAD AND BUTTER PICKLES
From an old Polish recipe.

4 quarts cucumbers, sliced
1 cups sliced onions
1/2 cup non-iodized salt
Ice water
2 pounds brown sugar
1 quart white vinegar
1 tablespoon mustard seed
1 teaspoon celery seed
1 teaspoon turmeric

Place washed and sliced cucumbers and onions in a large bowl. Cover with salted ice water and soak 3 hours. In a large kettle, bring brown sugar, vinegar, mustard seed, celery seed, and turmeric to a boil. Add drained vegetables and simmer 10 minutes. Pack in jars, with juice, and seal. Follow label directions for canning lids. Yield: about 8 pints

JOHN W. HAWLEY, Caseville, MI Age 58

I enjoy being a part of Green Thumb. I work for the Department of Public Works in Caseville, Michigan. My hobby is woodworking in my garage. My favorite times are spent with my family.

NO FUSS
SWEETENED DILL PICKLES

1 gallon hamburger dill slices
8 cups sugar
1 cup vinegar
2 teaspoons mustard seed
2 teaspoons celery seed

Drain pickles and rinse in cold water twice. Drain well and put back into jar. Bring all other ingredients almost to a boil. Pour over pickles and let stand 24 hours in the refrigerator. Yield: 1 gallon

LARETTA A. BAIRD, Montezuma, IA Age 74

FREEZER SWEET PICKLES

I like to pour syrup over the entire batch of pickles and put them into containers or ziplock bags with equal amounts of syrup. After thawing you may put them into pint fruit jars and keep them in the refrigerator. Grandkids love them.

6 cups cucumbers, sliced thin
1 large white onion, sliced thin
1 thinly sliced medium bell pepper
1/3 cup salt

SYRUP
3 cups sugar
1 tablespoon pickling spice
1 cup white vinegar

Combine cucumbers, onion, pepper, salt, and enough water to cover in a large bowl or crock. Soak overnight in the refrigerator. Next morning drain and wash well. Place in freezer containers. To make syrup, heat sugar, pickling spice, and vinegar until boiling. Remove from heat and pour over cucumbers. Freeze containers until ready to use. Yield: about 6 pints

MURLEAN WARD, Bastrop, LA Age 68

KOSHER DILL PICKLES

4 quarts fresh cucumbers
1/2 cup vinegar per quart jar
2 tablespoons sugar per quart jar
1 teaspoon salt per quart jar
Spices of choice: fresh dill, garlic, cloves, pepper

Wash, trim, and pack cucumbers in desired shapes (spears, whole, or slices); pack in sterile quart jars. Pour vinegar, sugar, and salt over cucumbers. Finish by filling jars with boiling water to within 1/4" of top of jars. Add any desired spices. Seal jars and process in water bath just until color begins to change. Remove from water bath; place in draft-free place to cool. When sealed, store in pantry. Yield: about 7 quarts

JAMES E. COOGAN, SR., Mena, AR Age 54

These pickles are very crisp if not overcooked. Use the same recipe to make pickled okra which is ready to eat as soon as it cools.

CLUB SAUCE
Use on hamburgers, hot dogs, or other meats.

12 large ripe tomatoes, peeled and chopped fine
2 large onions, peeled and chopped fine
2 taplespoons salt
1 teaspoon celery seed
1 teaspoon allspice
1 1/2 cups cider vinegar
6 large green peppers chopped fine

In a large, heavy saucepan or kettle, bring tomatoes, onions, salt, celery seed, allspice, and vinegar to a boil. Simmer for three hours, stirring often. Add green peppers and simmer for another 40 minutes. Yield: about 1 quart

NEWELL CASS, Nichols, NY Age 73

This recipe came from my wife's great-grand- mother. I tried making it and it came out great.

P.S. If I can make it, anyone can. I was a carpenter by trade!!

Garden Bounty

FDR alloted plots of land and provided vegetable seeds for people to grow their own food during the Depression. My father had a beautiful, bountiful garden. He was a true "green thumb." My mother canned the vegetables for winter and this spicy sauce was the family's favorite. We have enjoyed this recipe for four generations and I want to share it with my Green Thumb family.

Catherine Crantz

CHILI SAUCE

Try this on everything from hamburgers and meat loaf to fish and rice.

40 tomatoes
6 medium onions
8 green peppers
1 1/2 cups sugar
1 cup vinegar
1 teaspoon cinnamon
1 tablespoon allspice
2 tablespoons celery seed
1 teaspoon cloves

Drop tomatoes in very hot water to loosen skins; peel. Chop tomatoes, peppers, and onions. Add remaining ingredients. In a large kettle over medium heat, cook mixture until all vegetables are tender. Yield: about 1 gallon

CATHERINE CRANTZ, Kingston, NY Age 72

HOT DOG RELISH

4 cups ground onions
1 medium head of cabbage
4 cups ground green peppers
4 cups ground green tomatoes
6 sweet red peppers
1/2 cup salt
6 cups sugar
1 tablespoon celery seed
2 tablespoons mustard seed
1 1/2 teaspoons cider vinegar
2 cups water

Grind vegetables using the coarse blade on a food processor. Place in a large bowl and sprinkle with salt. Let stand overnight; rinse, drain and place in a large kettle. Combine remaining ingredients; pour over vegetables and heat to boiling. Reduce heat and simmer 3 minutes. Seal in hot jars. Yield: 8 pints

BERTIE H. ALEXANDER, Spring City, TN Age 84

SIMPLE SALSA

Delicious with corn chips, over broiled chicken breasts or scrambled eggs.

    1 regular size can tomatoes, chopped
    1/2 medium onion, chopped
    1 teaspoon garlic salt
    1 can chopped green chilies
    1 jalapeno pepper (optional)

Combine all prepared ingredients in a medium bowl. Let sit 12 hours.
Yield: 3-4 cups

PAT KORONIS, Picher, OK Age 61

WORLD'S BEST SALSA

This recipe can be doubled for large groups and takes only 10 minutes to prepare. When you start eating, you just can't stop!

    6-8 fresh ripe tomatoes, peeled seeded, and chopped (or 2 cans
        diced tomatoes, drained)
    1 can diced tomatoes with green chilies
    1/2 bunch chopped cilantro, or more to taste (this is the key
        ingredient!)
    1 medium vidalia onion or 1 small sweet onion
    Juice of 1/2 lime (or more to taste)
    1 teaspoon salt
    1-2 bags of regular flavor tortilla chips

Visit Ranger Morrison at Tennessee's Savage Gulf State Natural Area which is a host agency to several Green Thumb workers.

Combine all ingredients except chips in a large bowl. Let sit 30
minutes at room temperature. (Will keep refrigerated up to 2 weeks.
Cilantro loses its flavor in a day or two, so chop a little more fresh.)
Serve with chips. Yield: 6-8 servings

RANGER WAYNE MORRISON, Palmer, TN

TANGY TOPPER

    1 pound sharp cheddar, grated
    1/2 cup mayonnaise
    2 teaspoons mustard
    1 cup finely chopped pecans
    Bagel chips or crackers

Mix all ingredients together, blending well. Store in refrigerator in a
covered container. Very tangy--tastes excellent on bagel chips.

DIANE CHAPMAN, Magnolia, AR Age 58

BEET RELISH

4 cups beets, peeled
4 cups shredded cabbage
1 cup chopped onion
1 cup chopped red or green pepper
1 teaspoon horseradish sauce
2 cups sugar
2 cups white vinegar

In a large pan, cover peeled beets with boiling water and cook until tender. Drain. Grind beets, cabbage, onion, and pepper in a food mill or processor. Place mixture in a large pot or kettle and add sugar and vinegar; mix and bring to a boil. Cook for 10 minutes. Spoon into hot jars and seal. Yield: 4-5 pints

INEZ ROBERTSON, Sheldon, WI Age 62

QUICK CRANBERRY RELISH

1 16-ounce can whole cranberry sauce
1/2 cup chopped walnuts
1/2 cup light raisins
1/4 teaspoon ground cinnamon
1/8 teaspoon ground cloves
Additional walnuts for garnish

Combine all ingredients in a small mixing bowl. Cover and chill. Stir before serving; sprinkle with walnuts. Yield: 12 servings

CATHERINE PALMER, Age 72

CUCUMBER RELISH

5 cups chopped cucumber
3 cups chopped onion
3 cups chopped celery
2 cups chopped green pepper
1/4 to 1/2 cup salt
3 cups water
3 cups sugar
1/3 cup white mustard seed
1 pint white vinegar

Mix vegetables in a large bowl. Add salt, cover with water, stir, and let sit 8 hours. Drain and squeeze. Place in large pan or kettle and add sugar, mustard seed, and vinegar. Cook 10 minutes over medium-high heat. Place in pint jars. Yield: 5 pints

EVELYN ADAMS, Wise, VA Age 66

Rule of Thumb:

Heavily sweetened recipes foam when cooking, so choose a pot or pan with at least four times the capacity of the food being cooked in it.

Rule of Thumb:

Don't expect a recipe to require exactly the same cooking time every time you fix it. Pan size and seasonal variations in the water content of fruits and vegetables will affect cooking time.

PEAR RELISH

Grandma spooned this relish on black-eyed peas which had been cooked over an open fire.

1 peck (8 quarts) pears, peeled and diced
6 medium onions, diced
4 bell peppers, diced
1 tablespoon salt
1 tablespoon allspice
5 cups white vinegar
5 cups sugar

In a grinder or food processor, puree pears, onions, and peppers to a sauce-like texture. Place mixture in a large saucepan, add salt, allspice, vinegar, and sugar and bring to a boil. Reduce heat and simmer for 30 minutes. Pour into sterile jars and seal. Yield: 4-6 quarts

ANITA H. OVERTON, Branford, FL   Age 57

ZUCCHINI RELISH

10 cups peeled and chopped zucchini
4 cups chopped onion
1 large sweet red pepper, chopped
1 can green chiles, chopped
3 teaspoons coarse salt
3 1/2 cups sugar
3 cups white vinegar
1 teaspoon pepper
1/2 teaspoon nutmeg

Place chopped vegetables in a large pot and add salt. Let sit overnight. Drain. Add all other ingredients to drained vegetables and bring to a boil. Cook for 10 minutes. Put into hot jars, seal, and process 10 minutes. Yield: 5 pints

GENSIE D. FARRELL, Albany, KY   Age 78

Grandmother's Hearth

I loved visiting my grandmother Pearl Mae because she made the best black-eyed peas. She had this wonderful open fireplace where she prepared most of her meals. She didn't call it a fireplace though, she called it her hearth. She always said that the hearth was the heart of the home. I can vividly remember a big black iron pot that hung over the flames with the most delicious smells coming from it. Whenever we visited, I ran right to that black pot to see if she had kept her promise to have it filled with black-eyed peas. Grandmother Pearl Mae never made a promise she couldn't keep.

Anita Overton

-231-

**Red Corn
Cob Jelly**

Nebraska is one of
the great corn
states and we just
love corn--from
creamed corn to
corn chowder, we
cook it in a variety
of ways. Every fall
I look forward to
the harvest when
the big combines
shell the corn
kernals off the
cob. Combines are
harvest machines
that cut wheat,
but if a different
cutting head is
attached, then it
can shell corn
kernals. What is
left are the dried
cobs which are
used to make my
wonderful corn
jelly. If you are
unfortunate
enough to be a
city dweller, you
might want to
drive down to the
nearest cornfield
or look for corn
cobs at roadside
stands. If all else
fails, I invite you
to come to
Nebraska and I'll
give you a jar of
my red corn jelly.

Eve Comstock

CORN COB JELLY

This jelly sounds peculiar, but is very pretty and tastes somewhat like apple.

12 to 14 large corn cobs (preferably red ones)
3 pints water
1 package pectin (Sure-Jell)
3 cups sugar
2 or 3 drops red food coloring

Wash cobs. Put in large pot and boil for 30 minutes. Strain out 3 cups of juice; add pectin. Bring mixture to boil; add sugar; boil 1 more minute. Skim, cool, and pour into jars or glasses and seal with wax.
Yield: about 3 pints

EVE COMSTOCK, Inman, NE Age 60

BEET JELLY

I decided to experiment with this jelly; it turned out wonderfully.

8-10 beets, cooked, peeled, and sliced
4 cups beet juice
5 cups water
1 package Sure-Jell
1/2 cup lemon juice
6 cups sugar
1 small package raspberry jello

Drain cooked beets, reserving 4 cups of juice. In a large saucepan, cook beet juice and water 3 minutes. Add Sure-Jell and lemon juice and cook 3 minutes. Add sugar and jello; cook until completely dissolved, stirring constantly. Pour into jars and seal. Yield: about 10 cups

HELEN J. OCHS, Washington, IN Age 69

GREEN PEPPER JELLY

Yummy on crackers with cream cheese. May be canned as for jam or jelly.

6 large green peppers, stemmed, halved, seeded, and chopped
1/1/2 cups cider vinegar
4 pouches Certo pectin
2 teaspoons red pepper
6 cups sugar

Place 3 cups of prepared peppers, vinegar, and sugar in a large saucepan. Bring to a full rolling boil over high heat, stirring constantly. Stir in pectin; return mixture to a full boil, stirring constantly for 1 minute. Remove from heat. Skim off foam and ladle into prepared jars, filling to within 1/8" of top. Seal; invert jars for 5 minutes, then turn upright. Cool 1 to 1 1/2 hours. Shake jars to evenly distribute peppers throughout jelly. Yield: about 6 cups

MARGARET BREERS, Lakeport, CA

RHUBARB BLUEBERRY JAM

5 cups rhubarb, diced
1 cup water
5 cups sugar
1 cup blueberry pie filling
1 package raspberry jello

Cook rhubarb in water over medium heat until tender. Add sugar and boil for 2 minutes. Stir in pie filling and cool for about 10 minutes. Add jello and mix well. Pour into hot jars; process 15 minutes in boiling water or freeze. Yield: 12 servings

EVELYN RIPHENBURG, Asseo, WI Age 66

RHUBARB-PINEAPPLE VARIATION

5 cups rhubarb, diced
4 cups sugar
1 small can crushed pineapple, including juice
2 small boxes raspberry or strawberry jello

Boil rhubarb and sugar with pineapple and juice for 10 minutes. Remove from heat and add jello. Stir well. Put in jars; cover with lids; let cool and freeze. Yield: 8 small jars

JOAN NOAH, Neillsville, WI

Jelly Fit for a Queen

My husband always enjoyed food flavored with almost any variety of green peppers-- the hotter the better. He was born into the Basque family which helped to introduce curly sheep into the Territory of New Mexico. When I go to Elderhostel events, I take some of my green pepper jelly. I once attended a genealogical seminar at the University of New Brunswick in Canada. They served my green pepper jelly during a birthday reception for the visiting Queen Mother Elizabeth. I'm told she had a taste.

Margaret Breers

PRICKLY PEAR APPLE JELLY

There are abundant prickly pear apples in my area, and this is a recipe I remember from my mom. I am a retired 30-year fireman from Greenville, Texas.

5 pounds (about 56) large prickly pear apples
5 cups water
1/4 cup lemon juice
9 cups sugar
1 1.75-ounce package Sure-Jell pectin

Wipe spines from fruit with a paper towel or clean rag. Wash thoroughly and cut both ends of apple. To clear the stem-end, split fruit in half length-wise. Put apples in a kettle with water; simmer about 40 minutes, mashing fruit frequently. Strain through cheesecloth and measure 7 cups of apple juice into a large saucepan. Add lemon juice and pectin; bring mixture to a full rolling boil, stirring constantly. Add sugar; return mixture to a full boil. Boil exactly 1 minute, stirring constantly. Remove from heat, skim any foam, pour into small jars and seal. Yield: 10 cups

FINIS BURNS, Lone Oak, TX Age 64

STRAWBERRY JAM

Rule of Thumb:

Add 1/2 teaspoon of butter or margarine to jam and jelly mixtures to prevent foaming during cooking.

4 heaping cups strawberries, washed and hulled
1 tablespoon cider vinegar
4 cups sugar

Place strawberries and vinegar in a large saucepan; cover and bring to a boil. Boil mixture for one minute. Add sugar, stirring gently to blend. Cook 20 minutes at boiling point. Pour into clean sterilized pint jars and let cool. Melt paraffin and pour over the jam, about 1/4" to seal. This does best if only 4 cups are made at a time. Yield: 2 pints

SALLY BOOFER, Green Thumb National Office

CANNED GRAPE JUICE

PER QUART
1 cup grapes
1/2 cup sugar
Boiling water

Put grapes in a hot quart jar. Pour sugar over and fill with boiling water. Seal with lid and ring. Put jars in hot water bath and boil 10 minutes. Let sit at least 6 weeks before drinking. Strain before serving.
Yield: 1 quart

SALLY BOOFER, Green Thumb National Office

CHOKECHERRY SYRUP

Wonderful on waffles or ice cream. Makes a great gift.

2-4 pounds chokecherries
4 cups granulated sugar
2 cups light corn syrup
Dash of almond flavoring, optional

Clean chokecherries. Cover with water in a large kettle and cook 15 minutes or until soft. Press or sieve juice. Measure 4 cups of juice into a large kettle. Add sugar and corn syrup; stir to dissolve sugar. Cook on medium heat 10-15 minutes. Add almond flavoring if desired. Remove foam and pour into sterilized pint jars. Process in a boiling water bath 5 minutes or keep in refrigerator. For jelly, use the recipe on pectin packages for sour cherries. Yield: 2-4 pints

BONNIE WILSON-COWLES, Absarokee, MT Age 58

My dad introduced me to chokecherries when I was a kid in the 40's, and I've loved them ever since. However, the best part is picking the berries with family and friends while enjoying the first days of fall.

JELLY AND JAM TIPS

When making any jelly or jam, add 1/2 cup water for each 2 quarts soft fruits such as berries and grapes. Add water to cover, and cook until fruit is soft--10 to 20 minutes--stirring frequently. Mash fruit while it is cooking,

Strain mixture through cheesecloth. (If clear jelly is desired, do not squeeze cheesecloth.) Measure juice, heat to boiling, and add sugar.

A fruit must contain acid and the right amount of pectin in order to jell. The amount and quality of pectin in fruit varies at different states depending on ripeness.

If fruits are low in pectin, they may be combined with other high-pectin fruits, or a commercial pectin may be added. If using commercial pectin, follow exactly the directions given by the manufacturer.

Fruits that jell easily are apples, crab apples, unripe grapes, blackberries, cranberries, huckleberries, and plums.

CHRISTINE LARMORE, Sebring, FL

Rule of Thumb:

Contact a State or U.S. Department of Agriculture extension agent (they're listed in the telephone book) if you have questions about canning techniques.

EDITOR'S NOTE:

Sure-Jell and Certo are manufactured by Kraft Foods. Directions for preparing jars and lids, along with additional recipes, are included with instructions in the pectin packages. If you need further assistance, call their hotline at 1-800-437-3284.

House &
Garden Hints

HOUSE & GARDEN HINTS

CONTENTS

HOUSEHOLD CLEAN-UP

WINDOW CLEANERS

This recipe for window cleaner comes from a professional housecleaner. Most every household has these ingredients on hand.

    1/2 gallon warm water
    1 squirt dishwashing detergent
    2 tablespoons corn starch

Stir with hand to dissolve corn starch. Wash windows with sponge or cloth; dry with cotton cloth--an all cotton T-shirt works well.

Another professional cleaner recommends:

    8 ounces alcohol
    1 cap-full dishwashing liquid
    1/2 gallon water

Mix in a large bucket.

•Dry windows with wadded newspapers. Be sure to wear rubber gloves or you'll need hand cleaner to remove the ink!

PAINT REMOVER

To wipe paint off hands, arms and face, try using cooking oil instead of regular paint remover that often burns the skin.

GUNK REMOVER

Remove gummy residue from appliances, tools, bottles, windows, etc., with a dab of nail polish remover.

CLEAN AND GREEN

Place silk or plastic flowers in a large paper bag. Pour a generous amount of ordinary table salt inside. Close the bag and shake vigorously for about 2 minutes. The salt scrubs the flowers clean of dust and dirt.

Got the
Dishwashin'
Blues

I know that birds
have little birds
and frogs have
little frogs,

That pussy cats
have little cats
and dogs have
little dogs.

That proper
minks have little
minks and fish
have little fishes.

Then why don't
sinks have little
sinks instead of
dirty dishes?

———

Any housewife,
no matter how
large her family,
can always get
some time to be
alone by doing the
dishes!

———

Thank God for
dirty dishes; they
have a tale to tell.

While others are
going hungry,
we're eating very
well.

With home and
health and
happiness, I
shouldn't want to
fuss;

For by this stack
of evidence, God's
very good to us.

FURNITURE TOUCH-UP

Cover shallow scratches and bruises on dark furniture by touching with iodine. Polish when dry.

SCORCHED BOTTOMS OF GLASS POTS AND PANS

Cover the bottom of the pan with baking soda; pour vinegar over and leave overnight. Wash clean as usual.

HOMEMADE DRYER SHEETS
Soft and thrifty.

Instead of using expensive sheets of fabric softener in your dryer, mix equal parts liquid softener and water. Dampen an old washcloth with solution and toss into dryer. Since only half as much is needed, you'll save on liquid softener too.

STAIN Rx

•Pour seltzer or club soda on a food spill (like gravy or wine) on your carpet or clothes, then blot.

•Baking powder removes tea or coffee stains from both plastic and china pots and cups.

•Remove grass stains from white clothing by soaking in alcohol before washing. Or try using an oily-hair formula shampoo.

•For rust spots on clothing, nothing is better than the old reliable lemon juice and salt, plus sunshine.

OIL SLICKS

If you spill cooking oil on the counter or floor, sprinkle a heavy coating of flour over the spill, wait a few minutes, then just sweep or brush the flour into a dustpan.

BAY LEAF MAGIC

If cupboards become infested with weevils, scatter bay leaves on the shelves.

TIME SAVERS

SUPERMARKET SWEEP

When making out your shopping list, use a long business-size envelope; write your list on the back and insert your coupons inside. If you
are familiar with the lay-out of your store, arrange your list according
to the aisle you find items in. This is such a time saver. Clip coupons
together as you put the item in grocery cart, so you know you have
found everything. Try to have all coupons arranged so the checkout
person does not have to turn them--this saves time.

JUGGLING ACT

*It is possible to get all elements of a meal ready to serve
at the same time.*

Most foods can stand covered the same amount of time they took to
cook. Cook foods with high sugar or fat content first, they stay hot
longer.

Microwave dense foods or those with high moisture content which
retain heat (meats, rice, potatoes) next longest. Porous foods like
vegetables, fruits, and breads can be put in the oven last as they cool
more quickly than do dense foods and require shorter cooking and
standing time.

SPACE SAVER

Fold up electrical and extension cords and put in an empty bathroom
tissue roll. They fit neatly in a drawer or on a shelf.

SHOE DRYER

To dry wet tennis shoes, place them in front of the bottom grill of
your refrigerator. They will be dry by morning.

*I enjoy grocery
shopping and
try to buy
things when
they are on
sale, so when I
need them I
don't have to
pay full price.
This is good if
unexpected
company comes
for a meal!*

*Blanche
Slaughter,
Darwin, MN*

COOKING TIPS

GOOD IDEAS

• Use a cake rack with paper towels to drain french fries and other greasy foods.

• If soup tastes very salty, a piece of raw potato placed in the pot will absorb it.

• Spritz a sticky syrup bottle cap with non-stick vegetable spray for easy opening.

• Batters made with egg and water instead of milk are crisper.

• Use stuffing cubes in ground beef mixture for less dense, more moist meatballs.

• Use greased muffin tins as molds when baking stuffed green peppers.

• Never throw away unconsumed wine. Use it in cooking sauces, marinating, or salad dressings.

SKIM THE FAT AND CALORIES

• To cut calories and fat from recipes that call for whipped cream, use skimmed milk and your electric hand mixer. Stick with the skimmed milk; it beats up better than low-fat milk (1% or 2%).

• Use the following formula to reduce the fat in any recipe except pie crusts and cookies: for every cup of butter or oil, use 1/2 cup of the amount called for plus 1/2 cup applesauce.

VEGETABLE TRICKS

BROCCOLI

•Broccoli stems can be cooked in the same length of time as the flowers if an 'X' is made from top to bottom of stem.

•Drop pieces of lemon rind into the water of broccoli or cabbage to brighten the flavor.

CABBAGE/CAULIFLOWER

•When cooking cabbage, place a piece of bread on top before putting on the lid. There will be no odor.

•When cooking red cabbage, add a teaspoon of lemon juice or vinegar to the water to help retain color.

•Cook cauliflower, cabbage, or onions in a mixture of half milk and half water. Odor will be almost entirely eliminated and the liquid may be used in making cream sauce or soups.

CELERY

•To keep celery crisp, stand it up in a pitcher of cold water and refrigerate.

GREEN BEANS

•Vinegar will freshen the flavor of canned green beans.

ONIONS

•When preparing onions for cooking, make a cross incision in the stem end and the inner section will not slip out.

•Chop onions under running water to prevent teary eyes or light a candle close by to draw away the odor that causes tearing.

•Wrap onions individually in aluminum foil to prevent sprouting.

POTATOES

•A delicious way to prepare baked potatoes is to split them slightly lengthwise; wet, roll in table salt, and bake as normal. The salt makes a hard potato crust. Also try seasoned or coarse pretzel salts. Makes a great food for a potato bar.

•Place a couple of apples in stored potatoes to prevent sprouting.

BAKING ADVICE

Oh weary mother mixing dough,

Don't you wish that food would grow?

Your lips would smile, I know, to see

A cookie bush or a pancake tree!

•Put flour in a large salt shaker and use for dusting cake pans, meat, etc. It is less messy and wastes less flour.

•Sprinkle your cake plate lightly with granulated sugar before placing the warm cake on it.

•A soft new powder puff makes dusting a cake pan a breeze.

•Preheating cake pans produces better results.

•Improve cake texture by "burping" filled cake pans before baking. Gently pat the bottom of the pan to force air to the surface.

•Use thread instead of a knife to cut a cake.

•Use a knitting needle to loosen a cake baked in a tube pan. It does a better job of slipping around the center tube without tearing the cake.

CAN-TO-CUP CONVERSION

It is often helpful to have a list of various can sizes because so many recipes call for a can size instead of measurements. It is also good to know how many cups a can holds so you know what to buy.

CAN SIZE

6 ounce	3/4 cup
8 ounce	1 cup
#1 can, 10 1/2 ounce	1 1/4 cups
#300 can, 15 1/4 ounce	1 3/4 cups
#303 can, 1 pound	2 cups
#2 can, 1 pound 4 ounces	2 1/2 cups
#2 1/2 can, 1 pound 13 ounces	3 1/2 cups
46 ounce	5 3/4 cups
#10 can, 6 pounds 9 ounces	12 cups

BERTHA M. MARSHALL, Bowling Green, MO Age 70

CANNY CANNING

●Use only canning salt for pickling; regular salt will result in soft and discolored pickles.

●Put cut-up apples, peaches, and pears for canning into salted water to prevent darkening. Use about 1 teaspoon salt to 1 quart of water; drain well; rinse if desired.

HOME REMEDIES

●Reduce swelling of a bump or bruise by applying a bag of frozen vegetables. They are usually handy and conform to the shape of injured knees, ankles, etc.

●Epsom salts and warm water are a good treatment for swelling.

●When a baby has the croup, close the bathroom door and windows, turn the shower on hot and let it run for 10 minutes. Hold the baby in the steamy bathroom for 15 to 30 minutes.

●For cuts and bruises, use the juice from an aloe plant leaf. It helps speed the healing and reduce the chance of a scar.

●Keep some loose tobacco in your first aid kit to treat insect stings. Moisten the tobacco and apply it directly to the sting. A paste of meat tenderizer and water applied to the sting is also effective.

POTPOURRI
SIMMERING MIX
Makes your house smell great.

3 sticks cinnamon
1/4 cup whole cloves
2 sections orange peel
4 cups water

Bring to a boil in a medium saucepan and simmer for hours. Add more water as needed. This can be done on top of the stove or in an electric potpourri pot.

NELDA BIGELOW, Chestertown, MD Age 67

Texas Fruitcakes

Pick pears in late August. Slice in thin slices and place on a bed sheet. Place the bed sheet on the roof of the pump shed for a day or so in the hot August sun. Makes wonderful candied fruit for your Thanksgiving and Christmas fruitcakes.

from Lois Edwards' Swedish grandmother, Lily Anderson

IN THE GARDEN

Mother and Father always managed to have wonderful flower and vegetable gardens on a small city lot in Royal Oak, Michigan. My British parents shared their garden secrets and I now enjoy sharing my flowers and vegetables with others.

OLD ENGLISH COMPOST

Compost piles help to return nutrition to the earth.

Compost is vegetable waste of all kinds which is rotted down in a heap or pit. It is a blackish-brown crumbling material similar to humus. Use soft hedge clippings, tea bags or tea leaves, coffee grounds, vegetable peelings, fruit, lawn clippings, fallen leaves, soaked newspapers.

Add unprocessed animal or bird manure as an activator on top of every 6" layer. If the soil is acid, sprinkle limestone over every compacted foot of material. Build up gradually over several weeks. Keep the soil moist on top to keep the heat in.

Place a fence stake in the center of the pile until it reaches 4 or 5 feet in depth. When the stake is removed it will leave an airshaft. This pile will rot satisfactorily and will be ready in 6 months.

ALETA THOMPSON, Alpena, MI Age 60

MAGIC CABBAGES

I plant 6 early-variety cabbage plants. When they mature, I harvest by cutting the cabbage 2 to 3 leaf layers up from the root stem. The stem will produce a cabbage at each of the 4 to 5 leaf joints. I cut the cabbages at the end of July when they are 6 to 7 inches in diameter. By frost time the other 24+ cabbages are ready for harvest.

EDWIN E. MORSE, Hudson Falls, NY

WAGONS, HO

To mark straight even rows for vegetable planting, pull a child's wagon across your garden plot after it has been spaded.

LILLIAN D. JOHNSON, Montrose, MN Age 73

WEED CONTROL

A weed is a plant whose virtues have not yet been discovered!

Pour salted boiling water between the sections of your cement or brick walkway to kill weeds and grass. Inexpensive motor oil or plain salt is also effective.

POISON IVY REVENGE

Spray the infested area with a solution of 1 gallon soapy water and 3 pounds of salt. A few treatments will kill it.

PEST CONTROL

•Get rid of red ants--the biting kind--by spreading quick grits in affected areas. The ants eat the grits, the grits expand, the ants are gone.

•Sprinkle salt on slugs.

•If you're unfortunate enough to pick up chiggers while working outside, paint over the point of entry with clear nail polish. It suffocates them.

•If rabbits are nibbling your garden, dust inexpensive talcum powder on or around the plants. This works on tomatoes, peppers, potatoes, and other plants. If rain washes it away, just apply more.

•Hang aluminum pie plates from stakes all around the vegetable garden to keep the birds away.

CONTRIBUTORS TO THE HOUSE & GARDEN HINTS SECTION INCLUDE:

EVELYN ADAMS, Wise, VT Age 66
BUTCH BARKER, Redding, CA
RUTH BLEDSOE
JUANITA BRANCH, Norlina, NC Age 62
VELMA BUTT, Dows, IA Age 61
DALLAS L. GIBBS, Lebanon, MO Age 60
LILLIAN D. JOHNSON, Montrose, MN Age 73
ROSEMARY KAMPA, Grenville, SD Age 71
LITA LEVINE KLEGER, Green Thumb National Office
RHUY ANN LEWIS, Dodge City, KS Age 76
BARBARA MARCELLO, Reading, PA Age 60
ROSE OLIVER, Des Moines, IA Age 57
CAROL ROY, Brighton, TN
LISA SANDERS, Green Thumb National Office
DEB SKLAR, Green Thumb National Office
BLANCHE SLAUGHTER, Darwin, MN Age 58

Natural Fertilizers

My grandpa worked at the zoo and was forever carrying home buckets of "smelly stuff." He always had a garden that was the envy of the neighborhood. The zoo used to give him eggs from the zoo chickens, and his "banty" hen had some strange-looking babies! Grandpa also fed both left-over black coffee and coffee grounds to the shrubs around the house. They were always loaded with blooms.

Lois Edwards, Texas Green Thumb

Bury fish heads in your tomato garden for fertilizer.

-247-

INDEX OF RECIPES

-250-

-251-

If you would like information on Green Thumb's services in your area, if you would like to volunteer time or services, or if you are interested in employing an older worker, please call the national office or the nearest state office.

GREEN THUMB NATIONAL OFFICE

2000 North 14th Street, Suite 800
Arlington, Virginia 22201
Telephone: 703-522-7272
Fax: 703-522-0141
Voice Mail: 703-522-1223

BOARD OF DIRECTORS

Phil Klutts, Chairman, Oklahoma City, Oklahoma
Cy Carpenter, Minneapolis, Minnesota
Joe Rankin, Vice Chairman, Rall, Texas
Dr. Charles Toftoy, Arlington, Virginia
Ruth Ann Wefald, Manhattan, Kansas
Andrea Wooten, President, Arlington, Virginia

ALABAMA/ARKANSAS/TENNESSEE

P.O. Box 23920
Little Rock, Arkansas 72221
Telephone: 501-225-3520

CALIFORNIA

35 Maria Drive, Suite 865
Petaluma, California 94954
Telephone: 707-763-0652

FLORIDA

P.O. Box 330006
Atlantic Beach, Florida 32233-0006
Telephone: 904-241-8188

GEORGIA/NORTH CAROLINA/ SOUTH CAROLINA

P.O. Box 1354
Jesup, Georgia 31598
Telephone: 912-427-7708

ILLINOIS

P.O. Box 769
Harrisburg, Illinois 62946
Telephone: 618-253-3700

INDIANA
P.O. Box 687
Seymour, Indiana 47274
Telephone: 812-522-7390

IOWA
P.O. Box 4040
DesMoines, Iowa 50333-4040
Telephone: 515-243-2430

KENTUCKY/VIRGINIA/WEST VIRGINIA
P.O. Box A
Beattyville, Kentucky 41311
Telephone: 606-464-3675

LOUISIANA/MISSISSIPPI
1879 Leglise Street, Lot 2
Mansura, Louisiana 71350-4001
Telephone: 318-964-2191

MICHIGAN
P.O. Box 465
Mount Pleasant, Michigan 48804-0465
Telephone: 547-772-5308

MINNESOTA
P.O. Box 310
Wadena, Minnesota 56482
Telephone: 218-631-3483

MISSOURI/NEBRASKA
P.O. Box 414
Buffalo, Missouri 65622
Telephone: 417-345-2797

MONTANA/IDAHO
P.O. Box 2587
Great Falls, Montana 59403
Telephone: 406-761-4821

NEW ENGLAND
P.O. Box 1005
Gardner, Massachusetts 01440
Telephone: 508-630-1203

NEW JERSEY/MARYLAND
P.O. Box 8303
Trenton, New Jersey 08650
Telephone: 609-890-2121

NEW YORK
P.O. Box 5468
Cortland, New York 13045-5468
Telephone: 607-756-7509

OHIO
P.O. Box 366
Ottawa, Ohio 45875
Telephone: 419-523-4305

OKLAHOMA/KANSAS
P.O. Box 23437
Oklahoma City, Oklahoma 73123-2437
Telephone: 405-495-1415

OREGON/WASHINGTON
P.O. Box 50
Rickreall, Oregon 97371-0050
Telephone: 503-623-0237

PENNSYLVANIA
P.O. Box 3553
Shiremanstown, Pennsylvania 97371-0050
Telephone: 717-731-8350

PUERTO RICO
P.O. Box 41231, Minillas Station
San Juan, Puerto Rico 00940
Telephone: 809-727-8035

NORTH DAKOTA
1120 College Drive, Suite 101
Bismarck, North Dakota 58501-1214
Telephone: 701-258-8879

SOUTH DAKOTA
P.O. Box 509
Sioux Falls, South Dakota 57101
Telephone: 605-332-7991

TEXAS/NEW MEXICO
P.O. Box 7898
Waco, Texas 76714
Telephone: 817-776-4801

WISCONSIN
Clark County Court House, #107
Neillsville, Wisconsin 54456-1971
Telephone: 715-743-4636\

WYOMING/COLORADO/UTAH
1902 Thomes Avenue, #209
Cheyenne, Wyoming 82001
Telephone: 307-634-7417